THE
SAVE-BY-BORROWING
TECHNIQUE

THE
SAVE-BY-BORROWING
TECHNIQUE

BUILDING YOUR FORTUNE—FROM LOAN TO PROFIT

CARL E. PERSON

DOUBLEDAY & COMPANY, INC., GARDEN CITY, NEW YORK.

To
My Father

PREFACE

A person with a moderate ability to save, starting from scratch, has an excellent opportunity to accumulate a fortune exceeding one million dollars.

We will arrive at our goal, called the *"10th Multiple,"* in ten steps. This book explains how to put your money to work while you are accumulating it—and make more in the process than you can with insurance, traditional savings methods, random selections in the stock market, and most mutual funds. No guarantees are given. The 10th Multiple cannot be reached overnight—but it can be reached! What more could you expect, however, when you are called upon to save only a small amount, such as $20 per week?

Millions of savers have little chance of becoming wealthy because they are experiencing one or more *savings losses*. A "savings loss" is a needless depletion of savings caused by the lack of a fundamental understanding of savings procedures, and an unawareness of the most appropriate ways to put savings to work. Between those who are knowledgeable and those who are not there can be a one-million-dollar difference. The unknowledgeable savers have almost no hope of stemming their losses unless they become adequately informed about such savings institutions as stock markets, mutual funds, life insurance companies, savings banks, and savings and loan associations. For all of these people I have written this book, to point out how they can avoid savings waste amounting to many thousands of dollars. *The Save-by-Borrowing Technique* (for convenience I'll call it Save by Borrowing), showing the most effective way to save and invest, covers virtually every area of personal finance important to an individual or family. Written informally and not as a text, the book should prove invaluable to those having little or no experience in this field.

The average person, I believe, does not study the principles of saving and investment. He somehow picks up little bits of information (much of which is misleading) and believes this is sufficient. Ask him some basic questions about savings and loan associations, life insurance, mutual funds, and stocks—you will probably receive inadequate answers. My own experience tells me this is true. Only after I graduated from college and law school did I recognize and become concerned about my lack of a basic understanding of such matters. One day, out of curiosity, I started reading a well-known and excellent book on the stock market. From there, my interest led me to other books—books on banking, life insurance, stocks, mutual funds, real estate, and other areas of saving and investment. This reading and my own experiences have resulted in this book, in which I relate what I consider to be essential but frequently unknown information for persons who wish to watch their money multiply.

Save by Borrowing looks at the saving and increasing of capital from a unique, potentially controversial point of view: *borrowing*. In fact, many persons jump to the immediate conclusion that saving by borrowing is impossible, that it is clearly a contradiction in terms. But they soon find out it *is* possible. And I set forth the simple steps you can take to avoid the traps set for the unsophisticated. By implementation of the practical suggestions that follow, you will be able to prevent your savings program from suffering senseless losses.

I explain how a borrower can *force* himself to accumulate capital (one meaning of the word "save") and can reduce or altogether eliminate certain costs of saving and investment (another meaning of "save"). When a person saves by borrowing, therefore, he accomplishes two distinct types of saving—wherefore the phrase *Save by Borrowing*.

We will consider step-by-step a unique program for mandatory accumulation of capital—the most effective and profitable of them all. One can be assured he will complete his investment program as well as avoid the enormous savings losses resulting from unsuccessful voluntary plans. For example, of all the practical alternatives for mandatory saving, the Save-by-Borrowing method affords the strongest degree of coercion. When an individual borrows to put his investment plan into action, he will also be forced to save. It is the law which insists the saving be accomplished and will all but guarantee that money will be withdrawn from the saver's current earnings and returned to the lender in accordance with the loan agreement.

Borrowing to save overcomes problems inherent in most other programs of saving. The technique is simple to understand, flexible in application, and effective in results. Those who choose it can rest assured that only a major catastrophe could prevent them from missing any of their periodic payments. Isn't this a feature any reliable savings program should have?

A distinct advantage of borrowing is the *immediacy* which it affords. Borrowing in anticipation of saving avoids the delay experienced by those who accumulate savings *before* undertaking to place them in suitable investments. Within one or two days your "savings" for the forthcoming year are working for you through appropriate investment.

The problem of immediacy lurks in the innumerable books on business and investment offering techniques to make a fortune. "Money makes money" is a tacit premise of these books, yet they offer little help to the reader who has savings capacity but no savings. Save by Borrowing offers a real solution, instead of assuming (mistakenly, in many cases) the money needed to begin has already been accumulated. It requires no more than a capacity to save and a desire to get started right away on a long-range savings and investment program. The psychological advantage to the Save-by-Borrowing technique is of inestimable value: obviously, avoidance of delay minimizes possibilities of program abandonment.

I subject most popular methods of saving and investment to examination and criticism, to reveal how they compare with procedures described in this book as the Save-by-Borrowing process. Particularly, periodic investors in stock will be interested in the chart which compares three alternative methods of buying stocks:

1. Monthly purchases under the Monthly Investment Plan of the New York Stock Exchange (the MIP);
2. Year-end purchases out of savings accumulated in a bank account; and
3. Purchases by the Save-by-Borrowing method.

It should be apparent from the title which method is declared the winner—by a considerable dollar amount too.

An investor utilizing the MIP or other monthly purchase program often pays as much as three or four times the brokerage commissions paid by the investor who follows a Save-by-Borrowing program. Worse yet, to automatically reinvest dividends costs the MIP purchaser six times as much as the Save-by-Borrower. You will learn how to avoid these excess costs *and obtain the effect of purchasing stocks without paying any brokerage commissions.* Nor will there be any net interest expense.

Corporations and ownership of shares of stock in a corporation are discussed as an aid to persons unfamiliar with such concepts, together with basic and not-so-basic information about purchasing stocks. Much of this information is indispensable in planning and understanding a long-range savings and investment program.

Although it deals extensively with stocks, this book far from limits itself to them. Mutual funds (an indirect way of investing in stocks and bonds) are given full consideration. You will learn how the purchasers of mutual funds can be the victims of abuses. These abuses are carefully detailed to put you on guard. With no more than the basic information contained in the two mutual fund chapters these persons could have saved themselves many thousands of dollars. For your possible use, the names and mailing addresses of more than forty mutual funds which charge no sales commission, called "no-load" mutual funds, are offered. Also, I describe my concept of a reform mutual fund which would revolutionize the industry—and give investors otherwise unobtainable benefits.

Most people do not have even a working knowledge of life insurance. As a consequence, they are experiencing huge savings losses which they could avoid if they knew certain basic principles. For these persons life insurance is presented in a totally different perspective—different, that is, from the sales pitch given by so many life insurance agents. The setting is in the office of an overenthusiastic agent, from what we hear out to make a sale of the type of life insurance having greater value to himself than to the insured. How the potential purchaser deals with the hard sell can be your guide to overcoming a major obstacle to the accumulation of wealth. Comparisons show you what type of life insurance is most compatible with the goal of that 10th Multiple. What steps should you take if you are already committed to an undesirable life insurance savings program? You will find an answer.

The sophisticated saver and investor knows what to say to a financial salesman who comes knocking at his door. This is true whether the salesman is peddling mutual funds, life insurance, or some other investment product. *The Save-by-Borrowing Technique* affords you a working knowledge of diverse fields of finance, so that any choice of an investment medium will be your own, not the selection of the first salesman who happens to cross your path.

In essence, then, I show you how to declare your own war on poverty. In preparation you will learn how to force yourself to save with regularity a modest, pre-determined amount. This is just the beginning. The more significant battles are proper investment and the avoidance of needless commissions, which can be won by learning and applying certain rules. Victory comes when your savings increase many times over the total amount originally withdrawn from your earnings. It is within your reach.

Practical *information* about your personal finances and related legal rules is all I venture to present in this book. I do not *advise* you on the law or your legal rights; or the advisability for *you* to invest in, purchase, or sell or hold securities—whether specific or otherwise. Any worthwhile advice necessarily depends on the facts peculiar to your situation, of which I cannot be aware. My only advice to you, therefore, is as follows: When in need of advice you should consult your own attorney or investment adviser, as the case may be, who will be in a position to review your situation and render meaningful advice.

I do believe, however, that the information presented in this book —several unique points being unavailable elsewhere, as far as I know —can be of decided advantage, by affording you:

1. The unusual opportunity for an over-all look at essential principles in the difficult but potentially-profitable pursuit of accumulating a fortune; and

2. A background for you to more easily determine when you need additional information or should seek competent advice.

C.E.P.

CONTENTS

The Interest Deduction
Loss of Interest on Savings
Borrowing Advantages
The Dividend-Exclusion Loophole

Chapter Three BORROWING TO SAVE   **29**

Overcoming Aversion to Borrowing
Money Makes Money
Programs of Forced Saving
The Save-by-Borrowing Technique
Who Can Borrow?
Signature Loans
Passbook Loans
Life Insurance Loans
Loans by Small-Loan Companies
Margin Purchases of Stock
Calculating Interest Costs
Truth in Interest

Chapter Four 20,000,000 PART-TIME BUSINESSMEN   **49**

AT&T as a Part-Time Business
People's Capitalism
A Corporation Is a Person
Why Do Corporations Exist?
Absentee Ownership and Professional Management
Capital Structure and Distribution of Profits
How Much Is It Worth?
Going Public
Another Crash?
How You Buy Stocks

Which Costs Less: Par or Non-Par?

Words That Make Insurance Salesmen Shudder

For Those Who Have Bought Permanent Life
Insurance

Making Your Broker Like You

THE
SAVE-BY-BORROWING
TECHNIQUE

Chapter One

$1,000 BECOMES $1,024,000

I. HOW MUCH IS YOUR SAVINGS LOSS?

POPULAR WAYS TO LOSE YOUR SAVINGS

If you have the capacity to save and invest even a modest amount of money each week or month, the value of your ultimate accumulation could far exceed the *total amount* of wages or salary to be received by you during your lifetime.

If, on the other hand, you let a program of saving and investment become comparatively unimportant in your life, you forfeit the opportunity to realize your capital-accumulation potential. Well-planned and faithfully carried out, such a program can produce impressive growth and return—as we are about to see.

When reflecting upon how much capital you have been able to accumulate so far, think in terms of a businessman. He not only ascertains the amount of his profits, but tries to determine whether there were any business practices resulting in lower profits. In other words, you should examine your own saving and investment practices to determine whether you are experiencing any "savings losses." The chances are good to excellent that you are one of the unsuspecting millions suffering a needless loss of as much as $100,000 over the duration of an extended savings program.

Frankly, each of us bears a good part of the blame for opportunities missed when inefficiency is allowed to undermine the accumulation of savings. Other substantial contributors are the banking, mutual fund, securities, and life insurance industries, understandably promoting their respective interests to the possible detriment of the saver. These savings losses are all commonly experienced, but the important thing here is that they can be eliminated by the individual himself—and with surprising and highly profitable ease.

Generally speaking, a savings loss can be traced to one or more of the following three situations, each having achieved immense popularity among persons of minimal means attempting to accumulate wealth:

1. Failure to adhere to a voluntary savings program;

2. Payment of unnecessary commissions to life insurance salesmen, brokerage houses, and mutual fund salesmen;

3. Failure to appreciate the importance of rates of return on investments; and a misunderstanding of the nature of investments producing, on the average, a highly satisfactory rate of return.

THE HIGH COST OF SAVING

The second of the points above—by itself—can cause a loss of $33,-000 and more over the lifetime of a savings program. One thing is important for you to remember: Savings losses are not limited to the aggregate of unnecessary out-of-pocket expenses. Total savings losses can ultimately amount to many times more than the moneys originally wasted. If unnecessary sales and brokerage commissions total $75 per year, the *out-of-pocket loss* would add up to only $3,000 in 40 years. But the *accumulation loss* would then be in excess of $33,000. This assumes that, instead of throwing away the $75 each year, the victimized saver would have saved and invested the $75 each year at an average compound rate of return of 10% per year, after taxes. This long-range accumulation loss of $33,000—instead of the $3,000 out-of-pocket loss—represents the real cost to the saver, who makes a needless expenditure of $75 annually in the form of sales and brokerage commissions. By adhering to a well-reasoned savings plan, incorporating the most appropriate of available alternatives, you can protect yourself. Elimination of these needless expenses will allow you to avoid the high cost of saving.

Of particular importance to one who invests his savings in stocks is the cost of brokerage commissions. For savers following the Save-by-Borrowing technique, the cost of investment can be *reduced by two thirds*. And the investor can obtain the effect of immediate reinvestment of all dividends—no matter how small—at a brokerage cost of only 1%. This 1% is one sixth the maximum amount charged the more than 140,000 small investors making their purchases under the Monthly Investment Plan of the New York Stock Exchange.

Investors in mutual funds will be shocked to learn they have been paying needless sales charges, not knowing about the more than forty mutual funds charging no sales commission. For the convenience of the cost-conscious investor, the names and addresses of these "no-load" mutual funds are listed in Appendix A to this book.

Readers who have made mutual fund purchases under a *"contractual plan"* may be aghast to hear information which undoubtedly would have convinced them not to enter into such a transaction. Do *you* know what is so outrageous about a contractual plan and why it necessarily will produce a savings loss? The first of the two chapters on mutual funds gives you the answers.

The high cost of saving is a problem perhaps unknown to many, but resulting losses are of minor importance in comparison to the staggering savings losses caused by *improper investment orientation*. To maximize capital-accumulation possibilities, investments with a growth potential are clearly most desirable. For various reasons, savers have shied away from making the most appropriate investment decision. Hopefully, the reader will soon see how investments with a growth capacity can also have a fully adequate margin of safety for the long-run investor.

THE VOGUE OF COMPULSION

Compulsory saving is in vogue. The public has become accustomed to appeals by banks, life insurance companies, brokerage houses, and mutual funds for savers to follow a mandatory savings program of one kind or another. These appeals are convincing to the general public and, needless to say, profitable for the financial institutions.

A savings prospect can expect to be given many good reasons why he should save. All of us are continually receiving attractive mailing pieces, invitations, and brochures. Then, we are offered a painless method by which we will be "forced" to set aside periodically a certain amount of money.

An excellent illustration can be made with a typical life insurance

company. Suppose you respond to the company's newspaper advertisement by filling out a coupon and then mailing it to the company.
A life insurance salesman soon makes an appointment to see you.
In his sales presentation the salesman stresses that a primary virtue
of "permanent" life insurance is that you are forced to pay premiums, hence build up a *cash surrender value* (a measure of your
savings). The salesman explains that compulsory saving occurs
when, after receiving notice of premium due, the insured makes payment to the company. A portion of his premium payment is added
to the *"reserve"* for the policy, which increases the cash surrender
value of the policy after it has been in force, usually, for several
years. A policyholder feels morally obliged to pay the premium because he understands that his failure to pay could cause a lapse or
decrease of his insurance protection. By non-payment, an individual
assumes the risk that, in the event of poor health, he may not be
able to restore the original amount of protection except, possibly, at
a much higher premium.

Compulsory saving is a feature not found in life insurance alone.
Many other savings media employ some form of forced or automatic
withdrawals from current earnings. Payroll deductions encourage
employees to make periodic purchases of stock or United States
Savings Bonds. Also, an employee legally may claim fewer dependents than he is entitled to, causing him to overpay the withholding tax
and, hopefully, to establish his right to a tax refund, payable in the
succeeding year. Banks offer forced-savings programs such as Christmas Clubs (usually paying no interest, thus productive of savings
losses) and automatic transfers from checking to savings accounts.

One may also agree to make monthly purchases of mutual funds
over a protracted period, usually ten years. The mutual fund salesman deducts from the payments for the first twelve or thirteen months
a high percentage of the total commissions payable under the ten-
year plan. The sanction against premature termination of these buying programs is, the investor supposedly knows, an effective sales
commission of up to 50% of the total amount he has already paid
under the program.

Popularity of these and certain other methods of saving stems from
the compulsion they afford, forcing an individual to set aside a portion of his earnings. Many savers are painfully aware that, without

some degree of force, the slightest excuse could cause a setback which would prevent them from reaching their savings goals.

HOW TO SAVE BY BORROWING

A Save-by-Borrower also makes use of a compulsory system of saving, but one much more effective. After borrowing the amount intended to be saved during the next year, he invests the loan proceeds. By putting the "savings" out of reach, he is forced to pay off the loan out of current earnings, which completes the saving process. Borrowing to save is simple and quite effective. You may know people who are doing it. Ask *them*.

By the Save-by-Borrowing process you can declare your own war on poverty—and why not? Who else could do the best job? Attainment of financial independence marks the end of battle. But what is financial independence? Some people call it the 10th Multiple.

II. YOUR 10TH-MULTIPLE POTENTIAL

THE OLDEST MULTIPLE

Years ago an old, wise man performed a brave deed when he saved Rex, his beloved king, from certain death. As a reward, Rex instructed the ancient philosopher to make one reasonable request, which Rex vowed to fulfill. Several days later, the old man submitted his request. Rex, his face flushed with anger, demanded to know why the philosopher seemed to treat the generous offer with such lightness.

With seriousness befitting the occasion, the old man made assurances that he had not asked for less than adequate recompense. Accepting his word, Rex ordered that the old man be given his reward. Each day during February, Rex's exchequer paid the wise man a sum of money, beginning with one cent on February 1. Each payment thereafter was double the amount paid on the preceding day. On the last day of February, the philosopher received his twenty-eighth and final payment, the princely sum of $1,342,177.28, to the complete satisfaction of both sovereign and subject. Apocryphal it may be, but the story has innumerable counterparts in real life, one of which could concern you.

THE 10TH MULTIPLE AND COMPOUND MAGIC

Assume you have savings which are invested to produce an annual income of 4%. If the 4% return is *compounded by periodic reinvestment,* your savings in due course will undergo one or more doublings in value. As would be expected, any increase in the rate of return will increase the rapidity with which each doubling will take place. A descriptive name for this process of periodic reinvestment is Compound Magic.

Starting with only $1,000, Compound Magic can do astounding things for you. Let us invest $1,000 of your savings to produce an investment income. Whenever such income is received we immediately reinvest it, to make your investment grow until there is a doubling of your original $1,000 investment. If a doubling occurs ten times during your lifetime, it will make a millionaire out of you. Each of these doublings is hereafter referred to as a Multiple. Our goal, as shown below, is the 10th Multiple.

GOAL OF SAVE-BY-BORROWERS

The 10 Multiples	Total Accumulation
–	$ 1,000
1st	2,000
2nd	4,000
3rd	8,000
4th	16,000
5th	32,000
6th	64,000
7th	128,000
8th	256,000
9th	512,000
10th	1,024,000

An excellent opportunity exists for you to become wealthy, to acquire riches valued at the 10th Multiple. What do you need to get started?

- A willingness and earning capacity to set aside a comparatively modest sum from current earnings, say $20 per week;
- High investment returns, produced by adherence to sound investment practices, which you must undertake to learn; and
- A life span of sufficient length.

TWO THINGS YOU MUST HAVE

A confirmed skeptic may wish to ask, "How is it possible for the average person to reach all ten of the Multiples?"

The answer is easily given. It is only a matter of time and yield. A saver who sets his sights on the 10th Multiple must keep these two factors in mind. Time is something over which the investor has little control. Yield is different. Anyone, by intelligent investment, has an opportunity to obtain high investment returns or yields; and high yields, it should be remembered, are an absolute must for the investor who expects to attain the 10th Multiple.

Yield is ordinarily defined as the ratio of annual investment income to the amount invested, expressed as a percentage, and can be computed by dividing income by the cost or value of the investment. A $50 investment which returns $5 each year to the investor yields 10% per year. In the case of a loan, the lender's yield is also expressed as a rate of interest, such as 4% per annum, applied against the principal amount of the loan.

Gambling George always obtains high yields, having more than an average amount of luck. One long evening, with original capital of only $100, he won $1,000 in a friendly poker game. Desiring safety of his capital for a change, George deposited his winnings in a bank and was pleased to learn that the bank would pay him interest of 4% per annum, compounded annually. At the end of a full year, George rushed to the bank to present his bank book to a teller, who credited the account with $40. This amount represented 4% interest on the $1,000 deposit, paid by the bank for the privilege of using George's money during the year.

As a result of the interest payment, George's bank balance was increased to $1,040. At the end of the following year the bank paid the 4% interest on the $1,040 balance. This interest payment increased George's savings by $41.60, boosting his bank balance to $1,081.60. By this process, compounding or reinvestment of George's savings took place. George was beginning to learn that, when interest is compounded, interest payments are added to the amount on deposit so that the next interest payment will be a higher dollar amount, computed on the basis of the increased bank balance.

As an investor, you must take full advantage of Compound Magic if you are to achieve the 10th Multiple. Particularly, investment income (such as interest and dividends) should not be treated as spendable income. Assuming no such leakage in your accumulation program, reinvestment of investment income will afford you an excellent opportunity to achieve your savings goal. Although this compounding process is far from new, too many savers fail to realize its full potential. Before being exposed to the value of compounding, the reader should understand what amount we will be compounding.

A COMMON INVESTMENT FALLACY

Unless otherwise stated, all yields, interest, and rates of return mentioned hereafter are compounded annually. *The synonyms "yield" and "rate of return" include appreciation, if any, in capital value of the investment.* Keep this in mind. Any yield or rate of return for common stock investments includes any annual increase (or decrease) in market value of the stock as well as any distribution of dividends by the corporation. Inclusion of capital appreciation in the foregoing definition deviates from general usage, but is not illogical. In most instances of investment in common stocks, to cite only one example, the greater part of the profit is attributable to increases in capital value. For many investors it is fallacy, therefore, to be concerned almost wholly with the dividend rate rather than the prospects for capital growth.

THE COMPROMISE TAX

It would be utterly unrealistic to compound an anticipated investment return without prior deduction of income taxes expected to be paid. But what rate of tax should we use, to make our computations meaningful for the greatest number of readers? Let's work out some kind of compromise tax rate.

The average reader, we assume, will have his next dollar of *ordinary income* (such as salary, dividends, and interest) taxed at the rate of 20%. (A married couple having taxable income—after appropriate deductions and exemptions—of $8,000 to $12,000 would pay 22%. Assuming the couple are entitled to four $600 exemptions and have tax deductions amounting to 10%, their pre-tax income would range from about $11,600 to $16,000 per year.) Capital gains on investments held longer than six months ("long-term capital gains") would be taxed at one half the rate, or 10%. Accordingly, a Compromise Tax of 15% on a yield consisting both of ordinary income and long-term capital gains seems supportable.

Actually, our Compromise Tax applies to an even higher ordinary income tax bracket. A married couple filing a joint return would pay a 25% tax on ordinary income falling in the $12,000 to $16,000 tax bracket. Long-term capital gains would be taxed, then, at $12\frac{1}{2}\%$. Assuming that at least two thirds of the yield would be capital gains taxable at the $12\frac{1}{2}\%$ rate, the appropriate Compromise Tax would be no more than $16\frac{2}{3}\%$ ($\frac{1}{3} \times 25 + \frac{2}{3} \times 12.5$). But, as we shall see, $16\frac{2}{3}\%$ may be too much. Let the couple use instead the 15% Compromise Tax rate (which assumes contrary to fact a 20% tax on their next dollar of ordinary income).

To see how this works, assume that early in the program they obtain a return of $300 ($100 in taxable dividends and a $200 unrealized increase in capital value). The Compromise Tax of 15% would be deducted, amounting to $45. But only $25 would be used to meet the current tax liability, a 25% tax on the $100 of ordinary income. The remainder, $20, would be added to a reserve for future tax liabilities and accumulated for later payment of the $25 tax on the $200 of long-term capital gains.

A married couple below the $12,000 to $16,000 bracket at the outset of their savings and investment program may ultimately exceed such bracket, owing in part to increased investment income, *without* destroying the validity of the 15% Compromise Tax. In view of the preceding, a greater portion of the 15% Compromise Tax would be an excess deduction and, when added to the tax reserve and accumulated by investment compounding, could be drawn upon in later years when the tax bracket exceeded $16,000.

Further discussion of the Compromise Tax may be found in Appendix B, together with a schedule of applicable rates for federal income taxes. The discussion attempts to further justify the 15% Compromise Tax. Perhaps you are already convinced, but readers questioning any part of the preceding analysis of the Compromise Tax may wish to read the annexed material at some point.

To bring Gambling George's situation in line with our tax discussion, we must deduct $8 from the $40 of interest credited to his $1,000 savings account. This adjustment reflects the assumed 20% tax George was required to pay on the $40 of investment income. Payment of the tax reduced the yield to 3.2% after taxes; therefore, his savings account at the end of the first year should be increased by only $32, to $1,032. At the end of the second year, the 4% interest on $1,032 would amount to $41.28 and the account would be increased temporarily to $1,073.28. After payment of the 20% tax, amounting to $8.26, his bank balance would be reduced to a net $1,065.02.

YOUR EXPECTATIONS

Yield is a crucial factor in a modest savings and investment program to reach the 10th Multiple. Yield by itself means little, however, without a sufficient length of time.

If the limitations on time are not taken into account, anyone would be able to attain the goal of the 10th Multiple. Let us take a cautious individual who deposits his annual savings of $1,000 in a savings account which yields 4%. Should he live so long, he will become a millionaire at the end of 95 years, accumulating his fortune with a minimum of risk. Yet, who can reasonably expect to live 95 more years, even if he were willing to wait? He should assume that he will have no longer than an average remaining life span in which to achieve his goal. Even a newborn white female, who has the longest life expectancy, can expect to live only 74 years or so. (Your own anticipated life span may be determined from the abbreviated life-expectancy table [ages 21 to 50], based on the 1960 federal census, set forth in Appendix C to this book.)

Knowing that he cannot rely upon any significant extension of time, an individual must concentrate on *maximizing* his investment yield if he is to attain his savings goal. To a greater extent, this holds true for the person who sets his own time limit to become affluent enough to enjoy later years without worry.

To illustrate the power of yield: Assume Gambling George took his $1,000 out of the poker game and used the money to purchase real estate or common stocks. By skillful investment and reinvestment—and not a little bit of luck—it is possible for George to obtain an after-tax yield of 20% per year, compounded annually. ("Yield," as said before, includes dividends and capital appreciation.) He would experience one Multiple every 3.8 years and would accumulate almost $1,024,000 in 38 years. All this conceivably could be done with George's original investment of $1,000. It may not be very *likely* to happen—but it is possible.

If, in January 1954, George had been shrewd (or lucky) enough to invest in International Business Machines, he would have obtained, in the following 10-year period, a compound annual return of about 24.9%, after taxes. With an investment in Radio Corporation of America or Sears, Roebuck, the return would have been lower, about 18.5% or 19.3%, after taxes. These 3 stocks were the best performers among the 20 most popular with investors following the Monthly Investment Plan—an average return of 20.9% during the 10-year period.

STOP SAVING? YOU MUST BE CRAZY!

Rewards are *greater* for persons who can stick to their guns. By saving and investing $1,000 each year, you can obtain your goal of the 10th Multiple in only 30 years. The chart below illustrates the growth of your savings and affords a comparison of annual saving and investment ("Annual $1,000") with a one-shot investment of $1,000 ("Single $1,000").

Throughout this book we assume, unless it is otherwise stated, that savings earn no return during their year of accumulation. Thus, the chart shows that savings of $1,000 during the first year of the savings program will have only a $1,000 value at the end of the first year; thereafter, the $1,000 is assumed to earn the full return.

Examining the figures, we can see that $1,000 saved each year ("Annual $1,000"), when invested to yield 20%, would take the saver to the 5th Multiple at the end of 11 years. For the first 11 years, Multiple achievement is substantially faster than attainment of Multiples under the "Single $1,000" investment plan. Upon reaching the 5th Multiple, however, there is a leveling off.

Look again at the chart. The two middle columns, at their intersection with the 5th Multiple line (indicated by an asterisk), reveal

**COMPARISON OF SINGLE $1,000 AND ANNUAL $1,000
INVESTMENT AT COMPOUND RATE OF 20% PER ANNUM**

		Single $1,000				Annual $1,000		
Multi-ples	Total Ac-cumulation	At End of Year	No. of Years to Next Multi-ple	No. of Years to 10th Multi-ple		No. of Years to 10th Multi-ple	No. of Years to Next Multi-ple	At End of Year
–	$ 1,000	1.0	3.8	38.0		28.2	.8	1.0
1st	2,000	4.8	3.8	34.2		27.4	1.4	1.8
2nd	4,000	8.6	3.8	30.4		26.0	2.0	3.2
3rd	8,000	12.4	3.8	26.6		24.0	2.7	5.2
4th	16,000	16.2	3.8	22.8		21.3	3.1	7.9
5th	32,000	20.0	3.8	19.0	★	18.2	3.4	11.0
6th	64,000	23.8	3.8	15.2		14.9	3.6	14.4
7th	128,000	27.6	3.8	11.4		11.2	3.7	18.0
8th	256,000	31.4	3.8	7.6		7.5	3.7	21.7
9th	512,000	35.2	3.8	3.8		3.8	3.8	25.4
10th	1,024,000	39.0						29.2

this phenomenon. Starting together from the beginning, the Annual $1,000 plan will produce many thousands of dollars in excess of the Single $1,000 plan during the same investment period. But, starting at the 5th Multiple, the investment programs will achieve the 10-Multiple goal in 18.2 or 19.0 additional years, less than a year apart. We can go one step further. If both plans start together at the 4th Multiple ($16,000), completion of the 10 Multiples will be only 1.5 years apart, approximately.

Observant readers should be asking at this point, "What advantage is there in continuing to save $1,000 each year after an investor reaches the 4th or 5th Multiple?"

"Almost none" is the answer. After achievement of the 4th or 5th Multiple, assuming continuation of the 20% return, additional saving of $1,000 per year is not necessary as a practical matter. Annual savings after the 4th or 5th Multiple are relatively insignificant in comparison to the assumed annual investment return. Assuming high yields, the saving of $1,000 each year has a substantial effect upon Multiple accomplishment in only the earliest years of the 10-Multiple program. In the first through fourth years, the $1,000 in annual savings adds more to the accumulation than does the investment yield for the respective years. In later years, however, the $1,000 in savings becomes increasingly insignificant.

An individual who maintains an average rate of return of 20% has good reason to stop saving after 7.9 years, upon reaching the 4th Multiple ($16,000) or 11 years, if he is conservative by nature, upon achieving the 5th Multiple ($32,000). His switch to a non-saving investment program is equivalent to adopting a Single $1,000 investment program, but jumping in at the 4th or 5th Multiple. No substantial delay in reaching the 10th Multiple would be caused by such change from a saving to a non-saving investment program.

Saving becomes unnecessary, therefore, once an individual has a certain amount of capital, let us say $16,000 or $32,000. For this to be true, however, he must be able to maintain a high rate of return on his investments, say 20%. With this in mind, an individual should strive to reach the 4th or 5th Multiple as soon as possible. When this is accomplished, withdrawal from current earnings can cease and the individual is free to enjoy the full benefits of his employment compensation, having already provided for his future.

The only way to get this 20% yield is by purchasing sound investments with a good potential for capital appreciation. Diligent study of investments and proper application of the acquired principles will afford an individual a good opportunity to exceed the average common stock yield which has been, over the 14-year period ending 1964, approximately 12% after taxes, compounded annually.

When a person's investments yield only 10% per annum, he can stop saving at the end of 21 years, when he reaches the 6th Multiple ($64,000). Only 1⅛ extra years would be added to his 10-Multiple program, assuming continuation of the 10% yield. Look at the chart below to see where the two middle columns intersect the 6th Multiple line (indicated by an asterisk). It can be seen that the Single $1,000 investment plan has 29.08 years remaining, whereas Annual $1,000 has only 27.7 years left.

No guarantees can be made that you will be able to maintain a yield of 20% by investing in common stocks or even real estate. Some people are able to realize higher returns, but the average yield is

COMPARISON OF SINGLE $1,000 AND ANNUAL $1,000 INVESTMENT AT COMPOUND RATE OF 10% PER ANNUM

		Single $1,000			Annual $1,000		
Multi-ples	Total Ac-cumulation	At End of Year	Years to Next Multi-ple	Years to 10th Multi-ple	Years to 10th Multi-ple	Years to Next Multi-ple	At End of Year
–	$ 1,000	1.00	7.27	72.70	47.7	.9	1.0
1st	2,000	8.27	7.27	65.43	46.8	1.6	1.9
2nd	4,000	15.54	7.27	58.16	45.2	2.7	3.5
3rd	8,000	22.81	7.27	50.89	42.5	3.8	6.2
4th	16,000	30.08	7.27	43.62	37.7	5.1	10.0
5th	32,000	37.35	7.27	36.35	33.6	5.9	15.1
6th	64,000	44.62	7.27	29.08 ★	27.7	6.5	21.0
7th	128,000	51.89	7.27	21.81	21.2	6.9	27.5
8th	256,000	59.16	7.27	14.54	14.3	7.1	34.4
9th	512,000	66.43	7.27	7.27	7.2	7.2	41.5
10th	1,024,000	73.70					48.7

lower, at least for common stocks. To a very considerable extent, however, *you can exercise some control over your investment yields, through the skill with which you pursue opportunities in common stock or other equity investments.* A yield of 20% has been emphasized only as an indication of the opportunity which exists for savers who are willing to obtain high returns for taking some investment risks. Yields throughout this book are used for illustrative purposes only—and should be so regarded. Some people will do better, others will do worse. What you will do cannot be known until you have done it.

$1,000,000 DIFFERENCE

A thousand dollars saved each year and invested to yield 20% will accomplish the 10th Multiple in only 29.2 years. Compare this with $1,000 per year invested in permanent life insurance (the kind having an increasing cash surrender value). Life insurance investments generally yield about 3%. At the end of 29.2 years, the insured's accumulated savings would be approximately $46,000. This amount is some $8,000 less than the results achieved when equal amounts are deposited in a savings account which yields 4% per year; and almost $1,000,000 less than the results achieved when equal amounts are invested to produce a 20% rate of return.

YOUR SAVINGS EXPECTANCY AND THE INVESTMENT SPECTRUM

You may wish to estimate your present capacity to accumulate capital. But remember, it is at best an exceedingly rough guess, based only on past rates of return, with absolutely no guarantees for the future.

First, determine the timing of your individual investment program, guided by the life expectancy table referred to. Then, make a selection from the Investment Spectrum, below, where the various categories of investments are listed in order of descending yields. If your life expectancy is longer than the years required to reach the 10th Multiple, you have, based on past experience, an opportunity to become a millionaire. This assumes, of course, that you do your share in faithfully carrying out a $1,000 annual savings program.

When making your estimate, remember to take into account the Multiple reflecting your present investment worth. If you are now at the 4th Multiple ($16,000) you are 40% of the way up the ladder. However, because the first few Multiples arrive more quickly, it will take you in excess of 60% of the designated number of years.

If you are planning to save and invest, say, only $500 per year, your program would *not* take twice as long. Instead, the value of your *10th* Multiple is only half as much as the investment value indicated on the spectrum. In other words, only $512,000. You would need, therefore, an 11th Multiple to bring you up to $1,024,000, taking a few more years, depending on the rate of return.

An interested reader may desire to estimate his capital accumulation potential for an investment program unrelated in years or return to any listed in the Investment Spectrum. Appendix D may prove useful, containing a chart showing the accumulation value at 5 to 40 years for one who saves and invests $1,000 per year (or any other amount) and is able to maintain an average return, after taxes, ranging from 8% to 15% per year, compounded annually.

In the case of a Single $1,000 program, there is a very practical method—often called the "Rule of 70–72"—to estimate how long it would take for a sum of money to double in value if invested at a specified rate of return. (Ten doublings, of course, would take 10 times as long.) Divide the return into 70 or 72, whichever is more

INVESTMENT SPECTRUM

OPPORTUNITIES TO ACHIEVE THE 10TH MULTIPLE BY
ANNUAL $1,000 INVESTMENT AND REINVESTMENT OF
NET YIELD AFTER DEDUCTION FOR PAYMENT OF
ASSUMED 0%, 15%, OR 20% INCOME TAX

Type of Investment		Annual Yield Before Taxes	Compounded Annual Yield After Taxes	Investment Value at End of 43 Yrs.	Years to Achieve 10th Multiple
Cash		0%	0%	$ 43,000	1,024
Permanent Life Insurance	(1)	3.0	3.0	85,000	117
Municipal Bonds	(3)	3.6	3.6	99,000	102
Commercial Savings Account	(2)	4.0	3.2	90,000	112
U. S. Savings Bonds	(2)	4.15	3.3	91,000	111
Mutual Savings Bank Account	(2)	4.5	3.6	99,000	102
Savings and Loan Account	(2)	4.5	3.6	99,000	102
Preferred Stock	(2) (4)	4.5	3.6	99,000	102
U. S. Government Bonds	(2)	5.0	4.0	110,000	96
Corporate Bonds	(2) (4)	5.0	4.0	110,000	96
Convertible Debentures	(2) (4)	5.6	4.5	125,000	88
First Real Estate Mortgages	(2)	5.75	4.6	132,000	86
Real Estate Syndicate Shares	(5)	10.6	9.0	441,000	53
Mutual Funds	(5)	11.8	10.0	592,000	49
Common Stocks	(5)	14.1	12.0	1,081,000	43
Real Estate Transactions	(5)	26.4	22.5	28,000,000	–
Speculation in Stocks	(5)	29.4	25.0	59,000,000	–

(1) 0% Tax, ordinarily escaping the income tax.
(2) 20% Tax—Ordinary Income.
(3) 0% Tax—Tax-exempt Income.
(4) Equity feature, if any, not taken into account.
(5) 15% Tax—Long-term Capital Gains and Ordinary Income.

convenient. For example, $1,000 invested at 12% per year will become $2,000 in about 6 years (72 divided by 12). The 10th Multiple would take 10 times as long to achieve—60 years, as a close approximation.

The Investment Spectrum is not infallible. At the top of the spectrum the yields are fairly accurate; in the middle they are a reasonable approximation; but at and near the end of the list, where the indicated yields are highest, accuracy is impossible to achieve. The yield for common stocks, for example, being based on estimated performance in 14 preceding years, is at best only an indication of possibilities for the more fortunate investors.

During the 10-year period 1951–60, the average common stock listed on the New York Stock Exchange produced a yield (including dividends and appreciation in capital value) of about 14.8% before taxes or 12.5% after payment of the assumed 15% tax. This average return was not maintained during the 4-year period 1961–64. Standard & Poor's Index of 425 industrial common stocks listed on the New York Stock Exchange is highly representative of the average stock listed on the NYSE. During 1961–64, S&P's Index moved from 61.49 to 89.62, for an average compound rate of growth of about 10% per year, before taxes. Annual dividends averaged about 3% (before taxes). Therefore, the total compound annual return was about 13% before taxes—11% after deduction of the 15% Compromise Tax. Giving 10 units of weight to the 10-year, 12.5% return and 4 units to the 4-year, 11% return, we estimate a 12% annual compound return, after taxes, for the average industrial common stock listed on the NYSE, during the 14-year period ending in December, 1964. (The 12% figure was calculated as follows: $10 \times 12.5 + 4 \times 11 \div 14$.)

An investment in a typical common stock mutual fund would not have fared as well. Most funds have some uninvested assets: money from the sale of new shares and cash to be used for the repurchase of outstanding shares. A percentage of fund assets may be invested in "safe" securities, producing low yields, especially near market peaks. Also, management fees and expenses amount each year to about 1% of the value of the assets held by the fund. It is assumed, accordingly, that during 1951–64 an average common stock mutual fund had a yield of 10% after taxes, two percentage points below the indicated common stock yield. Sales commissions, if any, were not taken into account.

Debentures (which are unsecured bonds) and preferred stocks were assigned their average yields without any consideration of the possibility of capital appreciation resulting from any rights to convert to common stock. The actual yields, therefore, may be substantially higher than indicated.

Real estate syndications are business organizations set up to handle large real estate transactions. An individual can invest a comparatively small amount in a sizable real estate deal by purchasing a fractional interest in a syndication. An advantage to this type of investment is that the investor need not be (nor is he allowed to be) concerned with conduct of the transactions or management of the properties. In many instances 10% or 11% is the pre-tax yield (including capital appreciation).

Real estate returns are higher when an individual carries out the transactions himself. But to get those returns he must spend considerable time and possess a great deal of know-how. A yield of 22.5% (after taxes) was selected to reflect a combination of pure investment return and adequate compensation for services to be rendered by the investor. Had the investment been made by purchase of syndicate shares, the services would have been rendered by the syndicators or insiders, who would have been well compensated. Although there are real estate investors who average a 22.5% yield or better, no statistics are available, apparently, which reflect an average rate of return. The indicated yield of 22.5% is no more than an educated guess. By proper investment technique—and good fortune—however, a 22.5% yield can be obtained, there is no doubt.

Speculation in stocks occurs when an individual buys stocks to hold for a short period, in an attempt to make quick profits. Yield for this activity was arbitrarily set at 25% and should be considered under no circumstances an average return. Rewards and risks are greater in speculation than in investment in stocks for the long run. Anyway, an average return means little to you when, in one year, you lose 75% of your capital; and somebody else, to balance your loss and maintain the market average, obtains a return of 75%.

What the Investment Spectrum reveals is that higher yields are usually obtained at the cost of increased risks. Cash (which we consider an investment having no yield) and U. S. Savings Bonds are among the safest ways to invest your money, disregarding the possibilities of loss and theft. Corporate bonds, debentures, and preferred stocks do fluctuate in value to reflect changing interest rates, to discount possibilities that the principal amount invested will not be returned, and to reflect the changing value of any privileges to convert into common stock. Common stock investments can be expected to produce even greater fluctuations in value. But in the long run the stock market averages have always gone up and investors in common stocks have been able to achieve many Multiples.

After reading this book you must decide for yourself whether a certain amount of risk is desirable—in view of the possible rewards. Many people have so decided and have made tremendous profits. Of course there are others who have lost their proverbial shirts, especially during the Great Depression. An intelligent investor can minimize his risk while obtaining the higher yields. To do this he must understand and apply basic principles of investment. Two of the most important principles, as we will see, are *diversification* and *dollar-cost averaging*.

"What has the author himself been able to do with his Save-by-Borrowing program?" This is a question which, understandably, the reader may have on his mind.

The answer: As of the date of this book's publication, I have not achieved the 10th Multiple; in fact, I'm not even close. But this obviously is a goal set up for the future and pursued in the firm belief that given sufficient time it will be reached. I could have waited until reaching my goal, but then the book would probably be of little use to *you*.

Investment is a lifetime endeavor, and the investor has much to learn. Mistakes he will always make, but profits can be derived even from mistakes. And to encourage yourself along the way, recall that just $1,000 doubled 10 times amounts to $1,024,000.

Let's get down to business without any further preliminaries. One good way to avoid savings losses is to invest in stocks without paying any brokerage commissions.

Chapter Two

BUYING STOCKS
WITHOUT PAYING
BROKERAGE COMMISSIONS

FIRST-YEAR EXPENSES AND PROFITS

To many people, borrowing and investing bring to mind the "burdensome" costs of interest and brokerage commissions. The truth of the matter is that Save-by-Borrowers are able to avoid these expenses and obtain an extremely compulsory method of saving *at no net cost* to themselves.

In fact, there will be, on the average, a $47 "first-year" profit on each $1,000 loan, assuming a 12% compound annual return. This profit is derived after making provision for payment of interest, income taxes, brokerage commissions and odd-lot investment cost (known as the "odd-lot differential," to be described later) and taking into account the loss of an alternative investment opportunity. This repeating first-year profit is produced during each twelve-month period of loan repayment. No tricks are involved. It is simply a matter of *cost accounting*. Also, we will see the profitable operation of a certain tax "loophole."

In this book we assume that 100% of the $1,000 in annual savings (the savings *unreduced* by brokerage commissions or odd-lot differential) will earn the average rate of return. This is a proper assumption because, when using the Save-by-Borrowing procedure, the average investor pays no net brokerage commissions or odd-lot differential. In fact, he is left with a profit.

Furthermore, we have already seen that valuations in this book based on the investment of $1,000 each year assume that no return will be earned on the $1,000 during the year it is saved. Therefore, those first-year profits described in this chapter are extra—supplemental to the anticipated value of the $1,000 annual savings and investment program.

BORROWING AND BUYING

Assume you borrow $1,000 by means of a signature loan—a loan secured by nothing but your signature—which is to be repaid in twelve equal monthly installments of principal and interest. On the basis of a 4¾% "discount" loan, you will pay about $50 to obtain a net loan of $1,000. The true annual rate of interest is about 9.2%. A more elaborate discussion of borrowing is contained in the next chapter.

After depositing the $1,000 of borrowed funds in your checking account, you open a brokerage account with a stockbroker in whom you have a great deal of well-founded confidence. As a precaution, nevertheless, payment for your stock purchase will be made by personal check. The return of your canceled check will provide you automatically with a receipt for payment.

A discussion with your broker leads you to agree that the common stock of ABC Corporation, a hypothetical company, suits your needs.[1] Let us say that the current market price of the stock is $25 per share.

ABC Corporation now pays its common shareholders an aggregate annual dividend of $1.00 per share. Based upon the present price, the stock pays an annual cash dividend of 4%.[2] Every three months, therefore, each stockholder becomes entitled to receive a dividend check or checks amounting to 25 cents for each share of ABC stock he owns.

Other factors, such as a reasonable price-earnings ratio of 15 to 1, an excellent history of stock dividends and splits, an aggressive man-

[1] To prevent undue complexity, purchase of only one stock is assumed.
[2] The pre-tax dividend rate seldom will be exactly 4% per year and slight adjustments of the computations presented here will often be required. At the end of 1964, for example, the average dividend rate for dividend-paying stocks listed on the New York Stock Exchange was 3.3%, before taxes. The average year-end dividend rate for the 10-year period ending in 1964 is 4.2%.

agement, and an expanding industry, further convince you to buy the stock.

Your broker, knowing that you have about $1,000 to invest, suggests that you purchase 40 shares of ABC stock. You agree, and he immediately puts in an order to purchase this number for your account.

Since your order is executed at $25 per share, the total purchase price for the 40 shares is $1,000, plus an odd-lot differential of $\frac{1}{8}$ of one point (12$\frac{1}{2}$ cents) per share, amounting to $5 on the 40 shares. To these amounts your broker adds his commission, slightly more than $15. The total cost to make your $1,000 stock purchase, we see, comes to about $1,020.

So far, you have incurred $50 in interest expense and $20 in combined brokerage commission and odd-lot differential. But not for long. Investment yield and certain tax advantages should be given consideration.

THE INTEREST DEDUCTION

A taxpayer who, for federal income tax purposes, elects to take the 10% *standard* deduction does not benefit from the *interest* deduction. On the other hand, he will find an advantage to itemizing his deductions when these exceed the standard deduction of 10% of his adjusted gross income or $1,000, whichever is the lesser. Otherwise, the value of the $50 tax deduction for interest paid is lost.

When taken, the $50 interest-payment deduction generates a tax saving of $10, using the tax rate on ordinary income of 20%, assumed in Chapter One. As a consequence of using this deduction, the net cost of interest will be only $40.

LOSS OF INTEREST ON SAVINGS

We must not overlook the fact that the individual, instead of saving by borrowing, could have elected to save by *depositing* his twelve monthly payments in a savings bank account. By choosing not to do so, the Save-by-Borrower misses out on about $16 in bank interest, before taxes. We assume that the savings bank has a declared interest (or dividend) rate of 4.25% per year and the depositor would have his $1,000 in aggregate annual savings on interest-bearing deposit for an average of three eighths of a year.[3] Then, from the $16 of lost interest payments we should deduct the 20% assumed tax on ordinary income, reducing the interest loss to about $13.[4]

So far, to borrow and invest $1,000, we have seen a total economic cost of $73, as follows:

Net interest expense in taking out your loan	$40
Brokerage commission	15
Savings deposit interest loss	13
Odd-lot differential cost	5
	$73

Mentally circle this $73 amount. We will be coming back to it shortly.

BORROWING ADVANTAGES

Our Save-by-Borrower has enough foresight to select a stock which will produce the 12% rate of return. Thus, the stock will yield (including dividends and capital appreciation), after taxes, $120 on the $1,000 investment during the first year.

From this $120 we subtract the $73 mentioned previously (representing the total economic cost), leaving *a total economic profit of $47 for the borrowing year.*

By reason of the borrowing procedure, therefore, we see that certain advantages will accrue to you each year, when a $1,000 loan is being repaid. If you follow the technique, borrowing will do the following:

1. Make your interest payment of $40 net;
2. Pay the $15 brokerage commission;

[3] To be entitled to interest, savings must frequently be kept on deposit for a stipulated minimum period. We assume the savings bank requires three months. Thus, savings for the first quarter of the year will earn interest for only three quarters of a year. Second quarter-year savings will earn interest for only one half of a year. Third-quarter savings will earn interest for only one quarter of a year. And no interest will be earned by the savings for the fourth quarter. In effect, therefore, the saver will receive interest of 4.25% (before taxes) on $1,000 for only three eighths of a year ($\frac{1}{4}$ times the aggregate of $\frac{3}{4}$ plus $\frac{2}{4}$ plus $\frac{1}{4}$). To complete the computations, $\frac{3}{8}$ of 4.25% equals almost 1.6%—or $16 on $1,000.

[4] Interest rates are subject to change. An increase of savings account interest (before taxes) from 4.25% to 5%, for example, would increase the $13 net annual loss of interest to $15. Borrowing at 6% instead of 4¾% would increase the net interest expense from $40 to $48.

3. Pay the $5 cost of the odd-lot differential;

4. Reimburse you for the $13 net loss of interest which could have been earned by the accumulation of your savings in a savings account until the end of each year;

5. Provide you with an average, additional net profit of $47;

6. Most important of all, force you to save; and

7. Provide certain other advantages, set forth in this chapter and elsewhere in this book.

This $47 represents the net profit remaining at the end of the borrowing year, *after all costs incidental to borrowing and investing have been paid*. In 35 years, the annual $47 first-year profit could grow to $20,300, if invested at the rate of 12% per year, after taxes, compounded annually.

Actually, this is an understatement of the value of the Save-by-Borrowing process. The person who accumulates the $1,000 in a savings account, to be withdrawn to purchase stock at the year's end, will pay the same $15 brokerage commission and $5 odd-lot differential. Therefore, the Save-by-Borrowing process, in comparison to the savings-account process, produces an average annual net profit of $67. The value of this $67 at the end of 35 years, if invested at the after-tax rate of 12%, will amount to $28,900. *This* is the real profit to be obtained by the Save-by-Borrowing method.

Rates of return cannot be guaranteed, and, therefore, the reader may be wondering at what rate of return the borrowing operation would cease to be more profitable than using the savings-account method to accumulate the $1,000 with which to make the annual stock purchase. With an after-tax yield of 5.3%, the Save-by-Borrower will be at the break-even point if he takes an itemized tax deduction for the $50 in interest paid. If, however, the Save-by-Borrower chooses not to itemize his deductions, the break-even point will be higher, about 6.3%. (With a 6% installment loan and banks paying 5% interest, the two break-even points would be 6.3% and 7.5%.)

THE DIVIDEND-EXCLUSION LOOPHOLE

As an incentive for you to invest in stocks, the federal government has conveniently provided a certain tax "loophole." The dividend-exclusion loophole provides a profit, but only to persons who purchase stocks.[5] Borrowing is not essential to create the profit; however, to the extent he employs the Save-by-Borrowing method, a new investor in stocks can maximize his dividend-exclusion profits.

We now make certain assumptions. You are just beginning to apply our method and will receive in the current year no cash dividends from stock investments other than the $40 to be paid by ABC Corporation.

The dividend-exclusion loophole makes the $40 dividend payment non-taxable. A taxpayer filing an individual tax return has a $100 (maximum) annual dividend exclusion; and a married couple filing a joint tax return has a $200 (maximum) annual dividend exclusion.[6]

A related loophole: The interest deduction is available to Save-by-Borrowers even though the interest is paid to borrow money which is used to produce, as it turns out, non-taxable dividend income. No such interest deduction would be allowed, on the other hand, if the borrowed money were used to purchase investments producing wholly tax-exempt income, as in the case of tax-exempt municipal bonds.

The non-taxable status of the $40 dividend payment attributable to the $1,000 of borrowed money (hence a Save-by-Borrowing profit) does not last forever. It is operative *as to borrowing-attributable dividends* for almost two full years for individuals filing an individual tax return; and a little less than four full years for married couples filing a joint tax return. Thereafter, the borrowing-attributable dividends will be taxable.

Thus, during the first few years of a Save-by-Borrowing program, the dividend-exclusion loophole will increase the annual net profit (of $47) by the amount of the tax saving (up to $20 or $40). Part of this saving comes from the dividends produced by money borrowed to make the most recent annual stock purchase; and the other part comes from investments purchased by borrowed funds which have been repaid.

In comparison to a fixed-dollar investor who permanently accumulates his savings in a savings account, an individual Save-by-

[5] Dividends paid on deposits in a savings account do not qualify for this exclusion.
[6] The $200 maximum exclusion for a married couple assumes that each spouse has received at least $100 in dividend income.

Borrower's first-year dividend exclusion of $40 produces an $8 tax saving in the first year and almost $17 in the second year. In each succeeding year the tax saving amounts to $20. For married couples there will be a tax saving of $8 in the first year and more each succeeding year until a total annual tax saving of $40 is reached sometime during the fifth year of the program. The $20 or $40 annual tax saving will continue thereafter with the practical effect of a lifetime annuity.

**VALUE OF $40 PER YEAR INVESTED AT
A 12% NET RETURN OVER 40 YEARS**

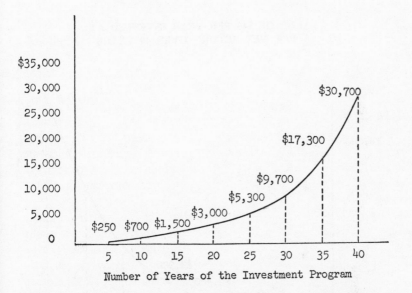

The annual saving—not granted to the savings-bank saver—should not be treated lightly. When $40 is invested each year for 35 years at a compound annual yield of 12%, after taxes, the investor will net a tidy profit of $17,300. The total saving for the $20 annual tax saving will amount to one half as much.

For readers who cannot plan on a program of saving for exactly 35 years, a graph is presented. The graph illustrates the approximate value of an accumulation of $40 per year over a period ranging up to 40 years, assuming the $40 investments earn an average return of 12% per year, after taxes, compounded annually.

The foregoing calculations have been based on the assumption that the Save-by-Borrower will be able to maintain the average after-tax return of 12%, including dividends and capital appreciation. Of course, this high average rate will probably change. Whether it will go higher or lower we cannot foresee, although most professionals believe it will be reduced.

To reflect the probability of a decline in the average rate of return, the following graph makes one change from the assumptions employed in the preceding graph—a 10% return.

**VALUE OF $40 PER YEAR INVESTED AT
A 10% NET RETURN OVER 40 YEARS**

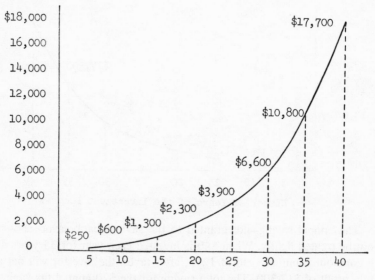

Number of Years of the Investment Program

Now that we have seen the advantages there are to borrowing, let us examine borrowing techniques more closely.

Chapter Three

BORROWING TO SAVE

OVERCOMING AVERSION TO BORROWING

Prejudice against borrowing has not vanished completely, in spite of our nation's credit-oriented economy. Borrowing for many people still borders on the sinful. Taking to heart the saying "He who goes a borrowing goes a sorrowing," some people firmly believe that one who cannot afford to purchase a desired item should not acquire it with somebody else's money. In support of their position, they warn that return of borrowed funds could entail unforeseen hardship. Further, the borrower would be obliged ordinarily to pay a premium (called "interest") for use of the money. Purchasing $100 worth of goods and services today with borrowed money may necessitate the foregoing of $110 worth of such items at some future date.

Whether borrowing is proper for an individual is a matter of degree. Rejection of borrowing should not be automatic, but should come only after due consideration of all the circumstances involved. All borrowing cannot be condemned. Who would hesitate to borrow money to purchase needed medical supplies or to pay for transportation to work? Let's see how one kind of borrowing actually works.

Borrowing has become quite popular recently among college students. In a few years, it will become widespread enough to make debtors out of a substantial majority of students by the time they graduate from the nation's colleges and universities.

Loans are made available to students by local banks, educational institutions, and philanthropic organizations. The loan proceeds help the student to defray living expenses, tuition, and costs of books and supplies. Gradual repayment of most of the loans commences soon after completion of schooling, when the graduate finally secures remunerative employment.

Borrowing to pay for an education is far from sinful. In fact, the loan transaction makes good economic sense. Using the loan proceeds to obtain a higher education or, perhaps, a better higher education, the borrower increases his earning power substantially. In the first few years after graduation, a portion of his increase in earnings is used to pay off the loan. After that, all of his increase in earnings is enjoyed by the former borrower.

The United States Congress and the legislatures of various states have enacted statutes to facilitate student loans. These laws provide that the loans will be guaranteed by the government or its agent. Little or no interest is paid by the borrower during his years of schooling. After graduation, he pays interest on the outstanding principal amount of the loan, frequently at the low rate of 3% per year.

Some students are over-enthusiastic in their support of student loan programs. They make out loan applications which contain false or misleading information about their needs. After obtaining the low-interest loans, they put borrowed moneys into savings accounts paying a higher rate of interest or invest the loan proceeds in stocks. Temptation to profiteer from the low-cost loans is too great for some people.

Even students who use the loan proceeds for scholastic purposes are able to derive secondary benefits from the loans. Some discharge their loans as slowly as possible after graduation. Interest of 3% per year on the unpaid balance is substantially less than the interest or the dividends and capital gains which the student can obtain by investing the moneys which otherwise would have been used to pay off the loan. In effect, delayed repayment of a student loan is a way to borrow money on exceptionally favorable terms.

By the purchase of dividend-paying stocks with the borrowed funds, student profits can be made quite easily. A dual tax loophole provides the incentive. One loophole is that dividends up to $100 per year may be received by an individual stockholder without being taxed; furthermore, a married couple may receive as much as $200, provided each spouse receives $100 or more in dividends. Secondly, interest payments, if any, on the student loans are deductible from the taxpayer's gross income, thereby creating a tax saving. This assumes the taxpayer will choose to itemize his deductions. In some cases he would not, when it would not be less advantageous for him to take the standard deduction of $1,000 or 10%, whichever is the lesser.

MONEY MAKES MONEY

Student loans can be a means of borrowing money to make money. The Save-by-Borrowing technique has the same objective. The technique is based upon the fact that the only practical way for many people to make money is to have money.

The technique does not require that an individual go deeply into debt. All he borrows is the amount he decides to set aside in a given year. The loan proceeds become the money which makes money for the borrower. During the course of the borrowing year, the borrower will make monthly payments to reduce his loan. By the end of the year, the loan will have been completely paid off. Then, the borrower takes out another loan in the same amount and repeats the process of repayment.

Psychology of saving and investment suggests that a person should start his investment program with a substantial amount of money. A person may withdraw and spend $20 or $30 which had been sitting in a savings bank account, but he dare not invade his sizable and growing investment fund, especially when the fund has been used to purchase real estate and stocks. Borrowing is a way for an individual to build his investment fund to this meaningful size.

A reader may have decided already that he should invest in real estate or common stocks—or perhaps buy into a business. His only problem may be to raise an investment fund. If he puts $1 or $100 into the fund, his opportunities for making capital profits seem somewhat meager. However, if he borrows the amount he decides to save during the next year, he will have an *immediate* investment fund of, let us say, $1,000. Now the reader can get started without delay on his money-making plans.

PROGRAMS OF FORCED SAVING

Who can say that he has never made a firm resolution to save a certain amount of money each pay period, only to see his savings program fail for some now-forgotten reason? "Emergencies" such as annual vacations, a new suit, and dining out have caused discontinuance of a countless number of savings programs. Motivation may have been strong at the outset of the program, but it was not strong enough to overcome the temptation of present enjoyment. The moral is that most of us cannot save regularly without coercion.

People go to all sorts of extremes to force themselves to save. One plan familiar to many readers is the Christmas Club account. A bank lends its collection facilities at no cost to persons who desire to set aside small sums each week. The weekly payments are often as little as 25 cents, 50 cents, or $1.00. Each "member" at the outset of the club year is given a payment booklet which indicates that fifty payments are to be made to the bank during the year. Each week the member makes his payment, and the bank teller stamps on the booklet that payment was received.

The "coercion" of this system is purely psychological. Members feel some kind of moral obligation to complete the savings program, realizing that funds will be needed at the year's end for the purchase of Christmas presents.

Near the end of the calendar year, each Christmas Club member is paid the total amount of his deposits. Ordinarily, no interest is paid to him. Banks claim that operation of the clubs is a non-profit service to the community. This may be true, especially with the smaller-deposit plans. Even if interest of 3% or 4% were to be paid on Christmas Club deposits, club memberships would not qualify as an acceptable method of forced saving. Payments are made only on a voluntary basis, and the money is at best a fixed-dollar investment during the year of club membership.

Payroll deduction for the purchase of United States Savings Bonds is another means by which a person can force himself to save. Similarly, a major objection is the fixed-dollar feature of the investment. Also, interest is below the rate paid by savings banks and savings and loan associations. Yet, Savings Bonds can pay an after-tax return as high as or even higher than savings accounts because of the exemption from state taxes and the bondholder's right to postpone recognition of income. By cashing in the bonds when his income tax bracket is comparatively low, such as during his retirement, the bondholder can reduce substantially his liability for payment of taxes.

All United States Savings Bonds Series E and H (whether issued before or after December 1, 1965) pay interest from that date aver-

aging 4.15% per year, compounded semi-annually. Bonds issued on
or after that date have an original maturity of 7 years. When an
investor desires to go after the 10th Multiple, he should not be thinking of investment returns of only 4.15%. Instead, he should have
his mind on equity investments. United States Savings Bonds, as
fixed-dollar investments, afford no opportunity for capital appreciation. As a consequence, they should be purchased only with the
emergency fund, you may conclude.

Other programs of automatic saving include "permanent" life insurance policies, by which the policyholder usually makes annual
or semi-annual payments of premiums to the insurance company. In
addition to the fixed-dollar objection to this form of saving, annual
or semi-annual payments are more difficult to meet than if they were
much smaller and spaced only a month apart. These smaller, more
frequent payments, although possible to make, involve additional
costs.

Some major corporations have stock-purchase plans for their employees, whereby regular deductions are made from the wages of a
participating employee. To a certain extent this type of automatic
saving is desirable, especially where the stock is of high quality and
can be purchased at discount prices or without payment of brokerage
commissions. But it is rarely wise for an investor to have his financial
independence contingent upon the fortunes of a single company.
Diversification and flexibility of investments are two missing elements in this method of forced saving.

THE SAVE-BY-BORROWING TECHNIQUE

How, then, can a person begin and force himself to continue an
extended program of capital accumulation? It is the thesis of this
book that anyone can do this—by borrowing. The actual saving process is technically simple and readily understandable.

Sit down with pencil and paper and calculate the amount you desire and are able to save in the forthcoming year. After reading this
book, you may wish to include in your figure any increase during the
preceding twelve months in cash surrender value of any "permanent"
life insurance you may have.

Some people use the borrowing technique as a painless way of
saving. By borrowing the annual after-tax amount of a pay increase,

the increase is allocated to savings before it is received and can be spent. In this way, the saver experiences no decline in spendable income for the year.

Moneys so borrowed are put to work immediately in whatever form of investment suits the individual. To purchase, improve, and sell real estate may be the borrower's investment decision. He may wish to invest in common stocks or mutual funds for the long run. Or short-term stock purchases in pursuit of quick profits could be his objective.

No matter what form of investment chosen, the borrowed funds enable you to begin immediately. The importance of time—a commodity which no one can purchase—cannot be overstated. To the extent that an individual puts his life span to work, in a capacity of capital accumulation, he will reap rewards. And as we've seen, an immediate and significant undertaking provides the incentive for the individual to begin a serious program of investment study, to make his investments perform as well as possible and outdistance the market averages.

There is a great advantage which results from being able to invest comparatively large amounts of money at one time: the cost of brokerage commissions is substantially lower. In fact there will be a $40 or $45 difference on a stock purchase involving $1,000. In addition, the investor should be able to put the borrowed funds to work immediately, to obtain an average rate of return, after taxes, in excess of 5.3% (or 6.3% if he does not take a tax deduction for interest paid). This will more than cover the cost of borrowing the funds.

Most important of all, as the loan is reduced by monthly payments, the saving program is actually being carried out. With each monthly payment there is a reduction of liability on the loan. At the end of the twelfth month, the loan is fully paid off, and the savings program for that year has automatically been achieved.

Saving by the borrowing process is "forced" or "mandatory" because of the legal obligations entailed when the loan is taken out. The borrower *must* make his payments to the lender each month. There is no element of choice here. Failure to pay would usually involve legal action against the borrower, and such a threat is exactly what many people need to force themselves to carry out their intentions to save regularly.

Of course, hard times may hit the borrower, and he may need to raise money to meet his monthly installment obligations. As a last resort, the borrower could convert some of his investments to cash to facilitate paying various bills. (A purchaser of consumer goods on credit ordinarily does not have his purchases to fall back on.) The chances are excellent, however, that the Save-by-Borrowing investor will strive to make payment out of his current earnings, rather than sell any of his investments. Investor's psychology is what makes the Save-by-Borrowing technique so effective.

Saving by borrowing is not immoral, nor is it without precedent. Our whole economy is based on credit. Making purchases with borrowed funds is taken for granted by many people. Real estate, department store items, automobiles, furniture, vacations, air travel, and meals are frequently bought on the installment plan. Credit purchases are so common that I saw a clerk in one of America's most famous department stores go into a slight state of shock when I informed him that I did not have a charge account with the store. I almost expected the surprised clerk to ask me how I expected to make my purchase.

If so many people can purchase products and services on credit when they need them, there is no reason why they cannot use credit to store their future claim for goods. Likewise, normal credit transactions involve current consumption, whereas the Save-by-Borrowing technique uses credit facilities to create a future claim for purchasable items.

At the end of each borrowing year, when the loan has been paid off, the full amount of $1,000 has been saved and the saver has created his claim for the future delivery of goods and services. Interest charges on each borrowed $1,000 do not run beyond full payment of the loan; and in the long run, interest costs are more than covered by first-year income on and capital appreciation of the investments. After payment of each loan, the full fruits of the $1,000 investment belong to the investor, increasing his claim for the future.

At the end of the first year of his Save-by-Borrowing program, when the first $1,000 loan has been paid off, the investor takes out a second loan for $1,000 and pays it off during the course of the second year. This process is repeated each year, involving the same borrowing costs and profits. His investment fund keeps growing each year, on the average, by the additional saving of $1,000, the borrowing profits and the accumulation of the investment fund. At no time does such borrowing exceed $1,000. In fact, the average amount of indebtedness during the borrowing year is much less—about $500— due to the monthly reductions of loan balance. Plainly, this borrowing is not designed to put an investor over his head in debt. Instead, it is purposive borrowing, intended to commit a person to a regular program of saving and investment.

For many who begin with and carry through this technique, there will come a time when they will be able to discipline themselves to save regularly, without the need for borrowing. For some people, this ability may come in one or two years. Others, however, may prefer to continue with the annual loans indefinitely.

Profitwise, it is desirable to continue with the annual loans. This assumes maintenance of an annual return (including capital appreciation) in excess of 5.3% or 6.3%, after taxes. This borrowing profit may even be substantial enough, on the average, to *dictate* that an individual maintain his annual loan program. Otherwise, the determinative factor will be whether the individual has learned to save regularly. If annual loans will be more effective in compelling regular saving, they should be continued.

Annual borrowing of $1,000 may be too much for you. Payments would approximate $87.50 per month for a total of twelve months, or about $20.20 per week. Instead, you may consider borrowing $1,000 every two years. Monthly payments would amount to about $46, approximately $10.60 each week, during a 2-year period.

A rule of thumb can be supplied to determine the amount an individual or family should save. Some people figure that 10% of income after taxes is a reasonable amount. Of course, you must be guided by your own circumstances.

WHO CAN BORROW?

The reader may wonder whether he will be able to obtain a loan. If he has obtained previously a travel loan, vacation loan, or other personal loan without pledging collateral security, his chances are better than those of persons who have never borrowed.

Not everyone is a good credit risk. When a bank has a limited amount of funds available to make loans, it will be very selective, lending only to people who are thought to be excellent risks. Later, the bank may have more funds to place and its loan policy will be less restrictive.

An evaluation of each applicant is made, and he is assigned a certain priority or credit rating. Many good risks are refused loans when the caliber of loan applicants runs high in proportion to the funds available. Save-by-Borrowers should bear in mind that it is not uncommon for successful borrowers to fail in their first one or two attempts. Keep trying.

Credit ratings are determined by the alliterative trio of capacity, capital, and character. Loan applications supply the information to loan officers by which certain conclusions concerning the applicant may be reached. Also, there are central organizations which gather data on individuals and relay the information to credit organizations upon request.

The *character* of the loan applicant is determined for the most part by his past loan experiences. If the applicant has a history of indebtedness and has never been delinquent in making payment, he rates an A-plus. The lending institution can foresee not only full discharge of the loan under consideration but the taking out and payment of further loans as well. With this thought in mind, the applicant should indicate to the loan officer that he intends to take out loans each year, in conjunction with a savings and investment program. Loan officers should look kindly on this. By stating the purpose of the loan, the applicant would help to assure the officer that the bank would ultimately be repaid.

Capacity of the borrower to pay off the loan is of major importance to the credit investigator. The borrower's ability to repay is based on his earning capacity. How much is he expecting to earn? Obviously, if he is unemployed, has a poor-paying job, or is in a seasonal position, his expected earnings are low or too speculative, hence his credit rating is low. Thus, musicians, waitresses, farm laborers, and domestic employees ordinarily have lower ratings than business executives, accountants, and teachers.

Even if an applicant's credit rating is acceptable, the bank will place a limit on the amount it will lend to him pursuant to an unsecured loan. For example, the bank may lend no more than the amount which, when added to all other outstanding unsecured indebtedness of the applicant, does not exceed, say, 20% or 25% of his anticipated annual income.

The third C, *capital,* relates to the question of whether the applicant has the wherewithal to provide support for his family and himself. A regular checking account, often requiring a minimum balance on deposit, would tend to suggest an affirmative answer.

SIGNATURE LOANS

What type of loan is recommended? Beginning Save-by-Borrowers may have no alternative to a "signature loan," made on the strength of the borrower's signature and not secured by any collateral (other than, possibly, an assignment of wages). In some instances the lender may insist that the borrower obtain the co-signature of a financially responsible party, to ensure payment of the indebtedness.

Loans of the signature type require that the borrower or his cosigner have a good credit rating, the borrower not posting any collateral security with the lender to which the lender may look for repayment. It is true that if the loan is to be secured by the pledge of stocks or other marketable securities, the true annual interest rate would be substantially lower. But the beginning Save-by-Borrower assumedly has no securities to pledge. Anyway, the regularity of saving could be jeopardized. Collateralized loans for Save-by-Borrowers ordinarily would not require monthly installment payments.

Regulation U promulgated by the Board of Governors of the Federal Reserve System prohibits banks from making loans *secured by stock* when the purpose of the loan is to purchase or carry any stock registered on a national securities exchange, unless the purchaser puts up a minimum amount of money or equity of his own. At this writing, Regulation U prevents Save-by-Borrowers from borrowing more than 30% of the cost of purchasing a registered stock, when the loan is to be secured by a stock (whether registered or not). Yet, Regulation U *does not prohibit* you from taking out an unsecured loan—or a secured loan if not secured by stock—for the purchase of stock of any kind. If a loan officer suggests otherwise, inform him he is wrong and refer the matter to his superior or to the law department of the bank. The regulation has been frequently misunderstood.

The reason for these rules is clear—to prevent recurrence of the 1929 market break. A severe drop in stock market prices would cause banks to further depress prices by throwing pledged securities on the open market, unless the borrower had a significant equity in the pledged securities. Regulation U requires a minimum percentage of equity, to safeguard the secured lender, the borrower, and the market generally. In the event of a drop in price, the borrower's equity affords a cushion of safety to the lending institution and prevents the bank from being forced to sell the stock in most instances.

Even when a borrower has stock available for pledge, he should consider whether the lower cost of interest is worth the inconvenience of substitution of collateral upon a change of investments or the risk that the pledged securities will be sold by the lending institution. Sale would occur if stock prices fell and the borrower found himself unable to comply with the lender's demand for additional stock or cash to further secure payment of the indebtedness. Sale at distress prices could involve substantial losses to the borrower. Also, a borrower should consider the fact that the secured loan may not require or contemplate payment in monthly installments; hence, the borrower loses the forced-savings effect which he is seeking in a loan.

Save-by-Borrowers should go to a commercial or industrial bank to obtain a signature loan. They will be charged interest at the rate of approximately $50 per year for a $1,000 loan, a nominal discount rate of 4¾% per year. Later we will see how this amounts to about 9.2% true annual interest on the outstanding balance of the loan, which averages about $500 during the course of the year.[1]

PASSBOOK LOANS

Passbook loans made by savings banks and savings and loan associations are much cheaper, though they are not especially helpful in saving by borrowing. In this type of secured loan, the borrower's savings book, evidencing an account of at least $1,000, is turned over to the bank as security for a $1,000 loan.

Savings banks now advertise that they will lend money at 2.88% interest and continue to pay 4.25% interest on the borrower's deposits. To many people this seems impossible. If the bank had only

[1] Calculated by use of the "constant ratio" formula, a simple method of computing annual rates of interest, the true annual interest rates set forth in this chapter are slightly higher than the actual true annual rates. For our purposes the difference is not material.

one depositor, who deposited $1,000 with the bank, how could the bank pay him 4.25% interest per year on his deposit when it lends the full $1,000 back to him and charges him only 2.88% interest? As soon as the loan of $1,000 is made to the sole depositor, the bank would seem to be left with no money with which to make up the difference in interest rates.

The answer is simple. The borrower makes monthly payments to the bank. At the end of the year, the full $1,000 has been repaid. On the average, the lender had use of about $500 over the year (which it can lend elsewhere to more than make up the difference). Accordingly, the 2.88% interest was almost twice as much as 2.88% (about 5.32%) of the $500 average outstanding amount of the loan. When the *discount* method of interest computation is used, as it ordinarily is, the true annual rate of interest would be higher, about 5.47%.

As soon as the bank receives each monthly payment, the money is put to work to produce income which, when added to the 5.47% of $500 paid by the borrower, would pay the borrower 4.25% on his $1,000 deposit and produce profits for the bank as well.

A passbook borrower pays interest of 5.47% to borrow his own money which continues to earn 4.25%. The difference, 1.22%, is almost pure profit to the bank, with no risk of loss whatsoever. Loans of this type are a gratuitous contribution to the bank for the borrower's privilege of using his own money.

This is perfectly agreeable to many people who argue that this is a good way for them to save—and, in fact, they probably are correct. Usually, however, the borrowed money is spent for consumer purchases, and the borrowing is merely a technique for restoring the savings account to its former level. Seldom is the passbook loan used to add to the saver's emergency or investment fund.

Passbook loans are disadvantageous in a Save-by-Borrowing program. To the extent that a person has emergency funds set aside in his savings account, he should not freeze them by pledging his bank book. If the funds are pledged, the borrower would have to obtain money from some other source, perhaps by sale of his investments at a loss, in order to obtain funds to cover an emergency.

If, on the other hand, the funds deposited in the savings account are part of an investment fund, they should be invested properly—in equity securities if so desired. In the long run, an equity investment is going to produce a return more than sufficient to pay the cost of borrowing someone else's money. Do not be fooled by the low cost of borrowing your own money. Invest your own money and save additional money by borrowing and investing somebody else's funds.

Readers may be asking themselves what should be done when a person, without borrowing, has $1,000 cash in his investment fund today for the purchase of stocks. Should he invest the $1,000 in stocks, then make regular payments into a savings account during the next year to build up his cash to $1,000 again, in anticipation of his next stock purchase?

Setting aside the problem of whether the saver could rely upon himself to carry through with his intentions to save, the answer is that at the end of 35 years he could be better off by $53,100 if he invested his $1,000 in savings, borrowed an additional $1,000 to invest, and repeated the borrowing process each year. A comparison in chart form, set forth in the final chapter, shows how this is so.

A word of warning. A person who contemplates investing a significant amount of money apart from his program of annual borrowing and investment must concern himself about timing his extraordinary purchases. It may be unwise for him to make his purchases when market prices appear to be nearing their peak. Instead, he may wish to wait for a drop in prices or split up his purchases over a considerable length of time.

It is up to the individual to decide how he should borrow. Loans secured by stocks involve the risk of forced sale of the stocks at a substantial loss. Also, the loans probably would not require payment by regular monthly installment. Passbook loans are either an ineffective employment of investment funds or an undesirable freezing of emergency funds. Signature loans may be more difficult to obtain and will cost more, but they avoid the difficulties inherent in passbook and other secured loans. At the outset, therefore, the beginner will probably desire to obtain a signature loan, which has fewer restrictions and perhaps a greater compulsion to discharge.

LIFE INSURANCE LOANS

A controversial subject is whether an insured should borrow against the cash surrender value of his "permanent" life insurance policy to invest in equity securities. If the borrowing takes place on an annual basis and the borrowed money is to be repaid by the end of each borrowing year, there seems to be little reason for argument. The amount at stake is too small. Borrowing, used only to facilitate the saving and investment of the annual $1,000, would average about $500 in outstanding amount and would never amount to more than $1,000 outstanding at any one time, irrespective of the increasing cash value of the policy. From the standpoint of *forcing* a person to save, however, there is little advantage to borrowing in this way. The borrower has no legal obligation to repay the money and is not even expected to make periodic payments to reduce the loan. All he need do is continue making interest payments. Repayment is nevertheless guaranteed. If the borrower dies without making full repayment, the outstanding balance of the loan will be deducted from the face amount of his policy before payment is made to the designated beneficiaries.

The real controversy is whether an insured should borrow money to remain on loan *indefinitely,* invested in equity securities while the loan is outstanding. It seems that most life insurance agents and company officers are dead set against this type of borrowing. But this is to be expected, a position taken out of obvious self-interest. The sale of permanent life insurance is more profitable to insurance agents, and it augments company reserves, a measure of a company's (hence its officers') importance in the industry. The insured has an entirely different orientation. Permanent insurance represents a fixed-dollar investment, upon which many savers cannot place total reliance. Borrowing against cash values for long-term investment in equity securities will be discussed in Chapter Eleven.

LOANS BY SMALL-LOAN COMPANIES

The borrower is strongly advised *not* to seek his loan at small-loan companies. Their rates of interest on the average outstanding balance of the loan usually approximate 24% to 36% per year (2% to 3% per month). These high interest rates are authorized by law as an incentive for small-loan companies to supply limited amounts of credit to poor credit risks. Many of these persons have only one alternative for obtaining a loan—a loan shark, who often charges interest at the rate of 520% per year (10% per week).

The alternative afforded by small-loan companies is beneficial to many people, but too costly for followers of the Save-by-Borrowing technique. A low ceiling on the amount which can be borrowed from a company is another reason for staying away, to avoid the inconvenience of multiple loans. The Save-by-Borrower is best advised to take out a signature loan from a commercial or industrial bank and pay a nominal interest rate of about $4\frac{3}{4}\%$, which is about 9.2% true annual interest, on the average outstanding balance of the loan.

Banks are ready and waiting to make loans, especially signature loans, for which the interest rate is higher than for secured loans. Daily newspaper advertisements often indicate an active solicitation of your business. Do not be afraid to talk things over with the bank's personal loan officer. His function is to put the bank's money to work. If you are a good credit risk, you should be able to find a bank which will lend you the money at a reasonable rate of interest.

MARGIN PURCHASES OF STOCK

Save-by-Borrowing, as explained so far, should not be confused with the margin purchases of stocks registered on a national securities exchange. When stocks are bought on margin, the purchaser borrows a portion of the purchase price from his stockbroker. To secure payment of the indebtedness, the purchaser pledges the newly purchased stock, which has a market value substantially higher than the amount of the loan. In 1965, the margin purchaser was required to put up "margin" or equity equaling at least 70% of the purchase price. Up to 30% could be borrowed from his broker.

If the market value of pledged stock declines so that the percentage of the purchaser's equity (market value minus loan obligation) drops below 25% of the loan obligation—the "margin maintenance requirement"—the broker must issue a call for additional margin. If the margin purchaser cannot meet the margin call with cash or collateral, the broker will be obliged to sell the pledged securities to obtain a discharge of the loan. This distress sale during a temporary decline in market value will result in substantial losses to the margin investor, who would wish to retain his equity interest in the pledged stock until its price could recover from the temporary decline. This is the major problem in purchasing stocks on margin.

Margin purchases are usually made by traders for speculative purposes. Accordingly, periods of stock ownership tend to be relatively short. The purchaser believes he can obtain higher profits on his investment fund, after payment of interest costs, by borrowing money to purchase more stocks than his investment fund would otherwise allow. When the margin requirement is set at 70% (as in 1965), the purchasing power of an investment fund can be increased by approximately 43%, but not without additional risk.

As the technique has been explained so far, a borrower need not worry about margin calls and distress sales. If the price of his stock falls, the Save-by-Borrower has no reason to fear that it will be sold out from under him. At his option, he could have taken possession of the stock certificates. Even if he did not, his broker has no authority to sell the stocks. All of the Save-by-Borrower's stock purchases, except to the extent his current $1,000 loan remains unpaid, will have been made, in effect, with his own savings. Furthermore, he will have pledged no stock to secure any portion of the current $1,000 loan. Regardless of how far the market price drops, the long-run investor will continue to hold his securities and worry, instead, about how he can raise additional funds to buy more stock at the temporary bargain prices.

CALCULATING INTEREST COSTS

You have already been exposed to the vagaries of interest calculation and have seen that interest is not computed the same way each time. The borrower must always be alert to protect himself from being deceived by quoted rates of interest. Looking back, could you have explained, before reading this chapter, how a passbook loan could be made at 2.88% interest when the bank continues to credit the passbook with 4.25% interest? Probably not. The reason is that the term "interest" is a chameleon, undergoing a change of meaning to suit the lending institution's purposes.

A useful way to think of interest is in terms of a percentage of an average sum of money which has been outstanding on loan for a full year. A thousand dollars borrowed at 5% interest and retained by the borrower for a full year would involve an interest cost of $50 by the end of the year. This method of interest computation, based on the use of *all* of the borrowed funds for the full year, is a *true annual rate of interest,* or *simple interest.* A prospective borrower, seeking to minimize his interest expense, must be able to reduce other methods of quoting interest to the true annual rate.

Interest is also quoted by the *add-on* method. An example is where an interest charge of, say, $50 is added to the principal amount of an assumed $1,000 loan. The total amount of $1,050 would be paid to the lender.

If payment of the add-on loan is made by twelve equal monthly installments (of $87.50 each), the true annual rate of interest would be approximately 9.2%.

Purchasers of automobiles on the installment plan should be familiar with the add-on method. To a $3,000 balance due, after down payment, on the purchase price of an automobile may be added a $400 financing charge, for a total of $3,400, to be paid in thirty-six equal monthly installments. True annual interest is slightly less than twice as much as the quoted rate for loans paid off in equal monthly installments.

Another way of calculating interest is the *discount method,* where the lender purports to lend you $1,000, say, but deducts his interest charge (we'll assume $50) in advance. Thus, the lender is charging $50 interest on only $950, the amount which the borrower actually receives. If the discount loan is paid off in a lump sum at the end of the year, the true annual interest rate is not 5% but 5.26%. Interest on a discount loan will always be slightly higher than the add-on method of interest calculation because, for example, the $50 interest charge pays for only $950 instead of $1,000 of borrowed funds.

If payment of the discount loan were to be made by twelve equal monthly installments—of $83.33 each—the true annual interest rate would be 9.72%, a little less than twice as much as 5.26%. Your signature loan will probably be a discount loan, involving the more costly method of interest calculation. Learn how to figure interest charges, then shop around for the most favorable rate.

Armed with a knowledge of how to compute interest costs, the reader should be able to protect himself from now on. When a department or furniture store charges 1½% per month on the outstanding monthly balance of a charge account, the true interest rate is 18% per year. Assume your life insurance premium is $100 per year and you have the option of paying $52 semi-annually (one payment due immediately and the other six months later). How much does the difference amount to on a true annual basis? You'll be surprised. It amounts to 16% per year. Only one half of the $100 premium is delayed in payment. Thus, there is a $4 charge for the delayed payment of $50, but for only one half of a year. This amounts to 8% for the half-year and 16% on a full-year basis. (Some of this higher cost is needed to offset the premium losses to be caused by insureds who will die during the year, before their full premiums for the year have been paid to the insurance company.)

In these and other instances of high interest costs, the credit consumer may be better off to pay cash, by drawing his money out of the savings bank or by obtaining a bank loan. However, by spacing the purchase of several insurance policies, the policyholder can split his due date for annual premium payments without incurring any charges for deferred premium payment. Of course, the splitting of policies will involve higher total premium costs, which would have to be taken into consideration.

For Save-by-Borrowing loans, to be paid off in twelve equal monthly installments, true annual interest rates for a range of nominal or quoted interest rates are listed in the following conversion table:

CONVERSION TABLE

Nominal Rate of Interest	True Annual Interest	
	Discount Loan	Add-On Loan
4%	7.7%	7.4%
4½%	8.7%	8.3%
5%	9.7%	9.2%
5½%	10.7%	10.2%
6%	11.8%	11.1%
6½%	12.8%	12.0%
7%	13.9%	12.9%
7½%	15.0%	13.8%

A close approximation of the true annual interest rate for add-on and discount loans, payable in twelve equal monthly installments, can be calculated by use of the following "constant ratio" formula, as adapted:

$$T = 1.846 \frac{I}{P}$$

where T = True annual interest rate;
      I = Interest charge expressed in dollars; and
      P = Principal amount of loan received.

For an *add-on* loan of $1,000 involving $50 in interest, true annual interest would approximate 9.2%

$$\left(\frac{1.846 \times 50}{1000}\right).$$

On the other hand, a $1,000 *discount* loan at the same nominal interest rate (5%) would have a true annual interest of about 9.7%

$$\left(\frac{1.846 \times 50}{950}\right).$$

TRUTH IN INTEREST

A break may be in store for borrowers. If the perennially proposed "Truth in Interest" bill is enacted into federal law, many lenders would be required to advertise the true annual interest rate applicable to transactions. This would go far to reduce confusion in the field of borrowing and consumer credit, and save millions of dollars in exorbitant, half-hidden interest charges. Borrowers would then be able to shop around, to compare financing and interest charges quoted on a uniform basis.

Now the Save-by-Borrower is on his way to the bank, to borrow $1,000 on a 4¾% signature loan (or at such other reasonable rate as may prevail in his locality). On a 4¾% discount loan he will be paying 9.2% true annual interest, approximately.

Readers have seen how money can be borrowed to buy stocks without payment of any net brokerage commission. But why should they want to buy stocks? The answer is that high rates of return can be obtained from investments in common stocks, which seem more desirable than other modes of investment. Failure to invest in common stocks, unfortunately, has cost many Multiples to millions.

Financial writers have suggested that this shortcoming has been caused by a public misunderstanding or ignorance of the true nature of common stocks and the corporate form of business. The next step, therefore, is becoming familiar with the characteristics of common stock investments.

Chapter Four

20,000,000 PART-TIME BUSINESSMEN

AT&T AS A PART-TIME BUSINESS

American Telephone and Telegraph Company is one of this country's most impressive organizations. A holding company, its numerous subsidiaries are responsible for about 82% of all the operative telephones in the United States; and it owns 99.82% of the stock of Western Electric Company and about 29% of the stock of Communications Satellite Corporation ("Comsat"). Employee stock-option plans and popularity of AT&T stock among the investing public have pushed 512,047,000 shares of outstanding AT&T stock into the hands of 2,674,141 shareholders. Each of these persons has a part interest in AT&T, an interest which can be considered his part-time business.

What type of return has this business produced for its owners? Let us consider the investor who purchased $100 worth of AT&T stock each month for a 10-year period ending early in 1964 and reinvested all dividends, for a total investment and reinvestment of $15,973. Of this amount, $12,000 represents savings and $3,973 represents dividends (without deduction of taxes). At the end of the 10 years, the market value of the purchased stock increased to $28,060, at the compound rate of approximately 18% per year before taxes.

Deducting the assumed 15% tax, we find a compound rate of return of 15.3% during the 10-year period. Assuming continuation of the $100 monthly investment and the 15.3% compound rate of return, these investors would achieve their 10th Multiple in about 39 additional years. The extensive position in Comsat stock may contribute to a high return for the future. Before we go on, a word of warning is in order. No recommendation whatsoever is being made as to the advisability of investing in AT&T stock or any other security which is mentioned by name in this book. Past performance does not necessarily indicate future performance. As circumstances change, the desirability of investing in a specific security may change. Nor do I take a position on the advisability of investing in securities generally. I do, however, present certain facts about investments, which you may find helpful in drawing your own conclusions. Undoubtedly, there will be many for whom investment in securities is desirable. On the other hand, there may be more—perhaps you are one—for whom security investment is inadvisable. As I said at the very outset of this book, advice in this field you should obtain from an investment adviser, who can talk to you, study your case and then render his professional opinion.

PEOPLE'S CAPITALISM

AT&T is the most striking example of public ownership of a business organization in the free world. General Motors Corporation and Chrysler Corporation are two other major companies having a widespread distribution of stock ownership. Time has come for our capitalist system to be called the people's capitalism, in recognition of the fact that more than 20,000,000 individuals have put a portion of their savings to work in American businesses by means of stock investments.

Of the remaining 175 million or so Americans, perhaps 3 million are *indirect* part-time businessmen by reason of mutual fund holdings. But the vast majority of persons has no such ownership interest in American business. Some cannot afford to risk their savings in this fashion. A great many persons, however, do have the economic capacity to make common stock purchases, but do not elect to join the ranks of shareholders.

It is quite possible that unwarranted fears and a misunderstanding of the nature of common stock investments are responsible for keeping untold numbers of persons out of the stock market. There may be many others who would purchase common stocks if they knew how to go about it. Let us now examine the fundamentals of common stock ownership.

A CORPORATION IS A PERSON

A corporation is not the magnificent edifice bearing its name. In fact, a corporation has no tangible existence. It exists only as a privilege to do business, granted by legislative enactment and evidenced by its corporate charter or certificate of incorporation.

The holders of *common stock* issued by a corporation are the owners of the business organization, but they do not own the business assets. Title to these assets is held by the corporation, a legal entity or person under the eyes of the law.

In most states, one person may own all of the "capital stock" or "common stock" of a corporation; and, in such case, he would be called the "sole stockholder" (or "sole shareholder") of the corporation. For many American corporations, the shares are distributed among millions or thousands of stockholders. Such corporations are said to be "publicly held." Corporations having their stock held by only a few persons are said to be "closely held."

To each of its stockholders the corporation issues a piece of paper called a stock certificate, which certifies that the person named thereon is the owner of a designated number of shares of stock of the corporation. Title to the stock may be transferred by endorsement of the owner's name on the back of the certificate (or by execution and delivery of a separate instrument called a "stock power") and delivery of the certificate to the new owner.

An interesting sidelight to stock ownership is the method by which banks, for example, take title to stock. Legal title is ordinarily taken in the name of a "nominee," usually a partnership of two or more bank officers or employees formed for this purpose. Upon sale of the stock, transfer of title is easier to accomplish than if title had been taken in the corporate name. No corporate resolutions to authorize the transfer need be passed by the directors of the bank; and certificates in evidence of the resolutions need not be submitted to the agent who transfers record ownership of the stock on the books of the corporation. No more is needed to transfer title than to have one of the partners (possibly a secretary or receptionist in the bank) endorse, in behalf of the partnership, the stock certificate and deliver it to the transferee.

WHY DO CORPORATIONS EXIST?

Corporations exist for the purpose of doing business; that is self-evident. But why should a corporate form of business organization be selected instead of a partnership? Two friends named Bob and Jim had to come to grips with this problem.

For several months Bob and Jim had toyed with the idea of making educational motion pictures based on popular "how to do it" books. Extensive public opinion polls firmly convinced them that instructive films would perform well at the box offices of local movie houses, assuming the educational material could be presented as a combined offering of self-improvement and entertainment. An important consideration, Bob and Jim agreed, was the anticipated shoe-string budget to produce such films.

Bob, a successful lawyer, spent most of his time in the courtroom. Jim attended to the business of his own employer, a major corporation. Neither person wished to curtail his current remunerative employment. Yet, they had an idea, a few thousand dollars to invest, and a desire to promote their idea.

Limited Liability. Early in their discussions, Bob and Jim decided they had to insulate themselves from any personal liability for debts incurred in conducting the business. Each had a home, a car, and savings which needed to be protected from creditors of the intended motion picture business.

Bob suggested that the corporate form of business be employed. Jim agreed, knowing that it would ordinarily protect its owners from personal liability. The law holds that a corporation is a legal entity, separate and apart from its owners—provided, however, that there is no abuse of the privilege. (Statutes of some states do provide the exception that major stockholders of a closely-held corporation are liable for payment of certain employee wages, for example.) Ordinarily, the only loss a stockholder can suffer by reason of his stock ownership is the loss resulting from a decline in value of his investment.

A *partnership* form of business organization was rejected. Bob and Jim both knew that any of the general partners in a partnership would be *unlimitedly liable* for all debts.

Joint-stock companies are a hybrid form of business entity. Until its change into a corporate entity in 1965, a well-known example was American Express Company. In all substantial respects except one, a joint-stock company is equivalent to a corporation. The one exception, however, is enough to classify the joint-stock company as a partnership: Each member ("shareholder") of the joint-stock company is unlimitedly liable for its unpaid debts, after exhaustion of creditor remedies against the company. For this reason, Bob and Jim decided not to do business as a joint-stock company.

Perpetuity of Existence. Permanence of the business organization was important to both men. A corporate form would afford the desirable perpetuity. If either of them were to die or become bankrupt, the corporate business could continue without interruption. A corporation survives the death, insanity, or bankruptcy of any of its owners. If, however, they formed a partnership there would be an automatic dissolution upon the death, insanity, or bankruptcy of Bob or Jim.

Transferability of Shares. Each of them wanted to have an easy way to sell his interest in the business in the event of dissatisfaction or financial necessity. The corporate form of business accommodated them, affording a convenient method of transferring an interest without interruption of the business enterprise. A shareholder need do no more than transfer title to his shares.

Divisibility of Interests. Another feature to the corporate form of business organization is the easy divisibility of interests. If Jim is to receive a 50% interest in the business, he would be issued 50% of the stock. Later, in absence of any agreement to the contrary, Jim would be free to sell or transfer any portion of his stock holdings, reducing his percentage of business ownership as he saw fit.

In a partnership, the process of transferring interests is not as easy. New partners cannot be admitted without the consent of the other partners.

Raising Capital. It was expected that in later months or years there would be need for additional capital in the corporation. A corporation affords a convenient means by which this capital can be raised. Upon approval by the stockholders or the board of directors, additional shares of common stock may be sold by the corporation. In its formative years, the corporation may have to resort to sale of ownership interests in order to acquire needed capital. When investment risks are great, prospective investors demand an opportunity to share in the growth of that company, to obtain substantial profits. This opportunity is offered by common stocks.

For more sophisticated financings, the corporation could issue bonds, debentures, preferred stocks—with or without the privilege of converting into common stock of the company. This flexibility makes the corporate entity highly desirable for a growing business.

Tax Advantages. Taxes were important for Bob and Jim to take into consideration. Each is in the 50% income tax bracket and therefore does not wish to receive unnecessarily any additional ordinary income. The corporation, not they, would be the payer of taxes on the business income. Beginning in 1965, the federal tax rate has been 22% on the first $25,000 of taxable income and 48% on all taxable income in excess of $25,000.

Bob and Jim agreed that it would be best for them to reinvest in the business all corporate earnings after payment of taxes. It was contemplated, accordingly, that for many years no distribution of corporate earnings would be made to the shareholders. A total accumulation by the corporation of up to $100,000 in earnings would involve no federal penalty tax, and applicability of such tax for accumulations in excess of $100,000 would depend upon the reasonable or reasonably anticipated needs of the business.

The advantage of keeping the earnings in the corporation had been worked out by Jim, the businessman. Assuming initial investment of a total of $10,000 and corporate earnings of 20% before taxes on invested capital, payment of the 22% corporate tax would reduce the net corporate profit to 15.6%. If the net corporate earnings are reinvested in (i.e., retained and used by) the corporation, to obtain a compounding of the investment return, the corporation would have a book value of $125,000 at the end of 13.9 years. Thereafter, corporate income would exceed $25,000 annually, and the 48% tax would be applicable to the excess annual income over $25,000, gradually reducing the compound rate of growth, after taxes, as the corporate earnings increased at the same pre-tax rate.

If, at the end of 13.9 years, Bob and Jim decided to sell their stock at book value, they would be required to pay a 25% long-term capital-gains tax on a $115,000 profit, reducing their cash proceeds from the sale of stock to about $96,000.

To have the business enterprise be taxed as a corporation would be more advantageous than to have it taxed as a partnership. Bob and Jim each expected to be in at least the 50% tax bracket through-out the 13.9 year period. Accordingly, to have them pay a tax of 50% or more on (and out of) the earnings of their business, if the business were taxed as a partnership, would reduce the net compound yield to 10% and reduce the book value of the business to about $38,000 by the end of 13.9 years. Adoption of the partnership basis for taxation would involve a total net loss of $58,000 to Bob and Jim. In complete agreement so far about use of the corporate form of business organization, they went on to discuss management of their business.

ABSENTEE OWNERSHIP AND PROFESSIONAL MANAGEMENT

The discussion did not dwell upon basics for long. It is well known by lawyers and corporate businessmen that shareholders (especially of publicly held corporations) are merely investors, usually not participants in the daily activities of the corporation. The shareholders ordinarily sit back and do nothing except cash dividend checks, read annual reports, and occasionally attend meetings of shareholders. Their absence from the scene of corporate action is not felt, however; corporate business, particularly in publicly owned corporations, is conducted by professional managers who are paid to work for the benefit of all stockholders. A board of directors is elected each year by the stockholders. This board does long-range planning for the corporation and appoints some or all of the corporate officers; however, routine business is conducted by the officers or other employees of the corporation.

Agreement was readily reached by Bob and Jim that neither of them need be active in the routine business of the corporation. Instead, as the shareholders of the corporation they would meet annually to vote for themselves as members of the board of directors. From this position they could oversee their business, appoint corporate officers to carry out the routine details, and if necessary make personnel changes or suggest alternative plans.

A retired producer and director of films agreed to become president of the company and commence production of the first motion picture film. As compensation he would receive a small salary and an option over some shares of stock of the company.

A housewife, permanently retired from full-time writing of screen-plays, promised to write a screenplay entitled *Conquering Tin Pan*

Alley, based on a (hypothetical) best-selling book about the song-writing industry—particularly, how songs are conceived and sold by song writers, then promoted into hits by Tin Pan Alley. Also, she agreed to accept appointment as secretary of the corporation. Compensation for her services would be several thousand dollars, and a stock option. With a good script, the company could obtain a distribution agreement and financing of the production costs.

Bob and Jim promoted the corporation, contributed the idea, and took enough money from their savings to get started. Then, they took a back seat, not to be involved in daily affairs of the business entity, except to keep an eye on expenses. The producer and housewife were the only persons qualified to conduct the routine business of the corporation. They would negotiate and make agreements in behalf of the corporation, and produce and arrange for distribution of the educational films.

As soon as the details of management were ironed out, Bob and Jim turned to consideration of the financial structure of their corporation.

CAPITAL STRUCTURE AND DISTRIBUTION
OF PROFITS

It was agreed that Bob and Jim would each receive, at the outset, one half of the 10,000 shares of common stock to be issued by the corporation, in exchange for a capital contribution of $5,000 apiece.

If the business does poorly, the stockholders may agree to dissolve the corporation and liquidate the remaining assets to themselves. First, however, all debts of the corporation would have to be paid. Whatever is left would then be liquidated to the stockholders in accordance with the proportion of outstanding shares of stock which each stockholder owns.

Bob and Jim do not think of loss, however. They are setting their sights on high corporate earnings. Soon, it is anticipated, the corporation will have income in excess of expenses. Years later, the earnings could build up to a point where the board would be willing to distribute some of the corporate earnings to the stockholders.

Corporations distributing earnings to their stockholders generally do so on a quarterly basis. Four times each year the board of directors meets to declare a dividend to the stockholders, which becomes a debt of the corporation to its shareholders.

The *dividend,* usually a cash distribution of a part of the corporate earnings, is made by mailing a check to each person listed as a stockholder on the corporate records. Each check is for an amount equal to the declared dividend per share multiplied by the number of shares owned by the stockholder. Thus, a 20-cent dividend per share would result in a $20 dividend to a stockholder for each 100 shares he owned.

The date as of which stockholders must be indicated as such on the records of the corporation, in order to receive payment of the dividend, is called the record date for share ownership, and is set by the board of directors when it declares the dividend. If no date is set, the date of declaration of the dividend governs.

Dividends are occasionally made in property other than cash. Pursuant to court decree, E. I. Du Pont de Nemours & Company distributed to its stockholders a substantial number of shares of General Motors stock. During prohibition, it was rumored that a liquor company was planning to distribute its holdings of liquor to its stockholders. Word spread quickly among thirsty members of the investing public and the stock price made tremendous advances. As it turned out, the liquor was not to be distributed, and the stock price toppled from its record high.

Another type of dividend—the stock dividend—results when a corporation declares a dividend payable in stock representing part ownership of the distributing corporation. Let us say that ABC Corporation declares a 5% stock dividend. For each 100 shares of ABC stock held by a stockholder he would receive 5 additional shares of ABC stock.

Theoretically, if the market value of ABC stock before the dividend was $100 per share, a total value of $10,000 for the 100 shares, the market value of 105 shares after the dividend would stay at $10,000, since the corporation has not distributed any of its cash or other assets. In other words, the stock distribution results in no depletion of the assets of the company.

As a practical matter, however, the market value of the 105 shares may go a little higher than $10,000. Stock dividends portend good times for the corporation. Also, investors seem to follow a bird-in-hand theory. They expect a continuation of the same dividend rate for each share of stock, making the total dividend payment for 105 shares greater than the total dividends received previously on the 100 shares. As a result, the stock price is apt to go up.

HOW MUCH IS IT WORTH?

A concern for stock values naturally accompanies stock ownership. Numerous methods of stock valuation can be used, but most important to an investor is the current market value, the price at which shares of the same stock have exchanged hands in an open market. For purposes of present valuation, the most recent market price is ordinarily the best indication although events may take place to cause the next sale to be made at a substantially different price.

"Closing" market prices for stocks traded on the New York Stock Exchange and American Stock Exchange are listed in the financial pages of many newspapers. These prices are an approximation of the amount for which a person could have bought or sold the stock if he had placed an order with his broker about five minutes before the close of the trading day, 3:30 P.M. on the New York Stock Exchange. A glance at these pages will inform a stockholder how his investment is performing. The stock may go up or down an "eighth" or a "quarter" of a "point," which means that each share has increased or decreased in market value by an eighth or a quarter of a dollar (12½ cents or 25 cents). For each 100 shares, this would amount to a change in price of $12.50 or $25.00.

An inexperienced investor may wonder why stock market prices go up and down; why it is that prices do not remain constant. Great fluctuation in prices does occur in spite of stabilization efforts by members of the stock exchange who, on the floor of the exchange, "specialize" in transactions concerning particular stocks and maintain an orderly market. Generally, as changes occur in economic outlook and expected earnings of a corporation, the market price of the stock will change. The previous balance of supply and demand is offset by the new factors. Immediate cause for a change may be rumors of a substantial sale or purchase of the stock by a leading mutual fund; a recommendation by an investment adviser who has a sizable following; a comment by a leading magazine or newspaper; election outcome; anticipation of a company announcement regarding dividends, stock split, merger, or earnings, among other things.

Earnings play perhaps the most significant role in stock valuation. Ordinarily, earnings are compared by the *price-earnings ratio*. You are apt to hear that a particular stock is selling at, for example, twenty times its earnings. This would be so when a share of stock has a $100 value and represents an interest in $5.00 of annual corporate earnings. If the earnings per share of the corporation are expected to double, the price of the stock may double also.

GOING PUBLIC

Bob and Jim were successful with their movie-producing business. In fact, they decided it was time for their corporation to undergo significant expansion. This was facilitated by having the corporation offer to the public, after appropriate registration and qualification, previously unissued common stock of the corporation, at $10 per share. The public was quick to pick up the stock; purchasers were willing to risk their capital in the relatively new enterprise, hoping to realize tremendous profits by getting in on the ground floor of a growing business.

By this public offering, shares of stock in the corporation became available to anyone wishing to invest his money in the new business. Although the stock still could not be purchased on a stock exchange, the stock now was available "over-the-counter," the market for stocks not listed on a national stock exchange. This market consists of a widespread group of brokers and dealers who negotiate transactions by an intricate network of telephones and teletypewriters.

During a few years of growth, the motion-picture company may establish an impressive earnings record. Also, the stock may become distributed among many stockholders. Then, the corporation may decide to "list" its stock for trading on a national stock exchange. Consideration would probably be given to listing on the American Stock Exchange (the ASE), where the requirements for listing are not as strict as the requirements of the New York Stock Exchange (the NYSE).

When a stock is traded on the NYSE or ASE, an investor is able to keep an eye on his investment in the stock; he can see in many newspapers the actual prices at which the stock has been selling. A further advantage to listing is that the price of the stock is apt to increase (frequently before listing is actually accomplished). Demand is generated by the publicity and the fact that many investors confine their stock investments to listed securities. Also, the shares become more readily convertible into cash, except in rare instances when trading is no longer permitted. Compare real estate investments, which cannot be sold too quickly. Note that although a stock may be readily marketable, it will not have a constant value. As one would hope and expect, stock values do fluctuate. It is possible, however, to purchase stocks having high or low probabilities of price fluctuation, to suit the individual preference of an investor.

At some later time, the corporation may be ready to list its shares on the NYSE. This may be done when the corporation meets certain conditions, including:

1. Net tangible assets in excess of $10,000,000;
2. Income of $2,000,000 per year before taxes; and
3. At least 700,000 common shares distributed to the public, among not fewer than 1,700 shareholders holding at least 100 shares apiece.

The NYSE is by far the most important stock exchange, handling almost 83% of the dollar value of sales taking place on all national exchanges. Sales taking place on the NYSE, accordingly, are most frequently reported by newspapers. Second in dollar value, sales on the ASE receive second billing.

ANOTHER CRASH?

You may be one of many who refuse to purchase stocks, basing your decision on the understandable feeling that you do not want to experience losses similar to those suffered in the market crash of 1929. Such fears can be eased to a considerable extent. In 1933, 1934, and after, federal laws were passed which have effectively regulated for more than thirty years the most important phases of securities transactions. Establishment of the Securities and Exchange Commission (the "SEC") occurred in 1934. Among other activities it is a watchdog over the public offering and sale of securities by means of interstate commerce or the mails. Also, the SEC oversees the national stock exchanges and their transactions.

Federal laws covering transactions in securities are comprehensive and complex, having been designed to eliminate or minimize most of the fraudulent and otherwise unsound practices contributing to the stock market debacle of 1929. The Securities Act of 1933, known to many as the "Truth in Securities" law, was drafted in accordance with a philosophy of full disclosure: the act requires generally that before securities can be offered to the public through mail or interstate commerce, a "registration statement" covering such securities must be filed with the SEC.

Part of the registration statement consists of a "prospectus," a printed statement containing information about the business and management which an investor should have available before deciding to buy the security. With certain exceptions, a full statutory prospectus must be delivered to a purchaser of securities newly offered to the public; this should occur at or prior to the delivery of the securities, if they are delivered through the mails or interstate commerce. False or misleading statements in the prospectus constitute grounds for a civil action by the purchaser against signers of the registration statement, directors of the issuing corporation, underwriters and certain others connected with the preparation or certification of the registration statement. Thus an innocent purchaser is especially protected against losses caused by fraud or misrepresentation.

The Securities Exchange Act of 1934 broadened the scope of federal regulation to cover transactions in stocks of a corporation having an equity security (such as common stock or preferred stock) listed on a national stock exchange registered with the SEC (including the NYSE and ASE). Abuses by the "insiders" of a corporation were curtailed in this way. The Act of 1934 calls for *"insider reporting,"* by which each director, officer, and beneficial owner of at least 10% of any class of a listed equity security of such company is required to report to the SEC when there has been any change in his beneficial holdings of *any* equity securities of the company, whether listed or unlisted. Upon publication of a change in holdings, the general investing public obtains a possible indication of what an insider thinks about the company.

Further, these insiders are required by law to turn over to the company any profits derived by them from a purchase and sale (or sale and purchase) of *any* equity securities of the company within a six-month period. These restrictions against insider trading decrease the opportunities for insiders to take advantage of information not generally available to lesser stockholders or the investing public.

In addition, the 1934 Act and SEC regulations thereunder established restrictions upon the solicitation of proxies. A *proxy* is a written authorization by which a stockholder intending to be absent from a stockholders' meeting can give his voting rights to someone else—a proxy. Solicitation of proxies is accomplished by mailing or delivering to each stockholder a proxy statement, which describes all business planned to be brought up at the meeting and lists the persons to be nominated for election to the board of directors. The stockholder is given the opportunity to instruct his proxy how to vote, but failure to do so ordinarily authorizes the proxy to vote as indicated in the proxy statement. Solicitation of proxies sometimes winds up in a proxy fight, where two or more groups or factions seek to elect their own slate of directors, to obtain or retain control of the corporation.

Finally, the 1934 Act requires the periodic filing of reports with the SEC by corporate issuers of listed securities and a small percentage of issuers of stocks traded only in the over-the-counter market. These reports are intended to be necessary or appropriate for the protection of investors.

In 1964, the 1934 Act underwent major amendment, extending federal regulation to perhaps 3,500 corporations not covered by the 1934 Act. With certain exceptions, companies having total assets in excess of $1,000,000 and at least one class of equity security held of record by 500 or more stockholders are required to register the securities with the SEC. Registration affords such stockholders the protection of the 1934 Act: company insiders are subject to insider reporting and insider trading restrictions; the company is obliged to render periodic reports to the SEC; and proxy solicitation rules apply.

The 1934 Act granted power to the Federal Reserve Board to regulate stock transactions taking place on *"margin."* A margin transaction involves the borrowing of money to purchase securities, the borrower pledging the securities to provide security for payment of the indebtedness. In 1929, when stock market prices started their disastrous decline, an enormous volume of pledged securities was thrown on the market by lenders exercising their power of sale to prevent further depreciation of their security. As a result, stock prices dropped to lower and lower levels, causing billions of dollars of loss to margin and non-margin purchasers of stock alike.

Now, however, margin (meaning, roughly, the investor's own contribution to the price of his stock purchase) does not come anywhere near the low figure of 10% not uncommon in 1929. A person using 10% margin lost his entire investment when a $100 stock dropped only $10, to $90 per share. But now, the Federal Reserve Board requires ordinarily that margin be no less than 70%, adjusting the percentage in accordance with demands of the economy.

Manipulation of securities transactions was curtailed by the 1934 Act, which outlawed devices known as wash sales, matched orders, and other market contrivances which created a false or misleading appearance of active trading in any security. Also, issuing or circulation of misleading statements about securities was barred. The SEC commenced regulation of potentially harmful practices such as short sales, stop orders, price-fixing, and price stabilization. Transactions in puts, calls, straddles, and other stock options were also brought under SEC control.

In retrospect, it seems unlikely that the 1929 crash will be repeated. Of course, stock prices remain subject to fluctuation, but "crashes" will be of smaller magnitude, and their effects will be of shorter duration. Fears about 1929 should not overshadow the many successful years that have elapsed since passage of the Securities Act of 1933 and the Securities Exchange Act of 1934. These acts appear to have made common stock investments, for the long run, reasonably safe, assuming adherence to fundamental principles of investment.

HOW YOU BUY STOCKS

One who desires to purchase some stock can do so quite conveniently, merely by selecting a stockbroker, then opening an account with him. The procedure is almost as simple as opening a savings account. Bank references will probably be required to satisfy the broker that you will be able to make payment for securities he purchases in your behalf. Once your account is established, you may order the sale or purchase of stocks by telephoning or telegraphing your broker. By all means select a reputable broker who possesses financial stability. This is essential for your protection. Your banker or friends and acquaintances who are experienced investors may offer some helpful advice in making your selection.

A modest investment is not unusual for beginners in the market; it may be advisable; and it is certainly nothing to be ashamed about.

Assuming you have decided to invest in stocks, what stocks should you buy? This is, of course, a major problem for all investors. Some rely upon their stockbroker to make all investment decisions for them. However, it is unwise in many instances to entrust precious savings to others. The account of a novice investor, who frequently has only a small amount to invest, may be turned over to a youthful and inexperienced "registered representative" (formerly called a "customer's man"), who may be no more than two or three investment books ahead of the novice. Advice from him would not be as valuable as the advice of an older, more experienced person. It goes without saying that the youthful representative should seldom be given carte blanche authority over your investments.

New investors should be aware that a registered representative has a financial interest in obtaining buy and sell orders from them. It has happened that a representative suggests needless changes in investments, merely to generate commissions for himself. "Churning the customer's account" is the term popularly applied to this reprehensible activity. The customer may be breaking even or losing money on the stock switches, but the registered representative and brokerage house do not suffer the same fate. Their earnings and profits are based mainly on the volume of sales, whether the value of the customer's account goes up or down.

A new investor who is really concerned with his personal finances should undertake to inform himself about principles of investment. At the outset of his investment program, his new knowledge may be a defense against an inexperienced or unscrupulous representative on whom he relies for advice; as he gains experience, the investor should take over the responsibility for making his own decisions. Suggested readings under a variety of topic headings are contained in the Bibliography.

Now that we have discussed various aspects of stock ownership, we go on to compare stocks and other equity investments with savings media of a fixed-dollar nature.

Chapter Five

ALL SAVERS ARE GAMBLERS

Saving is the storage of purchasing power for use at some later date. A savings bank deposit of today is a potential demand upon goods and services of tomorrow.

Deposit of money in a savings account is infinitely more convenient than storage of goods or services. One who wishes to set aside for future shoe needs cannot buy the shoes now and deposit them in a Bank for Shoe Savings. Commercially it is not feasible. Obsolescence of style, differences in size, and deterioration of product constitute major obstacles to success. Also, a depositor's needs or preferences may change; originally setting aside shoes for future use, he may decide later that he would like a radio or a toaster instead.

Money provides the desired flexibility. Early in history people recognized the impracticality of bartering, adopting money as a medium of exchange instead. Unfortunately, storage of purchasing power by saving of money has a major disadvantage.

An orphanage, for example, sets aside $400 in an emergency shoe-savings account. This amount is sufficient to purchase one pair of $4 shoes for each of the 100 children for whom the orphanage is parent and provider. Two generations of children pass through the institution, and all this time the emergency shoe fund has remained intact. Only the interest payments on the $400 deposit have been spent, to assist in keeping the orphanage open. Poor management and unfriendly alumni cause a dwindling of contributions and a worsening of the financial position of the home. Finally, 36 years after establishment of the emergency shoe fund, it has to be used for the purchase of shoes. As should have been anticipated, the fund is insufficient to provide new shoes for each of the 100 children. Assuming the present rate of inflation of 1.4% per year, the price of shoes doubled during the 36-year period, allowing the purchase of only 50 pairs of shoes.

Inflation is a phenomenon common to most countries, in one degree or another. It seems to be here to stay and will continue to take away the shoes.

THE WORLD'S MOST SUCCESSFUL THIEF

The orphanage story may sound far away, totally unrelated to matters which concern you. But the truth is that millions of savers, you among them, most probably, are suffering similar losses. Each year the more than $350 billion of savings held by mutual savings banks, commercial banks, savings and loan associations, and life insurance companies suffer a decline in purchasing power of about *$5 billion*. Surely, inflation must be the world's most successful thief.

Leading economists call for a stepping up of government spending, by means of borrowing, to nudge a sluggish economy forward or pull it out of the depths of a depression. Printing presses start to roll, turning out brand-new greenbacks, which are used to pay for the government purchases. As a complementary policy, availability of money is increased by the easing of credit restrictions. Then, gradually, the ever growing amount of circulating currency increases the demand for consumer goods and services, stimulating higher economic productivity. As the demand for workers rises, unemployment declines, and wages and prices increase. To the extent the increase in the supply of money exceeds the increase in supply of goods and services, some economists say, inflation has occurred.

Accompanying the higher cost of living we find increasing demands, both legitimate and illegitimate, made by organized labor upon a cost-conscious, perhaps obdurate, management. Shorter working hours, fewer working days, a sabbatical year every seven, featherbedding, higher pay, increased retirement benefits, a guaranteed annual wage, and other fringe benefits are the essence of labor's demands.

The government is understandably sympathetic with or terrified of the labor monopolies it established during the New Deal. Paying lip service to unworkable procedures of collective bargaining, the government invariably forces a settlement. No wonder labor confidently pursues its present policies. Organized labor may be awarded a good part of its demands, causing the price of goods and services and the cost of living index to move higher. To finish the cycle, the government makes credit easier to obtain, to permit continued purchase at higher prices of the union-made goods and union services. Refusal to do so would result in unemployment, making organized labor the victim of its own monopolistic practices. This could not be allowed to happen.

The price of goods and services may rise even higher than the increase in labor cost. Entrepreneurs frequently boost prices by more than the increased production costs. They do this to maintain their profit margin, a certain percentage of the cost of producing the goods or rendering the services. Some economists argue that an apparently inflationary loss is really no loss at all, that higher prices represent an improvement in the standard of living. Yet, from our own experience we may conclude that food, shoes, bus rides, coats, newspapers, and many other items have not increased in quality to the extent they have increased in price. To such extent, at least, inflation constitutes a real loss to many people.

Who are the victims of inflation? Pensioners, civil service employees, annuitants, and others who must rely upon relatively fixed incomes are hardest hit by the steady decline in purchasing power of the dollar. Their income does not increase with the growth of the economy; thus, they are prevented from purchasing their fair proportion of the increasing national output. Fixed-dollar savers, including persons having bank accounts, inevitably suffer losses. When a depositor's savings are returned to him in the form of inflated dollars, the depositor has suffered an economic loss. The share of the national output that his savings previously could claim has decreased in proportion to the length of time the savings were on deposit.

It is said that politicians look upon inflation as a way to keep debtors happy, allowing them to repay their loans with inflated dollars. Undoubtedly, there is a certain amount of truth to this indictment, even though it is difficult to believe that our nation's leaders could be so insensitive to the devastating effects that are caused by inflation. As a practical matter, there is little that legislators and politicians can do without incurring the wrath of organized labor and leaders of liberal persuasion.

But what about looking after the interests of savers for a change? Why is nothing done for them? They are unorganized and in less apparent need than certain other categories of voters. The need is real, nonetheless. Let us look at the "plight" of Joe, who had befriended an elderly gentleman. Quite suddenly, the old man died, bequeathing Joe $50,000. Joe rushed to a savings and loan association, where the rate of return is comparatively high, to store his new purchasing power. Thirty-six years went by, and he never touched the original amount, spending only the dividends (as they are called) for such diverse items as taxes, automobile repairs, and Christmas presents. At the present rate of inflation, his $50,000 of purchasing power of former years declined by 50%.

CONCERNING SAVINGS INSTITUTIONS — WERE YOU AWARE?

As a general rule, investments producing low yields entail less risk than those with high rates of return. To the extent an investor undergoes the risk that his capital may not be returned to him, compensation must be paid. Or, to put it another way, *if there is little risk of capital loss, a lender will receive correspondingly less for the use of his capital.*

Persons who put their savings in "permanent" life insurance, banks, and savings and loan associations, or buy bonds, for example, have *fixed-dollar investments.* Each dollar saved is promised to be returned with interest. A fixed-dollar investor obtains, he hopes, safety of his capital. He expects that, whenever desired, he will be able to liquidate his investment to obtain cash equal to the amount of the original investment. But does he fulfill his objective?

Savings Banks and Time Deposits. It is not generally known by savers that savings banks ordinarily have no legal obligation to pay over savings deposits upon a depositor's request. Savings accounts are "time deposits," meaning that the bank reserves (but will seldom exercise) the right to insist upon receipt of *prior notice* from a depositor of his intention to withdraw all or any portion of his savings. After expiration of the notice period, the bank becomes obligated to pay, and the savings may be withdrawn upon the depositor's demand (for a limited period of time).

Usually, notice must be given at least thirty days to six months prior to the date of withdrawal. Savings banks in New York State, for example, may require notice of at least sixty days. And the Commissioner of Banks in Massachusetts may require depositors to give up to a year's notice. Read the fine print in your savings bank book to determine the notice period which may be invoked to limit the withdrawal of your savings. Most savers probably are unaware of this notice requirement because, thankfully, it is seldom invoked. Delays in payment are rarely experienced, as they were in the 1930s.

In almost all savings banks, accounts are insured by the Federal Deposit Insurance Corporation (FDIC) or a state fund (Massachusetts, perhaps the only case). But there are some banks in which deposits are uninsured. Be sure, therefore, before making your deposit, that your account will be insured; and do not let your total deposits exceed the maximum amount of coverage. Insurance, however, does not change the nature of a time deposit. A depositor in an insured account still may be unable to get at his savings until they become "demand" deposits (at expiration of the notice period), assuming the bank does not go into liquidation beforehand.

S&LAs — Time Is Unlimited. A savings and loan association ("S&LA") chartered by the federal government is a mutual institution, owned by and run for the benefit of its depositors. In a mutual organization, all profits, after deduction of expenses, inure to their benefit, either in the form of dividends (or interest) or by additions to surplus for greater security. The depositor, technically, is a shareholder of the association. This is also true of most "state-chartered" associations (also known as "building and loan associations" and "homestead associations"). One who places his savings in an account with a mutual association is not its *creditor,* therefore. This difference may require him to wait an unlimited time before he can withdraw his savings.

Some state-chartered S&LAs are "capitalized," similar to a business corporation, so that the association is run for the benefit of its shareholders and *not* its depositors. In this case, the depositors are creditors of the association, and a delay in payment after due demand would constitute a default.

Savings in a mutual S&LA may *not* be as readily available as money on deposit in a savings bank. *Because the S&LA deposits are on time to an unlimited extent, they never become payable on demand,* and a delay in payment would not itself constitute a default. Unless legally insolvent, the association has the right to delay payment while it converts to cash its substantial holdings of unliquid investments.

Why Are S&LA Dividends Higher? A *mutual savings bank* (also run for the benefit of its depositors) and a mutual S&LA seem about the same to many persons, except for the frequently higher return (in the form of "dividends") paid by the association (when government regulations permit). What is the reason for this difference?

A savings and loan association ordinarily will lend a very high percentage of its members' savings on long-term loans (up to thirty years), secured by real estate mortgages. Long-term loans automatically command a higher rate of interest, the lender sacrificing the possibility of future participation in even higher interest rates. Because the association may have almost all of its funds tied up in such loans, its shareholders are required to relinquish the right to withdraw their savings upon due notice and demand, unlike persons who turn to mutual savings banks.

Associations specialize in financing the purchase and construction of lower-priced homes. Traditionally, they permit borrowers to make down payment of a smaller percentage (10% or 20% for federal S&LAs) of total home cost than would be required by a mutual savings bank under similar circumstances. Thus, a substantial portion of the higher rate of return earned by S&LAs is in compensation for increased risks. With *insured* association accounts, it should be said, the real risk is slight—a loss of return on invested capital until the savings are paid over to the account holder.

Mutual savings banks are not as heavily invested in real property loans as are associations. The banks customarily maintain a greater degree of liquidity, keeping a higher percentage of deposits invested in lower-yielding government obligations, for example, to ensure they would be able to meet depositors' demands for withdrawal.

For these reasons S&LAs often earn a high over-all return and can pay their members a return higher than that paid by mutual savings banks serving the same area. Yet, if S&LAs and mutual savings banks in your locality offer substantially identical returns, as may sometimes be the case, you would seem to have no real choice. Put your money in the savings bank unless you are willing to do your banking in an association located outside of your locality.

All Federal Insurance Is Not the Same. A S&LA member gives a *quid pro quo* for the higher return. He risks that his money will be withheld from him (and no return will be earned) for an extended period, in the event his association experiences financial difficulty. Coverage by the Federal Savings and Loan Insurance Corporation ("FSLIC") is not payable as quickly as FDIC (or state) insurance, which covers savings bank deposits. An association may take whatever time is necessary for it to liquidate its extensive investments secured by real estate mortgages. Unless the association is legally insolvent and a receiver or other public custodian has been appointed to liquidate it, FSLIC insurance is *not* payable. Compare this with FDIC coverage. As soon as an FDIC-insured savings bank fails to pay after due notice and demand, the bank is closed and the insurance is paid almost immediately. In actual practice, however, withdrawal delays have been almost nonexistent. Administrative procedures (including emergency loans to faltering associations) have been developed to prevent delays in payment of insured savings.

If you do decide to entrust your savings to a S&LA, protect yourself by making sure beforehand that your account will be covered by federal insurance. All federal associations are covered, but for state-chartered associations coverage is *optional*. State-chartered S&LAs are usually distinguishable from federal associations. A federal S&LA may, whereas a state-chartered S&LA may not, use the word "federal" in its name. Anyway, whether it is state-chartered or federal, an insured association will have on display a notice informing you that accounts are covered by insurance, and to what extent.

Why Commercial Banks Pay Less. All national (commercial) banks and certain state commercial banks are Federal Reserve members and, therefore, governed by Regulation Q of the Federal Reserve Board. This regulation prohibits a member of the Federal Reserve System from paying interest on *savings accounts* in excess of 4% per annum, compounded quarterly. But in 1966, when interest rates soared, commercial banks legally avoided the 4% maximum by paying $5\frac{1}{2}$% on deposits left for at least three to twelve months, usually, under a negotiable *certificate of deposit* (C/D), offered to small savers in denominations such as $1,000 or $2,500. Savings were siphoned away from S&LAs and savings banks which were invested in long-term, comparatively low-yield mortgages and often could not afford to pay $5\frac{1}{2}$% to attract or hold savings. To force rates down and to promote a more competitive situation for these institutions, federal legislation and regulations set a 5% maximum interest rate on the consumer-type (small-denomination) C/Ds issued by FDIC-insured commercial banks; a 5% limit on FDIC-insured accounts with savings banks; and a 4¾% to 5¼% limit on savings accounts with and savings certificates (similar to C/Ds) of FSLIC-insured S&LAs (the actual rate depending on locality).

Life Insurance Savings – "Uninsured Time Deposits." Life insurance savings can be obtained by borrowing against a policy's cash surrender value (one measure of "savings") or by surrendering the policy in exchange for the cash value. Yet, the *full* amount of savings may not be as readily available as other types of savings.

The other measure of "savings" is the *reserve* of a policy (roughly, the amount set aside by the company in excess of current insurance costs, to pay for future policy benefits). Unavailability of savings results from the fact that the cash value does not always equal the reserve of the policy. In some cases there will be no cash value until the second or third year after the policy has been issued, even though the policy reserve has been steadily increasing. Gradually the cash value will catch up to the reserve by, perhaps, the fifteenth or twentieth year, at which time the "full" amount of savings are available to the insured. This prevents the insurance company from suffering a loss, upon early surrender of the policy, on account of expenses incurred in putting the policy on the books of the company. The sales commission, examining doctor's fee, and other first-year costs have to be paid.

Also, to borrow your savings you will be required to pay interest of 5% per year (6% under older policies). This is about two (or three) percentage points higher than the amount the company will continue to credit to the policy reserves (and, in later years, to the cash value). Following the pattern of savings banks, life insurance companies need not pay over the cash value immediately upon request of the policyholder. Generally, the policyholder may be required to give notice of at least six months before the company will be legally bound to turn the "savings" over to the insured.

To conclude our examination of life insurance savings—for the time being—it should be emphasized that such savings are not protected by federal insurance, unlike most savings bank and S&LA accounts. It is absolutely essential, therefore, that a life insurance company be selected for its financial soundness, which is the best available protection.

How many insureds realize that their savings are in "uninsured time deposits"?

In all fairness, it should be emphasized that savings banks and insurance companies rarely exercise their right to demand a notice of withdrawal; that S&LAs infrequently fail to make payment upon demand; and that very few life insurance companies have gone bankrupt, causing losses to their insureds or policy beneficiaries. When safety is desired, however, the foregoing discussion should be kept in mind. Remember, the safest fixed-dollar investment of all is any obligation of the United States Government.

Regardless of the fixed-dollar system by which you store your savings, you inevitably will sacrifice yield and, usually, forfeit any chance of attaining the 10th Multiple. It cannot be emphasized too often, however, that fixed-dollar savings do play an important role in financial planning.

"Safe" or fixed-dollar investments are a must for some portion of the savings of an individual or a family. Furthermore, for persons having a small amount of savings, perhaps all should be in such investments.

The saver should have safe investments in an amount which would cover emergency situations such as medical treatment and temporary unemployment. Also, there should be enough for contemplated major expenditures such as tuition and an automobile. The amount will vary from one family or person to another, but consideration should be given to keeping, at a minimum, the equivalent of six months' wages in safe investments at all times.

Once having established your emergency fund, the remainder of your savings make up your investment fund, ready to go after the 10th Multiple.

POPULAR — BUT A SURE LOSER

The 1929 Crash wiped out immense paper fortunes and took the lifetime savings of innumerable individuals. Stock prices fell in many instances to 10% of the amount for which the shares had been purchased. Purchases on margin account, as explained previously, caused losses of 100% of the savings of many persons. As a result of these experiences, many investors to this day rely substantially upon safe investments, whether they be in bank accounts, savings bonds, or life insurance. They know that, as a practical matter, invested capital can be turned into cash upon demand, with no loss.

No one can seriously dispute the necessity of having a certain amount of fixed-dollar savings—but concentration on safe investments is often a financially devastating luxury. When an individual puts an excessive amount in fixed-dollar investments at best he can be called a gambler. He is betting that the dollar is not going to be subjected to the effects of inflation. As experience has shown, there is no gamble. He is sure to lose.

What is the answer? If fixed-dollar investments are ruled out as to a portion of the savings of many individuals, where should the savings be put? In equities is the answer.

HEDGING WITH EQUITIES

Typical equity investments are business ownership, common stocks, mutual funds, and real estate. An interest in property (as distinguished from a claim to a specified number of dollars) is the essence of an equity investment. The investor benefits from a rise or suffers from a fall in value of the property. Property ownership is *direct,* for example, when an individual is the outright owner of real property or a store; and *indirect* when a person owns, say, common stocks or common-stock mutual funds.

A fixed-dollar investment involves the right of an investor, derived from a contractual obligation of the other party to the contract, to have returned to him a set amount of money (the savings) plus interest at a stipulated rate. That is all the saver hopes and expects to receive.

The difference between fixed-dollar and equity investments can be further examined by taking a look at a transaction between Peter and Bill. Peter made an equity investment (unusual, perhaps) when he purchased 100 Kennedy 50-cent coins for $100, expecting the coins to further appreciate in value over the next few years. Bill, always looking out for a quick dollar, lent Peter the $100 with which the coin purchase was made, Peter promising to pay interest of 6% per annum. As a result of this transaction, Bill acquired a fixed-dollar investment. If the value of the Kennedy half-dollars ever exceeds the purchase price plus interest expense, Peter derives the whole profit. If, however, the coins drop in value, Peter bears the entire loss. Bill has no interest (or "equity") in their increase or decrease in value, other than as Peter's creditor, whereas Peter is legally obligated to repay the $100 plus interest no matter what happens to the coins or their value.

Equity investments, such as common stock, real estate, and mutual funds, are usually regarded as providing a "hedge against inflation." But what does it mean to hedge? In politics it is a qualification by which an individual can escape from an otherwise firm commitment. A candidate for office may say, ". . . Furthermore, I promise to vote for any *reasonable* extension of social security coverage." By the word "reasonable" the politician prepared an escape hatch for himself.

In saving and investment, to "hedge" is to take inconsistent positions, so that a decline in one position will be offset by an advance in the other. Thus, to hedge against inflation is to invest so that any decrease in purchasing power of one's savings dollar will be offset by increases in the dollar value of his investments. But when *all* of one's savings is in fixed-dollar investments, inflation will take its toll. It always has.

When an individual has invested his savings in equities, the value of the assets underlying his investments increases as the cost of replacement increases, due to rising prices. Also, business is more profitable during inflationary periods, causing the value of an investment to increase, to reflect the anticipated upsurge in earnings. In this way the equity investor is not hurt by inflation; he benefits from it.

But the equity investor is not always as well off as the cautious investor. Deflation increases the purchasing power of fixed-dollar investments. With equities, however, values can be expected to decline during a deflationary period. Savers should remember, though, that in the long run the economy expands. Increasing population, technological improvements, improved products, and new ideas will create investment opportunities and help to expand American business. As a consequence, the real value of equity investments can reasonably be expected to increase, while the real value of safe investments most probably will decline.

10TH MULTIPLES IN REAL PROPERTY

The effects of inflation have benefited millions of persons having an equity investment through home ownership. Real property values have gone up over the years as a result of increased building costs and an inflexible supply of land in a market of accelerating demand.

Even if an individual's real property holding has not appreciated in value, inflation may have caused it to maintain its original dollar value. Thus, the owner may have received some "free" housing during his ownership, after making appropriate adjustments for property carrying costs, interest rates, and devaluation of the dollar.

Constant reminder of the appreciability of real estate investments comes from the savings banks of the nation, pleading for homeowners to refinance their mortgages. In many instances, a bank is willing today to lend as much as or more than the house and land cost thirty-five years ago, recognizing that the dollar value has not declined. Thus, inflation has provided thirty-five years of free or inexpensive housing for the homeowner.

Who suffered a loss as a result of the low-cost housing? The persons whose savings were on deposit in the lending institution, perhaps the homeowner himself. Yet, he may be in a better position, thanks to his equity investment, than the bank depositors who rented their living quarters during the period.

Homeowners should have continued happiness. Constantly increasing numbers of persons desire to make use of land, but only a set amount of land is available to satisfy their demand. Land prices on the average are bound to rise as a consequence.

Real estate investment affords high profit possibilities. William Nickerson describes what he was able to do (and, presumably, what his readers can do) by the title of his bestseller, *How I Turned $1,000 into a Million in Real Estate in My Spare Time.* Save-by-Borrowers may decide to attempt the same feat.

Note, however, there are two major obstacles to successful investing in real estate. An investor must acquire a considerable amount of technical know-how concerning real estate transactions. Also, he must devote a great deal of time to his real estate investments. As compensation, an investor in real estate will earn a *much higher return,* on the average, than he would if he invested the same amount in the average common stock. From an economist's standpoint, we must bear in mind, income from the real estate investments which is allocable to the individual's personal services should be considered employment compensation, instead of profits from his investment.

Purchase, conversion, then sale or management of town houses has proved highly profitable for one New York City couple. On a strictly part-time basis, the couple purchased a Manhattan town house in 1960 for $40,000, spent "more than $45,000" for renovation, and sold the building in 1962 for about a $40,000 profit. Assuming that a good portion of the $85,000 cost was financed by a mortgage covering the property, the percentage of return on investment capital was stupendous. If they had an original equity of $20,-000, their long-term gain of about $40,000 amounted to a 200% profit before taxes and 150% profit after taxes. (This assumes they paid the 25% maximum long-term capital-gains tax.)

Other opportunities are waiting for them as well as for you. Engaging in part-time real estate transactions is an excellent way for a husband and wife to make Multiples. Between them time can be found to arrange for renovation and then lease of the properties. An advantage to real estate dealing is that much of the purchase money can be borrowed, giving the investor a great amount of leverage on his capital contribution.

You must realize, though, that a major obstacle with real estate investments is the problem of turning the investments into cash when the need arises. It may take months, especially during hard times, to find a purchaser or tenants. During periods of unproductivity, the cost of carrying the investment can prove burdensome. Insurance, taxes and repairs still must be paid.

Some alleviation of the three problems of (1) know-how, (2) time, and (3) liquidity of investment has resulted from the availability of shares in real estate syndicates. The syndicate managers have the know-how and spend their own time organizing the syndicate and acquiring the properties. Also, liquidity of the investment is enhanced, the syndicate shares being more readily salable than real estate, but still nowhere as quickly as stocks or mutual funds.

Real estate syndicates do not eliminate all problems. It still takes some skill to recognize a worthwhile investment. Average investors, without specialized study, are not able to pass adequately upon the merits of a proposed investment; nor can they protect themselves from questionable practices of some real estate syndicators. Furthermore, compensation of the syndicate managers cuts deeply into the profit potential.

RIDING MULTIPLE-CYCLES

"Multiple-cycle" seems to be a descriptive way of referring to any investment technique which makes use of both equity and fixed-dollar investments. This technique, when properly employed, produces many Multiples.

During inflationary times, money is comparatively easy to obtain, business is booming, and prices are on the upswing. The dollar value of assets underlying equity investments tends to increase. Equity investors are protected from loss of purchasing power, unlike fixed-dollar investors. At the end of the inflationary cycle, money becomes more difficult to obtain, business is contracting, prices are falling. The dollar value of assets tends to decline, usually faster than the declining cost of living. Such is the effect of a recession or depression.

Equity investments tend to reflect if not exaggerate the state of the economy, whether good or bad. In good times, they tend to provide the investor with purchasing power in excess of the rising cost of living, but during the lower regions of a depression, equity investments may reduce an investor's purchasing power far below the declining cost of living.

The reader is correct if he surmises that fixed-dollar investments provide somewhat different results. In time of depression, the purchasing power of a fixed-dollar investment increases, and the investor has greater real wealth than his counterpart who invests in equities. But as we have seen, during inflationary periods, the fixed-dollar investment shrinks in terms of real wealth, and the investor finds that he is able to purchase less as a result of increasing prices.

Perhaps the reader has anticipated how an informed investor can profit from periods of inflation *and* depression. Studying carefully the trend of the economy, he will take advantage of the increasing value of business assets by investing in growth stocks during anticipated inflationary periods, when he expects stock prices to go higher. But when he believes the prices are leveling off, readying to go into a decline, he will move out of growth stocks into so-called "defensive investments" (such as common stocks of food companies and public utilities). He lets these new investments increase in purchasing power until he believes the bottom of the depression or recession has been reached. In this way those sophisticated in the market can take advantage of a cyclical economy, increasing their purchasing power and wealth no matter which way the economy swings, as long as it does move. To put it another way, by the sale of growth stocks when an inflationary period is nearing an end, the increase in dollar value and purchasing power can be preserved; and, during a period of depressed prices, the investor protects his dollars until such time as his former investments (or their equivalent) may be repurchased for considerably less. When the repurchase is made, near the anticipated bottom of a depression or recession, the investor holds them while, hopefully, they increase in value, until the expected inflationary period nears an end. By riding this "Multiple-cycle" an investor can undergo his 10 Multiples more readily. *Cyclical investment* is the usual name for this investment technique.

Intelligent investing in equity securities to take advantage of economic trends requires a good deal of understanding, which can be acquired from study and application of investment principles to your own investments. For those who are eager to learn and apply investment principles and can accept a certain amount of risk, there are great financial rewards available. This is true even for those who have only a modest amount of money to invest. Study alone will not give you a complete education, however. Unless you have a financial stake in your own decisions, obtained by actual investment, your learning may be unrealistic.

Professional investors who manage the investment funds of certain non-profit institutions have adopted a sliding scale to determine what percentage of fund value, at a given time, should be invested in common stocks. As common stock prices increase, a certain portion of such investments is sold in order to reduce, periodically, that percentage. By this *sliding-scale method,* the investment managers anticipate that the funds will be shifted to defensive or fixed-dollar investments by the time, if ever, the market undergoes a major "technical readjustment"—or, perhaps, a crash.

Investment in equities can produce losses, but is this not true of fixed-dollar investments? We see, therefore, that *all savers are gamblers*. Fixed-dollar investors are betting, whether they are aware of it or not, that inflation will not occur, but most equity investors believe that inflation is inevitable and back their conclusions with their savings.

Chapter Six

SPECULATIVE MULTIPLES

FOLLOW THE LEADER

Widespread interest was aroused by Nicolas Darvas' bestseller, *How I Made $2,000,000 in the Stock Market*. The author, an internationally known dancer, reported how he made profits in excess of $2,000,000 by means of his intriguing "box system." He merely follows the lead set by persons unknown to him who, with increasing demand, are bidding up the price of a stock. Timing of his purchases depends upon the movement of stock price from one box (defined as a range of market prices) to the next.

The underlying premise of his box system seems logical. If a stock, on increasing volume of sales, has been increasing in market value for a number of weeks, the laws of probability suggest that the stock will continue to appreciate in value. It could be profitable, therefore, to buy the stock and hold onto it until the price falls (or, I assume, the price remains inactive during a certain length of time). "Cut your losses and let your profits run," a market adage, has been systematized by Mr. Darvas.

Losses will result from declines in value occurring soon after purchase of a stock. But profits from extended price advances may be greatly in excess of such losses. Rewards are as great as the risks. Darvas reports that his profits, after deduction of losses, totaled $2,450,000 in only 7 years, which included his years of self-instruction. Eliminating his comparatively unprofitable years, it appears that he took about $36,000 or $37,000 (slightly more than the 5th Multiple) and turned it into a pre-tax profit of $2,250,000 (which is more than the 11th Multiple) in only a year and a half.

His box system has certain difficulties, but is interesting to read about. This is not to say that I necessarily recommend adoption of the Darvas system by Save-by-Borrowers.

MARKET DEVICES

Stop Orders. Let us assume shares of stock of a hypothetical company, ABC Corporation, are purchased on the New York Stock Exchange. Then, by prior arrangement, the stockbroker places a "stop order" with the appropriate specialist, a member of the exchange who on the floor of the exchange makes a market for the purchase and sale of ABC and other stocks. The stop order directs the specialist to sell the stock at the best possible price in the event the market price drops to a specified level. In this way, profits are given some degree of protection and losses can be minimized.

As the price of the stock increases, the purchaser adjusts the stop order to a higher level, so that the set-off price of the order trails closely behind the increasing value of the stock. If the price falls more than a few points below the highest price obtained, there will be an automatic sale of the stock.

Let's go back to see how the purchaser made up his mind to buy ABC stock. He noticed, during a period of several weeks, an increasing demand for the stock as evidenced by a steadily growing volume of sales. At the same time, the price moved from 50 to 56 per share. He determined then that if the stock price moved up and out of its current trading range, further advances in price should result. Thus, he bought the stock at 57 per share, after it moved into the higher trading range.

The purchaser instructed his broker to place a stop order with the specialist right away, to be set off if the market price dropped to 54, in which case the stock would be sold immediately for whatever price the market would bring. If the stock increased in price to 60, say, the stop order would be changed to 57 or so. Additional adjustments would be made if the stock price advanced further.

The system contemplates that the stop order be kept closely behind the increasing value of the stock, to protect paper profits. If the stock price falls several points, ending the record of regular price advance, the stock is automatically sold for whatever price the market will bring. This may be sound practice. Once a continuous and rapid advance shows weakness, there is far less reason to believe that the price will advance, if at all, at the former rate.

Stop orders, one must bear in mind, cannot be guaranteed to maximize profits. If they are set too closely to the current market price, a temporary decline of a modest amount which precedes a major price advance would force an undesirable sale of the stock. In such a case, the investor either undergoes the expense of "round-trip" commissions and taxes to repurchase (and ultimately resell) the stock, or he loses out on the major price increase. On the other hand, substantial losses would occur if the stop order were set too far from the current price. As one would expect, determination of the set-off price is a primary difficulty to be faced by an investor making use of stop orders.

Investors wishing to utilize stop orders in a "round-lot" (e.g., 100-share) transaction should know that since April 1961, they have been banned on the American Stock Exchange (the ASE). ASE officials may have reasoned that too many of the orders were in effect; if the stock price dropped several points, to the level that would set off many of the stop orders, there could be a chain reaction setting off additional stop orders, followed by a wholesale dumping on the market of tens or hundreds of thousands of shares. A disastrous decline of the stock price would be a possible result. The ASE does permit their use, however, in an "odd-lot" (e.g., 99-share) transaction. Except in certain instances, stop orders are permissible on the New York Stock Exchange, whether in round-lot or odd-lot transactions.

Limit Orders. As a means to obtain some protection when a stop order cannot be utilized, an investor could direct his broker to place with the specialist a "limit order" to sell the stock. This order would be exercised only if the price declined to the predetermined level *and* the obtainable price were equal to or higher than the price set in the order. Thus, if the limit order to sell is set at 60, it would be executed only if the price of the stock dropped to 60 and the seller were able to obtain a price of 60 or better.

In most instances, a drop in value to the predetermined level would cause the stock to be sold pursuant to the limit order. However, when the market price of a stock drops below the limit price without a sale of the stock, the limit order has proved ineffective to protect the investor. His stock would remain unsold.

Unless an investor settled for a stop order covering an odd lot (say 99 shares) of an ASE-traded stock, he would have to fall back on a limit order. But it may be possible to back up a limit order by an informal agreement with the broker (or registered representative) to have him immediately sell the stock at the market price if the limit order failed. The limit order probably entails, however, too much risk for an investor who seeks to obtain the protection afforded by a stop order. It is wholly dependent upon the broker. Especially in time of crisis, when the special attention would probably be needed, the broker may not be able to remember the investor's request or follow his stock.

TRADING

Mr. Darvas reports that he made more than $2,000,000 by *trading,* the speculative activity of making frequent purchases and sales of stocks with the objective of realizing quick profits. Risk of loss was greater than if he had purchased stocks for investment, to hold for the long run, but the profits he made seem adequate.

Trading the stop-order way may result in a longer holding period for stocks than is customary with ordinary trading activities. The average trader is "in" and "out" of the market quickly, hoping to net 1 or 2 "points." In non-technical language this means that the trader customarily buys and sells stock within a short period of time, to obtain profits of $1 or $2 (one or two points) per share. This would amount to a profit of $100 or $200 for each 100-share lot. To realize such profits, the trader must sell his stock for a sum in excess of the desired spread of 1 or 2 points. The excess is necessary to pay brokerage commissions, the New York stock transfer tax, and the SEC fee.

The trader does not buy for long-run capital appreciation. He feels that capital should not be kept tied up this way but should be kept in the active pursuit of quick profits. Attempting to capitalize on the ups and downs of stock values, he hopes to profit no matter which way the stock values go. All that matters to the trader is that a stock be active, and that he be successful in predicting the time and direction of movement. The pattern of a stock as it moves from 30 to 100 could look something like the chart on the next page.

As the stock moves upward in value from 30 to 48, a "perfect" trader could profit by becoming the owner of the stock when the stock is at 30 and holding onto it during the advance to 48. Then, he would sell. When the stock drops to 38, an intermediate low, the trader would buy the stock again, to benefit from the forthcoming advance to 64. As the stock moves from 30 to 100, a total of 70 points, the ideal trader would pick up 112 points, 42 points *more* than the 70-point advance from 30 to 100.

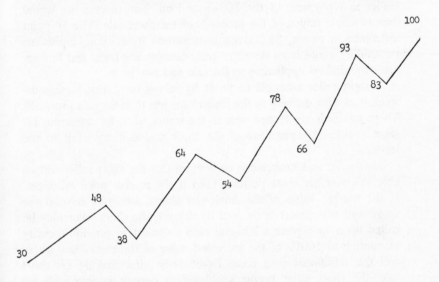

WHAT IT MEANS TO SELL SHORT

The trader could go on to double the 42 extra points. He would accomplish this by selling twice as many shares as he owned when the stock reached each of the intermediate highs (48, 64, 78, and 93). Assume the trader bought 100 shares of stock when it was selling at 30. When the stock reached 48, the trader would make a *"long sale"* of the 100 shares which he actually owned. In addition, he would sell an extra 100 shares, which he did *not* own, by means of a *"short sale."* In order to avoid legal difficulties, the trader must inform his broker that he is selling short. The broker borrows the 100 shares from another customer, usually; and the broker (or, occasionally, the lending customer) obtains in effect an interest-free loan of the sale proceeds during the borrowing period.

A few days after the sale takes place, the borrowed stock is delivered to the purchaser, who pays the purchase price in cash. These sale proceeds are then, in essence, held by the broker (or his lending customer) without payment of interest as security to guarantee return of the same number of borrowed shares.

If a stock which had been sold short at 50 declines in value to 40, the trader could buy 100 shares of the stock at 40 for delivery to the lender in repayment of the 100-share loan. The short seller would then obtain a return of the proceeds of the short sale. The 10-point difference in prices, $1,000 on a 100-share transaction, represents the trader's profit from the short sale, disregarding taxes and brokerage commissions applicable to the sale and purchase.

A short seller attempts to profit by selling first, then buying the stock back (for delivery to the lender) for less than the sale proceeds. These proceeds are turned over to the trader when he closes out his short position by purchase of the stock and delivery of it to the lender.

The lender and broker can be assured that the short seller will be able to cover his short position even if the market price advances. If the market value of the borrowed shares increases beyond the amount of sale proceeds on security deposit, the short seller may be called upon to deposit additional cash sufficient to provide security amounting to 100% of the increased value of the stock. But where will this additional cash come from? Soon after making his short sale, the short seller becomes obliged to deposit margin with his broker—cash (or marginable securities having a loan value) equivalent to 70% of the short sale proceeds. This is the present requirement of Regulation T promulgated by the Federal Reserve Board, which regulation governs credit extended by brokers. (Its counterpart, Regulation U, regulates credit extended by banks.) The broker will draw from this 70% margin deposit to provide any additional security required for the lender. Whenever the short-seller's equity —original margin deposit minus any increase in market value of the borrowed stock—drops to 30% of the market value, the broker will call upon the short seller to put up additional margin (a margin call). If the short seller fails to comply, he will be forced to cover (at a loss), by buying the stock and delivering it to the lender, thereby closing out the short sale.

One who buys stock can suffer a loss no greater than the amount he paid for the stock (disregarding any loss of subsequent appreciation). His potential losses are limited and ascertainable. But how does a trader protect himself from unlimited losses which could occur if he sold a stock short at 20, only to see it climb to 30, then 40, then 50, and so on? As can be seen, the loss potential is not calculable and could be extremely high. Stop orders are a means, but not a guarantee, to cover this situation. The short seller merely instructs his broker to place a stop order, with the appropriate exchange specialist, to "cover" or buy the stock at the then market price if the price reaches a predetermined higher level. By use of this covering order to "buy on stop," a short seller's losses can be limited, as a practical matter.

We see, therefore, that a trader desires to be "long" in a stock when its price is advancing and "short" when its price is falling. In this way he would get maximum benefit from fluctuations in prices. An increase in price from 30 to 100 represents a 70-point increase. A look at the chart on page 85 will show that profits would amount to 154 points if the trader owns the stock during all advances and is short the stock during all declines in price.

There is nothing mysterious about short sales. It is merely an inversion of the purchase-sale sequence employed by persons who believe the market price for the stock is to go up. When it is believed the market price will decline, the short seller makes profits in similar fashion.

Short sales can produce quicker profits. It frequently takes one or two months for a stock to advance 5 points, but a 5-point decline in the same stock may occur in only one or two days. A trader's difficulty, of course, is to determine whether a stock is going to move up or down. One who can forecast this a sufficiently high percentage of times can make trading a lucrative activity.

THE HIGH COST OF TRADING

A trader, often holding his investments for six months or less, pays income taxes on his short-term capital gains at the rate applicable to his ordinary income, instead of the 25% maximum. This is one of the high costs of trading. Traders must obtain a higher pre-tax yield, therefore, to achieve the same after-tax yield as one who holds his investments for the long run. There is another high cost. Brokerage commissions can cut deeply into the profits of investors in stocks.

The commission schedule (representing the lowest amount an exchange member can charge for purchases or sales taking place on the NYSE or ASE) follows:

	Brokerage Commission	
Price of 100 Shares	*Fixed Amount*	*Percentage of Price*
Less than $100	(As agreed upon)	
$100 to $150	$ 6 minimum	
$150 to $400	$ 3 plus	2%
$400 to $2,400	$ 7 "	1%
$2,400 to $5,000	$19 "	$\frac{1}{2}$%
$5,000 to $36,000	$39 "	$\frac{1}{10}$%
$36,000 and over	$75 maximum	

The brokerage commissions above are applicable to each *round-lot transaction* (ordinarily 100 shares, but 10 shares for a few very high-priced or inactive stocks). If 200 shares are purchased, the brokerage cost is twice as much as the cost of a 100-share transaction, there being no volume discount.

If fewer than 100 shares are purchased—an "odd-lot transaction" —the fixed amount in the chart above must be reduced by $2 (although the $6 minimum remains).[1] But this reduction is offset by an additional charge, the odd-lot differential. Shares of stock having a market price per share of less than $40 (ASE) or $55 (NYSE) cost an additional 12½ cents per share in an odd-lot transaction, as compensation to the odd-lot dealer who sells that amount to the investor's stockbroker. If the market price is more than the $40 or $55, an odd-lot differential of 25 cents per share must be added to the market price. This is only a simplification, the actual rules being quite complex.

Save-by-Borrowers who purchase $1,000 worth of stock each year would probably be making odd-lot purchases. If the stock sells for $25 per share, a total of approximately 40 shares would be bought, at the additional (odd-lot) cost of $5. Accordingly, the total cost of the stock would be $1,005 plus the brokerage commission of $15.05 ($5 plus 1% of $1,005), amounting to $1020.05. (The extra

[1] For transactions involving at least $100, there is a maximum commission of $1.50 per share, but this too will give way to the $6 minimum commission on the entire transaction.

5 cents is also an odd-lot cost, representing the broker's 1% commission on the odd-lot differential of $5.)

For shares sold by him on the NYSE or ASE, the seller pays a New York State stock transfer tax and a Securities and Exchange Commission fee. At times, we'll refer to the tax and fee as the "transfer taxes."

The New York State stock transfer tax, when applicable, can be determined from the following schedule:

Price of Each Share	Tax on Each Share
Less than $5	1½¢
$5 but less than $10	2½¢
$10 but less than $20	3¾¢
$20 or more	5¢

Upon sale in New York of 100 shares of stock at $18 per share, the New York State stock transfer tax would apply, amounting to $3.75 (100 times 3¾¢).

Minimal in amount, the SEC fee is 1 cent for each $500 and fraction thereof in cost. Accordingly, a $1,005 sale price would involve a SEC fee of 3 cents.

See if you understand how to calculate the tax and fee to be paid by the seller of the 40 shares of stock for $1,005. He would have to pay:

New York State stock transfer tax	$2.00
SEC fee	.03
	$2.03

Traders among the public are at a disadvantage, compared with members of the stock exchanges and certain persons with an affiliation, who pay no brokerage commissions or reduced ones. (They are required to pay the same transfer tax and fee, it should be observed.) A trader having this advantage will show a profit with either fewer successful trades or a smaller gross profit margin on successful trades.

Brokerage commissions and transfer taxes can constitute such a high percentage of stock costs that you are apt to lose much of your investment fund if you engage in trading, unless you are a thoroughly experienced investor and are knowledgeable about the principles of technical analysis. Two excellent books on technical analysis are listed in the Bibliography.

Even an experienced trader assumes high risks. Recurrent brokerage commissions and stock transfer taxes applicable to frequent purchases and sales of stock may make deep inroads into his investment fund (more aptly called "speculation fund") unless he possesses and exercises a reasonable amount of skill. Fortunately, not all of his trades need be profitable. His successful trades at least should recoup the losses from his other transactions. Anything left over will be his profit.

By referring to the schedules of brokerage commissions and transfer taxes, we can determine the cost of trading in 100-share lots of a stock selling for $50 per share. Upon purchase of the stock, the ordinary trader would pay brokerage commissions amounting to $44, as follows:

$\frac{1}{2}$% of the $5,000 price of the stock	$25.00
$19.00 fixed amount	19.00
	$44.00

When the trader sells his 100 shares of stock, he must pay the transfer tax and fee and another round of brokerage commissions (hence the term "round-trip commissions and taxes"). The total cost of selling the 100 shares, assuming the shares have not changed in value, would be $49.10, computed as follows:

$\frac{1}{2}$% of the $5,000 price of the stock	$25.00
$19.00 fixed amount	19.00
New York State stock transfer tax	5.00
SEC fee	.10
	$49.10

See how costly the speculative activity of trading can be when a trader fails to obtain a satisfactory percentage of successful trades. Purchase *and* sale of 100 shares of stock at $50 per share would involve a commission, tax and fee totaling $93.10, approximately 1.8% of the $5,000 invested.

If the trader makes ten different $5,000 speculations, his stock failing to either decrease or increase in value, he would pay ten times $93.10, or a total of $931.00, in commissions, taxes and fees. This unsuccessful trader would suffer losses equivalent to 18% of his original $5,000 investment.

An investor should be aware that the percentage cost of commissions is much greater with lower-priced stocks. Take, for example, a stock purchased by a trader for $3 per share. He would need a $\frac{1}{4}$-point (25-cent) spread to make any profit on the 100 shares. (The profit would turn out to be $5.49.) If he sold the stock at $3\frac{1}{8}$ or less, he would suffer a loss. The $\frac{1}{4}$-point spread for a $3 stock represents an increase of $8\frac{1}{2}$% which must be attained before loss can be avoided.

At the other extreme, each share of the common stock of International Business Machines once sold for about $450. Round-trip commissions and taxes would amount to $155.90, which is only $\frac{34}{100}$ of 1% of the $45,000 cost of the stock. Whereas an increase in market value of $8\frac{1}{2}$% for the $3 stock was needed to prevent a loss on one complete trade, the same percentage increase on the $450 stock would provide enough profit to pay for *24½ round-trip transactions*. As can be seen, commissions are not too costly percentagewise when a person deals in high-priced stocks.

INVESTING FOR PERCENTAGE APPRECIATION

There is a basic difficulty, however, with high-priced stocks. A 10-point increase on a $500 stock is only a 2% appreciation in value. On the other hand, if the stock sold originally for $40 per share, the 10-point advance in price would represent a 25% increase in value.

If stock prices, whether low or high, increased in equal proportions, it would be best to restrict trading activities to high-priced stocks, the percentage cost of commissions being considerably less. However, stocks may not increase in value by equal proportions.

The value of a share of stock ordinarily reflects the anticipated earnings allocable to the share. Small companies can more easily double their earnings than corporate empires, such as General Motors. Thus, it would seem that stock values of smaller companies tend to double more quickly than those of the more substantial companies. Smaller corporations generally have lower stock prices than major companies and one would naturally expect a greater percentage of price fluctuation in lower-priced stocks than in higher-priced stocks. This is the rationale in support of the theory that the *square roots of stock-market prices tend to make equal arithmetic movements*. If this is true, it means that a stock selling for 81 will tend to advance to 100 (its square root 9 advancing to 10) at the same time that a stock selling for 16 will tend to advance to 25 (its square root 4 advancing to 5). The lower-priced stock thereby increases 56% in value while the higher-priced stock advances only 23% in value.

If the theory of "arithmetically progressing square roots" is well-founded, a Multiple-seeking investor who can spot good investment opportunities should concentrate on medium-priced stocks. He would avoid the high percentage cost of commissions applicable to the lower-priced stocks and take advantage of the theory that moderately priced stocks undergo a greater percentage appreciation in value than higher-priced stocks. A buying range of 20–30 probably would achieve this objective.

Traders especially should consider adopting a philosophy of *percentage appreciation*. Instead of purchasing stocks to obtain the maximum number of points on each share of stock, they could concentrate on maximizing the percentage appreciation in value of their investments. There is a difference.

Many traders would probably be content to obtain a net increase of two or three points, for example, disregarding the amount of money tied up in the stock to produce the increase. A two-point net increase on a $100 stock represents a 2% appreciation. Yet, if the investor had invested his money in, say, a $20 stock and had obtained a net increase of only one point, his percentage appreciation would be 5%, $2\frac{1}{2}$ times the percentage increase on the other investment. Especially for traders, the concept of percentage appreciation is significant. At times stocks can be expected to rise a point or so for purely technical reasons, irrespective of the "real" value of the stock. In such case, for a given number of dollars, the trader could maximize his return by purchasing stocks in the middle-to-lower price range. The lowest-priced stocks are not appropriate for percentage-appreciation purchasing because of the high percentage cost of brokerage commissions.

INTELLIGENT SPECULATION

Whether a person trades or invests, he should be attempting to maximize the rate of return on his investment fund. This rate of return, as defined previously, is based upon dividends *and* appreciation in capital value. Dividends seldom exceed 7%, and, for the past ten years (ending 1964), have averaged only 4.2% per year for dividend-paying common stocks listed at year's end on the New York Stock Exchange. To many people, dividends are insignificant and do not enter into their determinations to buy or sell. This is true particularly of traders, who expect the stock price to fall by the amount of the dividend.

To obtain a high rate of return on his investment fund a person must invest for substantial capital appreciation but assume a correspondingly high degree of risk. In other words, he should speculate (if this be the correct term to use) intelligently.

Stocks which are likely candidates for significant increases in market value are often more risky, speculative stocks. For investors who are willing to take a chance, however, the profits from one speculative stock investment can amount to their lifetime investment goal.

Xerox (then known as Haloid) was a speculative stock in 1947, selling for 75 cents per share (adjusted to reflect later capital changes). In 1965, the stock reached a high of 215 per share, increasing to 28,666% of the prior market value. An investor who put $4,000 in the stock in 1947 has been amply rewarded, so he will say. His $4,000 speculation increased to about $1,146,640 (disregarding dividends, commissions and taxes).

You may be wondering whether in the future there will be other Xeroxes. Undoubtedly. And one who looks hard enough will find them. As would be expected, an excellent prospect for substantial capital appreciation is investment in the stock of relatively small, well-managed companies while they are undergoing growth. Take a long look at some of the stocks sold "over-the-counter." Also, look at stocks traded on the American Stock Exchange, the proving ground for many growing companies. Many corporations will list their common stock on the ASE for a temporary period only, until the company grows to the point where it can meet the more stringent listing requirements of the New York Stock Exchange, also known as the Big

Board. General Motors and Du Pont are among the major organizations which got their start on the ASE.

PRICE-EARNINGS RATIO

An investor should not automatically shy away from a company which pays no dividends. Instead, the investor should investigate the earnings record of the company, and ascertain the number of times the market price of the stock exceeds the annual earnings. This factor, of primary importance to investors, is the *price-earnings ratio.*

Formerly, a low price-earnings ratio was common, in the neighborhood of 10–1. Now, however, the average ratio is about 20–1 for stocks listed on the NYSE. Some stocks, IBM for example, have had price-earnings ratios of 80–1 or higher, indicating that investors are willing to pay high prices in anticipation of substantially increased earnings (and stock prices) for the future.

It may be unwise, however, for an investor to risk his money in stocks having a price-earnings ratio in excess of, say, 20–1. When stock prices are tumbling, these often suffer the worst declines. In 1962, prices fell approximately 30%. IBM, selling for 579 per share, dropped to 300, for a decline of almost 50%.

HOW IMPORTANT ARE DIVIDENDS?

A high cash-dividend rate need not be a major concern. In fact, it may deprive a growing company of funds which could be used to undergo expansion and meet competition. Instead of purchasing stocks to obtain annual dividends amounting to a 3%, 4%, or 5% return on invested capital, many investors make their purchases almost wholly on the basis of prospects for appreciation in market value of the stock, disregarding dividends (except as a negative factor, possibly). They are well aware that substantial capital appreciation is the only way to obtain a yield sufficient to achieve the 10th Multiple.

An investment in a young, aggressive company using most of its earnings for research and development and to purchase new plants and equipment may have much better prospects for high return over the years—more so than an investment in a fully matured corporation distributing most of its earnings to its shareholders.

For tax reasons, some investors do not wish to receive cash dividends unnecessarily. Upon receipt of dividends they would be obliged to pay federal income taxes, possibly at the highest bracket of 70%. By investment in stock of corporations retaining their earnings, this high tax would be avoided, and compounding of the business income would occur automatically.

To the extent a Save-by-Borrower receives cash dividends, compounding of his investment return could occur only by reinvestment, after payment of individual income taxes and brokerage commissions. The total cost of brokerage commissions and taxes easily could take away 25% or more of the earnings distributed by the company.

The beneficial effect of a corporation paying no or low dividends should be apparent. Assume all earnings are retained by the company for an indefinite period instead of distributed to the stockholders, only for them to reinvest. The annual retention of capital by the corporation, employed in an income-producing capacity for the benefit of the stockholders, would be approximately 33% greater (assuming a 25% combined tax and commission cost). This is of tremendous importance over the long run, during which the investor can postpone payment of taxes and avoid brokerage commissions by holding onto his investments in stocks of growth companies.

The 33% higher amount of annual reinvested capital would produce approximately 33% more earnings, which in turn would be capitalized each year to afford the investor a compounding of earnings. Over the years, the difference in investment values, theoretically at least, would be many times greater than the alternative of dividend payment and reinvestment. When the investor finally decides to sell his appreciated stock and pay the long-term capital-gains tax, he will pay no more than 25%, if he has held the stock for longer than six months.

To encourage corporations to declare dividends with respect to corporate earnings, federal income tax law penalizes corporate earnings in excess of $100,000 which cannot be justified by reasonable or reasonably anticipated needs of the corporate enterprise. Yet this tax law does not inhibit legitimate growth of the corporation and seems less of a reason for the declaration of dividends by many companies than the desire to maintain good shareholder relations.

The desire for dividends sometimes will force the trustee of a trust to invest in high-dividend, low-growth stocks, to fulfill the purposes of the trust. The settler of the trust may have expressed his desire to provide an adequate income to beneficiaries during their lifetime but may have been unwilling (perhaps ill-advisedly) to give the trustee power to invade the corpus of the trust.

There is a way to deprive a trustee of the discretionary power to invade corpus, yet enable him to invest in growth stocks without injuring income beneficiaries of the trust. The trust agreement could have a *percentage-payout* provision, based on a formula involving asset value at commencement of the trust year and capital appreciation and dividends during the year.

A percentage-payout provision could require, for example, that the trustee pay the income beneficiary (1) all cash dividends; plus (2) trust corpus (in cash) which, when added to the dividend payout for the year, would amount to a total trust payout of, say, 6% of the trust value at the start of the trust year; plus (3) 20% of the capital appreciation, if any, of the trust assets during the trust year. With such a provision, a trustee could feel free to seek capital growth of the trust assets, instead of restricting his stock purchases to the low-growth, high-dividend stocks.

Upon termination of the trust and distribution of the assets to the trust remaindermen, the original assets would have increased in value substantially higher, on the average, than if the trustee had followed a policy of investing to obtain a high dividend yield.

Investors who now rely on dividend income for part or all of their support could adapt the foregoing percentage-payout provision to their own needs. A precedent for giving income-seekers an opportunity to invest in low-dividend, high-growth stocks is found in the mutual fund industry. Many mutual funds will, upon prior arrangement, make regular cash payments to their investors. To the extent that dividends are insufficient to cover the desired payment, it will be covered by a sale of one or more mutual fund shares of the investor.

REGULAR AND INVERSE MULTIPLES

The speculative quality of many ASE-traded stocks explains why it is not uncommon for their values to experience a Multiple in appreciation or depreciation. Value of a stock may appreciate 100% (a regular Multiple) or decline 50% (an inverse, half Multiple). At random, I selected 50 common stocks from a list of common stocks traded on the ASE. Of the 50 stocks, 18 had achieved a high price which was at least double the low price during a recent 14-month period ending early in 1964. Most of the 18 stocks made at least one "regular" Multiple during the 14-month period; and the remaining few stocks declined in value, making at least one "inverse" (half) Multiple.

A speculator could have realized one or more Multiples or half-Multiples (regularly or inversely), assuming that his transaction was timed so as to buy at the low price and sell—whether long or short—at the high price. As said previously, a sale of stock prior to its purchase constitutes a short sale, a procedure by which a trader hopes to profit from an anticipated price decline by selling the stock first, then buying it (closing out his position in the stock) at a lower price.

Multiples may be realized more quickly by purchasing speculative stocks. The risks will be greater in many instances, but usually equal to the profit potential. By purchase of stocks having a low price-earnings ratio, however, the investor could lessen the risk of loss. Furthermore, a low dividend rate, or none, may maximize his opportunity for capital appreciation.

CYCLICAL STOCK TRANSACTIONS

Speculative and growth stocks experience greater changes in value than *defensive stocks*. Defensive common stocks represent an equity interest in companies providing goods and services less vulnerable to changes in the economy. Foods and utilities are good examples. The more volatile issues, including airlines, chemicals, and automobiles, are cyclical in nature, and temporary declines in value of 50% can be expected. Proper timing of sales and purchases of cyclical stocks can produce a high rate of return for investors.

Ideally, an investor should buy the more volatile issues at their low and sell them at their high, during each cycle of prices. Accomplishing this ideal is impossible, of course. The most an investor can do is analyze economic and market indicators, estimate the direction and extent of movement of particular stock prices, and hope to benefit from a major portion of the price change. Success in cyclical investment can substantially increase the rate of return on an investment fund and more quickly reach the 10th Multiple.

TECHNICAL ANALYSIS

A *technical analyst* (also known as a "technician") makes predictions about future price movements, basing his predictions on "technical indicators" such as price trends, outstanding short interest, and volume of sales. His decisions are not an indication of the underlying value of a stock, about which he may be little concerned. Instead, he spends much of his time poring over charts and graphs which reveal the informative trends of stock prices and sales volume. From their charts, the technicians (also called "chartists") claim they can predict when a stock price is going to rise or fall. Their predictions have to be true only part of the time for them to realize substantial profits.

As an example of technical analysis, consider the stock market action of stock in ABC Company. Last June, the stock was selling for $50 per share. In July, the price began rising until it reached $60 per share, when a great many investors were attracted to the stock and began purchasing it, hoping for a ride to even greater highs.

Profit-takers were at work, however, selling their own stock in the quantities demanded by the newly attracted purchasers. The market price leveled off at 60–62, then declined when the supply created by the profit-takers exceeded the demand of the new investors. The support for a price advance beyond 60–62 was exhausted by the overabundance of supply.

During the next two months, the stock price continued to decline. Meanwhile, technicians were reviewing their charts and determining that if the price of ABC stock dropped back to 50, there would be a large demand for the stock. Investors would buy the stock at 50 to get in on profits which they missed by failing to buy ABC stock when it previously sold for 50.

A technician will base his conclusion on a belief that many people do not like to buy stocks after they have gone through a price rise. After all, why should they pay 60 for something they could have obtained for only 50 not too long ago? Whether this attitude is foolish or not, the technician realizes this type of thinking does occur among many investors.

When ABC stock drops to a price nearing $50 per share, the technician is alerted. He may place a stop order at $51\frac{1}{4}$ to buy the stock, just to ensure that he does not miss the anticipated advance in price. The order is executed. To minimize his losses, he may have directed his broker to place a stop order to sell the stock if it drops to 48¾, in event his predictions do not come true and the stock price continues to fall. Let us say, however, that his predictions come true and the price advances. When should he sell?

A great many people bought ABC stock at 60–62, but were disappointed when the stock dropped in value. They were unwilling to sell their shares at a loss, however, when the price was falling to 50–51. Such an attitude can be very costly, especially when the stock price keeps dropping. Be that as it may, the technician believes he knows the attitude of the average investor in ABC stock and gets ready to capitalize on it. He believes there are a substantial number of persons waiting to sell when the market price again reaches 60–62. This anticipated excess of supply may prevent the stock from going above 60–62. Accordingly, the technician sells his stock and takes his profits when the stock reaches 58¾ or so. He may then proceed to other areas of quick profit, returning to ABC stock if it breaks through the *resistance level* of 60–62.

As you can see, there is a school of stock market analysis that may be worth your while to study.

THE AGE OF THE COMPUTER

Projects have been undertaken to program computers with such variables as stock prices, sales volume, dividends, taxes, and other economic data. Sponsors of the projects are trying to determine whether a computer can be programed to predict price changes with a high degree of reliability. Unless the stock market is completely irrational, it would seem that computers should prove better at predicting stock trends than human beings (some of whom are pretty good at it). It is only a question of identifying the variables, some important ones of which may not be known today. In due course, I believe, enough of the variables will be found and their relationships ascertained to make computer predictions a valuable tool for investors.

Use of computers to predict stock market action would give project insiders a competitive advantage. Problems would arise, however, if the information, when turned out by the computers, were made known to the investing public. When the computer was bullish and emitted a "buy" signal, demand for stocks could shoot prices sky high; on the other hand, when the computer made a bearish forecast and said "sell," prices could drop to new lows. Whether the factor of computer recommendations could be programed would have to be determined.

If computer advice could be relied upon, the fortunes to be made by insiders would be beyond estimation. Who knows, a bestseller may come out any day now entitled *How My Computer Invested $1,000 and Made $2,000,000 in the Stock Market in Thirty Minutes*.

I am engaged in a related project, based for the most part on price-percentage changes over relevant periods. I believe it is possible for a computer to point out which group of stocks on the average will outperform the trend of the market, whether up or down. Far from being perfect, the computer would be no more than a tool, to afford the investor a marginal advantage.

Even without computers, an investor can learn and apply the rules of stock market timing. If he does, he will have an excellent chance to obtain high stock market profits. Guarantees against loss are not to be found. But there are techniques for minimizing risk and maximizing profits.

The small investor, like the big-timer, can slowly divest himself of his equity investments as stock prices advance to record highs and be sitting with a high proportion of defensive or fixed-dollar investments when stock market prices start to decline. After a substantial decline, he can start reinvesting in equities, and be fully invested in equities when prices start moving upward again.

Through a system of timing, an investor should be able to obtain yields in excess of the estimated 12% after taxes produced during 1951–64 by the average stock traded on the NYSE. Proper timing techniques could increase an investor's yield to 15%, say. At this rate of return, a person saving and investing $1,000 each year would achieve the 10th Multiple in about 36 years.

We will see now what the average investor reasonably could have realized by a regular program of saving and investment, assuming in many instances a reinvestment of dividends. Instead of trading or speculating, we assume stock purchases for the long run, without use of any timing techniques except periodic purchase of stock in equal dollar amounts. To the extent that an investor took the trouble to learn and apply rules of stock selection, he probably would have obtained stock market profits in excess of the average.

Chapter Seven

10 MULTIPLES AN EASIER WAY

TECHNICAL, CYCLICAL, AND FUNDAMENTAL SCHOOLS

Three major schools of investment are open to investors. Technical analysis, as we have seen, is based on statistical data not directly related to fundamental values of the stocks. The technician does not necessarily care whether the "real" value of a stock will ultimately rise. He spends his time figuring out ways to make a quick profit from price movements, whether up or down, anticipated for the near future. The discipline may be too demanding for non-professionals, however.

Cyclical investment is an intermediate approach. Metals, chemicals, or other cyclical stocks are purchased during periods of rising prices, but the cyclical investor hopes that by the time inflation has reached its peak he will have switched to fixed-dollar or other defensive investments, to protect the real value of his savings during the oncoming recessionary or deflationary period.

The most popular school, and by far the easiest to follow, is *fundamentalism,* which teaches the investor to buy sound stocks and hold them for the long run. A fundamentalist will purchase stocks when they are selling substantially below the fundamental value he assigns to the stock. Such values are calculated by considering, among other things, the financial statements of the company, competition, sales records, labor conditions, managerial ability, and the prospects for the industry and economy generally. The assigned fundamental value relates directly to the expected earnings for the company. When he believes the price of a stock does not adequately reflect anticipated earnings, he will buy the stock and hold it indefinitely, during which time he hopes it will increase considerably in market price. Further increases in value may be achieved as expected earnings for the company increase.

"Hold onto the stock no matter what happens, unless there is a fundamental reason to sell" is the fundamentalist's advice to an investor. "In the long run, a sound stock is bound to recover any paper losses and realize new highs."

Such has been the experience of many of today's leading stocks. General Motors, AT&T, and Xerox have all suffered tremendous price declines at one time or another. Yet each of these stocks hit a new high in 1964 (AT&T) or 1965 (G.M. and Xerox). The average price for railroad stocks took until 1964 to push beyond its record high set before the Great Depression. And the average may go much higher. Highway congestion and the need for mass transportation, "piggy-back" movement of vehicles, elimination of featherbedding, and the great amounts of land held by railroads may each contribute to an increase in rail stock values. It would seem, though, that many other industries offer a substantially higher capital-appreciation potential.

Unsound stocks may never recover from high market prices of preceding years. An investor must be careful, therefore. His task is to remain invested in stocks having good prospects for undergoing significant increases in earnings. When one of his stocks fails to meet this test, he will eliminate it from his portfolio, to make way for a better investment.

Fundamentalism is convenient for a novice investor. Also, it is relied upon by many investors who have no time to study investment principles conscientiously. To help fundamentalists in their search for good stocks, some brokerage houses distribute stock analyses to their customers at no cost. As a further aid, some houses make available an updated list of stocks they recommend for various investment objectives. At the least, these publications offer some direction in the search.

Finally, the investor makes his selection and purchase. Following fundamentalist teachings, he retains permanent ownership of his stock purchase, unless there is good reason why he should sell. A reason may be pointed out to him by a periodic letter from his stockbroker, although when written by a major firm the letter may be the immediate cause of a predicted decline in price.

Fundamentalism is a school for "rocking-chair" investors, as a result of the comparative ease with which profits can be made. Often, there is little or no effort on the part of the investor. It may be disheartening for you to review the immense profits which you, as a long-term investor, could have realized in years past. Yet, if you believe the profits of the past are an indication for the future, you may decide to obtain some of the profits for yourself, without further delay.

A long-term investor may run into psychological problems, at times, especially when the market values of his investments fall below cost. It so happens that during a temporary setback in prices an investor can pick up bargains in stocks, to make the best out of a bad situation. In general, however, the stock market averages have always gone up. But, in order to benefit from advances after a severe decline, an investor must be able to hold his investments, *without liquidation,* during periods of economic difficulty. An adequate emergency fund will minimize possibilities of forced liquidation and give assurance that investments can be retained until, on the average, they recover in market value.

Assuming the investor obtains adequate diversification of his investments and takes advantage of dollar-cost averaging, protective devices discussed later in this chapter, the risk of loss to him can be minimized and the rate of return on his investment may put him within striking distance of the 10th-Multiple objective.

GROWTH STOCKS

Growth of an industry from infancy to adulthood produces along the way many Multiples for its investors. When you are looking for sound investments, you would do well to determine which are the well-managed and aggressive companies. Some of the most famous fortunes of the world were produced by the expanding oil industry, for example. The names of J. Paul Getty and John D. Rockefeller come to mind. Railroads were responsible for the Harriman and Vanderbilt fortunes. Chemicals, airlines, automobiles, steel, and other major industries have produced immense wealth for their investors, especially the earlier ones. But opportunity here is far from depleted. Industries not yet in existence will have their names added to the list of fortune-producers.

As a practical matter, the only way for one to become rich is to invest in sound common stocks, holding onto them as long as they remain fundamentally sound. When, however, an individual puts all his resources in fixed-dollar investments such as savings accounts, savings bonds, and life insurance, he should resign himself to financial insecurity, and dependence upon social security, if available.

Let's digress for a moment. Social Security is not the final answer to the financial needs of our older citizens. It is true that a Social Security payment of $200 per month to a husband and wife is similar to an investment of $48,000 producing an annual rate of return, after taxes, of 5%. Many people will find this income inadequate, however, and work past their normal age of retirement.

Persons who find it necessary to continue working past their retirement age are dismayed to learn that they may not be entitled to full Social Security benefits, even though they have paid the Social Security tax for so many years. As the law now stands, Social Security benefits paid to a person before he reaches the age of seventy-two are reduced when his earnings for a month exceed $125. For every additional dollar over $125 earned in the month, his monthly benefit will be decreased by 50 cents, unless his earnings for the month exceed $225, in which case he will be entitled to *no* benefit for the month. Therefore, by earning $100 more than $125 in a single month, he will lose $50 in Social Security benefits (which would not have been taxed), and still be required to pay a tax—at his ordinary income rate—on the full $100 of excess earnings. As strange as it may seem, persons in high income tax brackets actually *lose* money by earning the extra $100.

Social Security is commonly considered as *insurance* against the contingency of old age. Yet, after years of "premium payment" and occurrence of the contingency (reaching old age) the "insured" may obtain no benefits. It appears instead that a primary purpose is to encourage older workers to retire from the labor force, to make room for younger workers. Certainly Social Security was not intended to benefit only the needy. You can have a monthly investment income of $1,000,000 and still receive the full, unreduced amount of Social Security benefits. This may not be just, but it is the law. Certainly it is no deterrent to having a sizable income from investments.

RAPIDITY OF MULTIPLE ACHIEVEMENT

Rapidity of Multiple achievement is usually proportional to the degree of risk an investor is willing to assume. Riches produce greater riches, the wealthy being able to afford to take a calculated risk to obtain a higher return on their investments. Whether you are willing to invest your capital where the returns are higher is a decision only you can make. Risks can be minimized, however, if you study and apply the principles of investment in stocks, whether you follow the fundamental, cyclical, or technical school.

Multiples can be reached more quickly by skillful short-term trading, as long as the income tax bracket of the trader is comparatively low, but when the applicable tax rate is high, he may be better off seeking long-term capital gains, to be taxed at the maximum rate of only 25%. Also, the fundamental approach to investing seems to be the safest. In other words, it seems best for the average investor in stocks to buy good stocks and hold them for an indefinite period.

Let us now turn to investment results, to see the ways the 10th Multiple has or could have been achieved, by investing for the long run. A good example of a long-term investment is a testamentary trust of Benjamin Franklin, who died in 1790. In his last will and testament, Franklin made a charitable bequest in trust of 1,000 pounds ($4,440) to be used to lend money at 5% interest to married skilled craftsmen under 25 years of age, residing in Boston, Massachusetts. After 1886, loans were made no longer. Later, the trustees began to invest the trust funds in stocks. Notwithstanding various trust expenditures for administration and charitable purposes, the trust is worth more than $1,500,000 today.

AVERAGE RETURN FOR NYSE STOCKS

A thorough and reasonably accurate computation of investment results has been and is being conducted by The Center for Research in Security Prices, of the Graduate School of Business, of the University of Chicago. An electronic computer has been programed with a massive amount of information, including income and stock transfer tax rates, commission schedules, stock prices, capital changes and dividend distributions, relating to the period from 1926 to the present. Findings reveal that an investment in 1926 of an equal amount of money in each stock traded on the New York Stock Exchange would have produced, during the following 35 years (through 1960), an annual compound return of 8.46% before capital-gains taxes, including dividends and capital appreciation.

This return was based on monthly reinvestment of dividends, after they were reduced by brokerage commissions, odd-lot differential, and federal income taxes. The study assumed the investor at all times during the 35-year period had a tax status applicable to the then economic equivalent of an individual in 1960 who was in the $10,000 income tax bracket. It was further assumed that the investor sold all his stock holdings at the end of 1960, paying the appropriate commissions, transfer taxes, and long-term capital-gains tax, which reduced the compound rate of return to 8.2%.

The 8.2% after-tax return is quite high, considering that it covered the depression of the 1930s. Upon elimination of the years covering the Great Depression and the Second World War, the researchers found that the average rate of return was substantially higher than 8.2%. From December 1950 to December 1960, the average *after-tax* return, based on the same assumptions, was 13.09%.

An individual who saves and invests $1,000 per year at the compound return of 8.2% would realize the 10th Multiple in less than 57 years. However, if the return of 13.09% for the 10-year period ending December 1960 could be maintained by an individual, he would achieve the 10th Multiple in only 40 years.

Older readers may say to themselves that they cannot wait the 57 or 40 years necessary to reach the 10th Multiple. They may not have to wait. These figures assume that an investor commences his program from the very beginning, having no more than his first year's borrowing of $1,000. Older readers, however, are apt to have accumulated savings amounting to several or more Multiples. Proper investment of these savings could lessen considerably the number of years necessary to reach the goal.

A Save-by-Borrower who has already reached the 4th Multiple ($16,000) would be able to achieve the 10th Multiple in 46 additional years at 8.2% or 31 years at 13.09%. This assumes, of course, that he could maintain the indicated rate of return. He may not be able to, even if the average rate for all stocks is higher than the indicated rate—which is unlikely—or perhaps he would be able to, despite a probable rate lower than the 13.09% average. Once again, the rate to be achieved depends so much on individual ability and judgment.

The 1951–60 return of 13.09% for all common stocks listed on the New York Stock Exchange does not reflect the 1962 decline, nor the bull market of 1963–64. To update these statistics we looked to Standard & Poor's Index. During the four years 1961–64, which cover both such periods, the average price for S&P's 425 industrial common stocks increased approximately 45.75%. This amounts to a pre-tax rate of growth (excluding dividends) of approximately 10% per year. To this figure we added about 3% in pre-tax dividends paid to the stockholders and presumably reinvested. The total compound annual return during the years 1961–64, inclusive, seems to approximate 13% before, or 11% after, payment of taxes. Computers may soon give us the over-all return on all NYSE common stocks for the 14-year period 1951–64, inclusive. But we have already seen how by giving appropriate weight to the 13.09% and

COMPLETION OF 10 MULTIPLES ASSUMING $1,000 ANNUAL SAVING AND INVESTMENT AT 12%

Present Value of Investment Fund		Number of Years to Complete 10th Multiple
In Multiples	In Dollars	
–	1,000	41.6
1	2,000	40.6
2	4,000	39.2
3	8,000	36.6
4	16,000	33.2
5	32,000	28.5
6	64,000	23.5
7	128,000	18.2
8	256,000	12.1
9	512,000	6.1

11% returns, the 14-year results should approximate 12%, compounded annually, after payment of the Compromise Tax of 15%.

Assuming that an investor maintains this 12% return, by investment of $1,000 annually he will achieve his 10th Multiple in 43 years. If, however, he starts off at the 4th Multiple ($16,000) he will reach his goal in only 33 years. The following chart shows how many years it would take, assuming the investor begins his $1,000 annual saving and investment program at any Multiple from 1 to 9.

WHAT ABOUT FIXED-DOLLAR INVESTMENTS?

Compare the average common stock investment with the situation where a person invests his savings in life insurance policies or savings accounts, generally paying an after-tax return of 3% per year. It would take 117 years for him to achieve the 10th Multiple, investing $1,000 per year. At the end of 43 years, the investor would have a cash surrender value or bank accounts amounting to only $85,000. This is approximately $1,000,000 less than the results realized when the investor obtains an after-tax return of 12% on his investment.

If 12% is a return over the next few decades which an intelligent investor has a good opportunity to obtain for himself, there would seem to be a sufficient cushion to minimize his over-all risk and make common stocks desirable for a substantial portion of his investment fund.

The value of common stock investments cannot be overemphasized. Multiples are there waiting to be realized, as compensation to persons willing to accept some risk. The cost of investing in fixed-dollar investments is too high: comparative safety is purchased at the expense of an excellent chance of attaining financial independence.

Do you believe you can avoid gambling by staying out of the market? You cannot. By casting your lot with fixed-dollar investments you are betting in effect that stock market prices are not going to advance substantially in the long run, and you are very apt to lose your bet.

LIFE INSURANCE STOCKS OR LIFE INSURANCE?

In 1947, some investors concluded that stocks of life insurance companies would make excellent investments. Through research they may have discovered that the antiquated life expectancy tables in use did not reflect substantial increases in life expectancy, meaning substantial profits to the stockholders of stock life insurance companies. Long after insureds should have died and insurance benefits should have been paid (according to the assumptions on which premiums were based), they continued to pay premiums to the life companies. Also, the investors could predict that as the field of medicine made advances, the disparity between mortality table predictions and actual death experience would grow greater. Furthermore, investment income on reserves held by the life companies exceeded the rate of return guaranteed to the holders of non-participating policies, resulting in additional profits. Consequently, investors could reasonably anticipate that the market values of life insurance stocks would go much higher in future years. Their conclusions were well-founded.

A certain clerk for a major stock life insurance company may have gone through this thinking process when he made his investment decision. Instead of buying permanent life insurance from his employer he bought shares of stock in his employer, and left an estate valued in excess of the 10th Multiple.

The stock of Franklin Life Insurance Company, of Illinois, is a good example of capital appreciation in the life insurance industry. For each $10,000 invested in 1951, the investor had stock worth approximately $474,000 at the close of 1961 (excluding dividends and taxes). Or take another example: If in January 1952 one had chosen to invest his $10,000 in United Services Life, of Washington, D.C., his investment would have appreciated to $2,158,400 (excluding dividends and taxes) by the close of 1961.

Second-guessing is easy to do. The reader may wonder what the average life insurance stock did during the same period. A $10,000 investment from January 1952 to January 1962 in Standard & Poor's Life Stock Index would have appreciated to $77,600, and in the Alfred M. Best Life Stock Index the $10,000 would have grown to $90,600. From 1942 to 1962, a $10,000 investment in the Best

Index would have appreciated in value to $431,000. It is probable that, even now, certain life insurance stock investments will perform similarly in the future. Ferreting out the sound stocks from the many stocks available could prove highly rewarding.

HOW WELL HAVE SMALL INVESTORS DONE?

The answer to this basic question: some have been doing very well in the past years with their stock market investments. The Monthly Investment Plan of the New York Stock Exchange (known as the MIP) contemplates purchase of no less than $40 worth of a favorite stock every three months, with the privilege of immediate, automatic reinvestment of dividends no matter how small the amount. Purchases in such small dollar amounts are made possible by the use of fractional shares of stock.

Merrill Lynch, Pierce, Fenner & Smith, Inc., the nation's largest brokerage house, published statistics on an assumed $100 monthly investment in each of the 20 stocks most popular with its MIP customers. From January 1954 to January 1964 these 20 stocks averaged an annual compound rate of return (including dividends and capital appreciation) of about 16% before, and 13.6% after, payment of the Compromise Tax. Brokerage commissions on the stock purchases were deducted before arriving at the final investment valuation. At this 13.6% rate, continued investment of $1,000 per year would reach the 10th Multiple in only 29 additional years. Once again, it is highly doubtful whether this high rate will be maintained in the future.

STOCK INSURANCE

Our hypothetical Save-by-Borrower is a small investor, having only $1,000 with which to purchase stocks each year (exclusive of reinvestment of dividends). If all of the $1,000 is used each year to accumulate stock of one company only, he runs the extremely undesirable risk that he may lose a substantial part of his invested savings. The company may lose a material patent suit; managerial abilities may decline; research and development may be unrewarding; or the company may suffer from other business maladies. An over-concentration significantly increases the possibility that his investments will undergo a tremendous increase in value or a spectacular decline, a risk which a prudent investor is usually unwilling to take.

What should the Save-by-Borrower do? He has only $1,000 to invest. Should he buy $10 worth of stock in each of 100 corporations? To do this he would have the immense task of selecting the 100 stocks that would appear to give him the best investment opportunity. Many hours of his time would be spent collecting dividend checks, keeping records, and reinvesting the dividends in the 100 stocks. Another problem would be the prohibitively high cost of brokerage commissions applicable to the 100 annual stock transactions.

Diversification can be as foolish as over-concentration. Diversification to the extent of 100 stocks, even if feasible, may be undesirable, ordinarily producing no more than average investment results. An ambitious, conscientious investor may not be satisfied with such results. Why should he accept an average rate of return if, by careful selection of stocks, he can avoid potentially bad stock investments? And further, by careful selection he has an excellent opportunity to obtain investments producing far superior returns.

Finally, it should be obvious that our investor would find it impossible to invest approximately $10 in each of 100 good stocks. Fractional shares of stocks ordinarily being impossible to purchase, the Save-by-Borrower would have insuperable problems in splitting up his $1,000 into 100 investments of equal size. Most of the high-quality stocks would be out of his price range.

We return once again to the problem of how to invest the $1,000. For many small investors, diversification beyond four, five, or six stocks seems undesirable. Fewer than four may be too daring. By investing in, say, five fundamentally sound stocks, an investor would not be hurt too severely if one or two of his investments took a turn for the worse. His other stocks could be expected to offset the loss in whole or in part. Thus, by diversification our Save-by-Borrower has some degree of insurance against total or substantial loss.

By proper diversification of his investments, he can rely upon the law of averages, making it highly unlikely that permanent, devastating misfortune would hit each of the five companies, diversified as to product and location. For diversification among the five stocks, the Save-by-Borrower could buy some cyclical and some defensive stocks. Also, he could invest in different industries, different areas of influence. Stock in a company which has a substantial part of its business in several diverse industries could be an attractive investment.

With the foregoing in mind, the Save-by-Borrower may wish to purchase stocks in only one or two different companies each year, until he has diversified his holdings to the desired extent, say five stocks. It will take the investor several years to obtain full diversification, but the point is that until such time the total amount of his savings at risk will be less significant.

He obtains further diversification by making his annual stock purchases in equal dollar amounts. This prevents the investor from making a significant percentage of his investments when stocks are over-priced. Over the years, the cost of his stock investments will be balanced between the comparatively high and comparatively low prices.

When ready to make his annual purchase, the investor may decide to break from his original order of stock purchase, to pick up one or two stocks which appear underpriced in relation to his remaining stocks. He should wonder, however, whether he is able to determine which stocks are truly underpriced. The higher-priced, seemingly less attractive stocks may keep on moving upward in price, becoming a lost opportunity to the investor who deviates from a program of orderly stock purchase, trying to outguess the market.

Thus, we see that a program of *diversified concentration* enables an investor to select a few fundamentally sound stocks, which should outdistance the market averages, but protect his investment fund from the severe, permanent losses which could result if his investment judgment turned out to be erroneous. This is a highly important protection afforded to Save-by-Borrowers investing for the long run.

The diversification resulting from periodic purchase of the same dollar value of stock deserves a closer look.

DOLLAR-COST AVERAGING

Dollar-cost averaging affords an extra margin of protection to Save-by-Borrowers, making investment in equity securities especially attractive. An average rate of return of 12%, produced by dividends and capital gains alone, is substantial, and is responsible for the decision of many millions of persons to invest in common stocks. Yet an extra profit in excess of the average rate of return is to be made by a Save-by-Borrower or anyone else who invests periodically the same dollar amount in equity securities.

This extra profit comes from the self-imposed limitation inherent in a program of regular investment of a constant-dollar amount. With a fixed amount to work with, the investor prevents himself from purchasing too many shares of stock when the market price for the stock is comparatively high; and when the stock price is comparatively low, his constant-dollar stock-purchasing program enables him to buy enough shares of stock to more than offset the loss in number of shares which occurred when he made his stock purchase at the higher price. The dollar-cost averaging profit is the excess of shares over the number needed to offset this loss, if and when the price of the stock returns to the level at which the investor began his dollar-cost averaging program.

As an illustration, let us consider the case of a new Save-by-Borrower, who makes his first investment by purchasing 40 shares of a stock which is selling at $25 per share. His total cost is $1,000 (disregarding brokerage commissions and odd-lot differential). One year later, after the stock has moved to $40 per share, he makes his second $1,000 investment, this time acquiring only 25 shares. By the end of the second year of his program, his stock dropped in price to $10 per share, giving him the opportunity to purchase 100 shares with his $1,000 of borrowed money—his third $1,000 investment. Soon thereafter, the stock value returned to $25 per share, where it remained for a few months (before undergoing the average rate of appreciation in capital value).

Some readers may have believed that, when the stock price returned to $25, the Save-by-Borrower experienced neither gains nor losses. After all, the investor's loss (caused by purchasing stocks at $15 more than $25 per share) was exactly offset by his profit (caused by purchasing stocks at $15 less than $25 per share). Actually, our investor could sell his stock and realize a handsome profit, even though the stock is selling for only $25 per share, the price of his first purchase. To obtain this profit when the value of the stock is only $25 per share, the investor's three $1,000 purchases must have averaged more than 40 shares each.

By his second purchase—25 shares of stock at $40 per share—he suffered a 15-share loss from the 40-share average he needed to maintain; however, through his third investment, 100 shares at $10 per share, he obtained 75 shares in excess of the needed 25. This offset the 15-share loss and left *a profit of 60 shares* to boot. When the value of the stock returned to $25 per share, our Save-by-Borrower had an excess profit of $1,500 (25 times 60), before the stock made its average advance in capital value.

The profits produced by dollar-cost averaging are extra profits because they are in addition to dividend payments, and capital appreciation which the average stock undergoes. The $1,500 profit from dollar-cost averaging was computed when the stock price returned temporarily to $25 per share, the price first paid for the stock by the Save-by-Borrower.

When dividends and capital appreciation (above cost) are added to dollar-cost averaging profits, the results are quite impressive. Although this is only a rough guess, extra profits may equal 5% of the accumulation value projected on the basis of an assumed rate of return. All he must do is invest $1,000 (or some other fixed amount) each year in fundamentally sound stocks and hold onto his investments for an indefinite period, as long as the stocks remain sound. Adding the assumed dollar-cost averaging profit to the 12% return, the $1,000 annual investor should reach his 10th Multiple about two years earlier.

Dollar-cost averaging, as we have seen, takes advantage of temporary price fluctuations. If an investor purchases the same amount of stocks at prices equally above and below the cost of his original stock purchase, he will be able to show a profit even though the stock price is the same as or a little lower than the cost of his original stock purchase. A profit will be shown as long as the average cost of his stock is lower than the market price. Of course, *if the investor does not purchase at such different price levels, dollar-cost averaging will produce no profits.*

Bearing in mind that the average stock market price has always gone up in the long run, we see that dollar-cost averaging takes advantage of temporary declines in market prices, making it worthwhile for an investor to remain in sound investments, to continue with his buying program, and wait for the market to reach new highs.

Benefits from dollar-cost averaging can be obtained only if the investment program is carried out faithfully. It cannot be overemphasized that, especially during bad times, the investor must continue to hold his fundamentally sound stocks and make new purchases. Otherwise, the investor probably would be selling out at a loss, when the average cost of his investments exceeded their market value.

An investor in common stocks should think ahead, to estimate his future cash needs. He should estimate the amount of *cash* he will need *after* five years, say, to cover anticipated expenses for home, business, and travel, and the children's educations and weddings, for example. Also, he should consider his prospects for retirement and to what extent he should switch his investment fund to savings accounts and bonds, for example.

If, to switch to cash or fixed-dollar investments, he sells some common stock holdings when their value is below cost or substantially below their high market values, the investor will suffer a loss —of original savings or of recoverable capital appreciation. To avoid this, he may plan to liquidate an appropriate part of his investments *several years before* the time his savings will be needed in cash or near-cash form; but he should liquidate only if stock prices are favorable, waiting several years if necessary. In this way, the investor will have a grace period in which to wait for market prices to return to a favorable level, in the event they are too low at the start of the conversion period. If the trend of the market is still upward when he starts converting, it may be desirable to sell out gradually, over the course of one or more years.

An investor, to obtain full benefits from dollar-cost averaging, must plan to maintain his periodic purchases for at least five or six years. Continuation of the plan is virtually assured if the investor adopts the Save-by-Borrowing technique, but only if he has the requisite extra income during the period. When times are most troubled and he is least apt to have extra money to save, stock bargains will be the best—he must not miss out on them.

Save-by-Borrowers may wonder whether it would be advisable to make a number of small stock purchases throughout the year, to maximize their dollar-cost averaging profits. The answer seems to be no. Studies have indicated there is little difference between monthly and annual purchases. What does makes a difference, however, is the trend of the market. If he knows the market price of his stock is to go down, an *omniscient* annual investor would not invest at the start of the year, but at the *end,* when the price for that year had reached its lowest point. If he knew the price was to rise, he would purchase at the *outset* of the year, to benefit from the full advance in price. But, of course, who can be omniscient? Save-by-Borrowers, not having this advantage, should assume market prices are on their way up, which has been and should remain true in the long run. Thus, by making their stock purchases at the *start* of each year, they would be putting themselves in the best position to receive full benefit of the average annual advance in market prices.

Previously, it was stated that an investor should weed out bad stocks and substitute fundamentally sound stocks. Does this necessarily ruin dollar-cost averaging benefits? No. Stock prices have an apparent tendency to rise and fall together; and a substitute stock could be purchased at an equivalent price level. Dollar-cost averaging is a benefit derived from fluctuations in prices, no matter what specific stocks the investor buys. Accordingly, the dollar-cost averager should have soundness as his standard; no dollar-cost averaging benefits need be lost even though an investor finds it necessary to switch to different stocks.

A phenomenon of dollar-cost averaging is that its profits are made only if the stock decreases in value. This assumes, however, that the stock price rebounds to a certain extent. It is natural for you, as an investor, to want the value of your stock to go up, but when the value goes down, additional shares of stock can be bought at bargain prices. So, don't complain. As long as your stocks are sound, you are bound to benefit ultimately.

To obtain full dollar-cost averaging benefits, a Save-by-Borrower should keep purchasing no matter how high or low the stock prices go. If they seem too high, he should remember they may keep going higher and higher. As a compromise, however, when prices are "too high," the dollar-cost averager may decide to purchase defensive stocks, which are less apt to decrease in value. On the other hand, when stock prices are substantially lower, sound cyclical stocks are a good investment, being bound to undergo a substantial increase in value.

Reinvestment of dividends has a dollar-cost averaging effect also. Based upon our conclusion to invest at the outset of the year, we find it desirable to obtain a reinvestment of dividends as soon as they are paid. The next chapter discusses an excellent method, perhaps the only suitable way, by which you can obtain the effect of automatic and immediate reinvestment of dividends.

Annual investment of the same amount of money is an easy way to time your stock purchases, providing extra profits and an excellent safeguard for you. This technique of purchase timing should be of noteworthy success over the years of your investment program.

LIFETIME POKER GAME

There are exceedingly attractive profits to be made by investing in common stocks. This book does not tell you which stocks to purchase, nor whether you should follow the technical, cyclical, or fundamental school. You must make your own decisions when the time for investment rolls around, and the decision should be based upon your needs, disposition, and a thorough understanding of the principles of investment. The more you learn about the subject of investments, the greater the opportunity you will have to beat the averages, to obtain the 10th Multiple more quickly.

You might think of your stock market investments as a lifetime game of poker. But what a game! Many of the cards are marked, the marks becoming clearer with continuous study and play. Start playing, then, and let yourself become familiar with the markings. By learning and keeping informed about economic and stock market indicators, you can stack your own deck of cards, and the odds will swing heavily in your favor.

Everybody does not obtain average profits, this is true. In the averages there will be losers as well as winners. But by following generally accepted rules of investment, such as dollar-cost averaging and diversified purchases of fundamentally sound stocks, you can minimize the possibilities of loss and back winners a good percentage of the time. The degree of success depends upon the skill and determination of the investor. The rewards will be an earlier completion of your 10-Multiple program, a reduction in risk to your investment fund, and an opportunity to retire with complete financial independence. But the process is a long one, be well prepared.

Many persons desiring to invest in equity securities are not sure when to make their purchases. One may feel, for example, that he should not make an investment unless it is with a substantial amount of money; therefore, he lets his savings account increase during the year until $1,000 or so has been accumulated, enough to make a stock purchase seem warranted. Another investor may open up an account with a broker without any delay, to make his investments under the Monthly Investment Plan of the New York Stock Exchange (the MIP). We turn now to analyze the MIP. How long will it take for you to spot its major weaknesses? Also, how does the MIP compare with the Save-by-Borrowing technique? We soon shall see.

Chapter Eight

DON'T GET CAUGHT IN A "POOR TRAP"

I. ALLOCATION OF ENJOYMENT

Thankfully, not everyone is actively seeking the 10th Multiple. Philosophies differ, as you might expect. Enjoyment for many people is sought and obtained on a daily basis, with a complete disregard for the future. "After all," a devotee may argue, "there may be no tomorrow. Unless I do what I want today, I may never get another chance, or by the time the chance arrives, I may not derive as much pleasure as I can get today."

Others, adopting a more conservative approach, readily admit they could be experiencing more pleasure today, but they quickly point out that some pleasure should be stored for the future, as a form of insurance against the unknown. For such reason they are willing to withdraw from current enjoyment a certain amount of earnings, let us assume $1,000 per year.

The cost in terms of current enjoyment is quite high, as most savers will admit. Therefore, the saver has a right—no, a duty to himself —to see that his savings are put to work in a most effective manner, to offset the lost enjoyment of today with the prospects for comfort, happiness, and peace of mind available to him in the future.

To make saving worthwhile in these terms, the Save-by-Borrower owes it to himself to make his savings do the maximum amount of work. Accordingly, all inefficiencies in his program of periodic saving and investment must be eliminated if he is to have a fighting chance to reach his goal.

For the comparatively impoverished saver, the path to the 10th Multiple is strewn with "poor traps." These include the costs normally paid by the small investor which can be avoided by a certain amount of knowledge and planning.

We turn now to poor traps, to see where some of them are located and how they can be avoided.

II. SMALL INVESTORS HAVE PROBLEMS

THE POOR PAY MORE

Poor traps are set in virtually all fields of commercial enterprise. Examples are easy to find.

When he buys an automobile, the comparatively poor individual tends to shop around for a sound used car. After many hours or days of search, he winds up at "Honest ——'s Used-Car Lot," to select, then purchase, an "A-1" car. Several miles after leaving the lot, our buyer realizes that he has been taken. He asks himself, however, "What else could I have done?" A new car would have been too expensive—or so he thought.

New tires, a complete brake job, several towings, a new automatic transmission, and a rebuilt carburetor double the cost of his car. Higher gas and oil expenses add to the real cost of the used-car bargain.

At the end of the year, the motor turns over for the final time, and the car is junked for $15. Now the mistake is clearly visible. He would have been better off if he had bought a new car. For $66 per month (and almost no down payment) he could have owned and enjoyed a new car; and, after paying off a 36-month installment obligation, he would have been able to sell his car and reduce to about $45 the cost per month of use (exclusive of insurance, parking, etc.). Instead, he wound up paying about $50 per month of use for a piece of junk.

Too often, a cost-conscious used-car buyer will make this terrible mistake. Another purchaser, however, may have no choice. Poverty may prevent him from buying a new car. Not having a good credit rating, he may not be able to borrow the purchase money. As one of the poor, he will pay more.

False economy results when a purchaser shops around for low prices but disregards quality. Many is the time a purchaser would be better off paying a higher price. A $150 suit may last three times as long as a suit selling for one half as much. And at no additional cost, the purchaser of the higher-quality suit would obtain a garment having a better appearance.

Of all this the poor purchaser may be aware, but he still insists that he cannot afford to pay the higher initial cost. Instead, circumstances force him to keep paying and paying.

The high cost of a poor man's purchase can be seen in apartment rentals too. On a square-foot basis, tenements in the slums of New York City often rent for substantially higher amounts than luxury apartments on Manhattan's fashionable East Side.

That poverty is expensive can be seen in the field of borrowing. A person of low economic status is often a poor credit risk; therefore, he may be required to pay interest to a small loan company at a true annual interest rate of 24–36%. A wealthy borrower, in contrast, should be able to obtain a (secured) loan at only 5% or 6% true annual interest.

The cost of being poor is inordinately high. In fact, for a person who can afford to invest only $83 per month, the cost may equal $46,900 over a 35-year savings and investment program if he fails to follow fully the Save-by-Borrowing method. A comparison in chart form, found in Chapter Twelve, shows how this can be so.

Complaints about this high cost of investment are seldom heard from persons charged the most. By now they are accustomed to the overcharge and, presumably, accept it as inevitable. With eagerness they run to the cleaners, unwilling merely to be taken. But who are these people?

DISCRIMINATION ON WALL STREET

Discrimination is found on Wall Street, where the small investor in stocks is required to pay a higher rate of brokerage commissions than the investor who buys his stocks in substantial dollar amounts. To invest $100 the small investor must pay a 6% brokerage commission; to invest $1,000 he would have to pay only 1.5%. (Both rates are applicable to an odd-lot price.)

Although the small investor pays a substantially higher percentage in brokerage commissions than wealthy, more significant investors, the small investor may not be paying his fair share. Execution by a stockbroker of a $100 order for stock seems to require about the same amount of work needed to execute a $1,000 order. It is arguable, therefore, that the small investor should pay an even higher commission, on a percentage basis, for the services of his broker. After all, why should the $100 investor pay only $6.00 for the same brokerage services for which the $1,000 investor is charged $15.00?

Complaints may seem justified, therefore, when heard from investors of large dollar amounts. If a broker does not incur expenses substantially in proportion to the amount of money involved in a stock transaction, why should his brokerage commission be based (in part) on a percentage of such amount? Furthermore, why should a purchase of 1,000 shares of stock, which involves at most a few minutes more work than a 100-share purchase, entail a brokerage cost ten times as much as the 100-share purchase?

Reforms may be coming, but not because of the complaints by the investors of large dollar amounts. Their resort to the Third Market has proved much more effective. The Third Market[1] is a small, informal group of heavily capitalized "over-the-counter" securities dealers who maintain a market for certain stocks listed on the New York Stock Exchange. Substantial investors, including some pension funds, insurance companies, and mutual funds, frequently turn to the Third Market when seeking to buy or sell big blocks of certain NYSE-listed stocks.

Competing against members of the NYSE, who by exchange rule are forbidden from charging below the minimum schedule of brokerage commissions, a Third Market dealer can make to a substantial investor a highly attractive offer. The substantial investor benefits not only from the Third Market competition against the membership of the NYSE, but from the competition among the Third Market dealers as well.

To a prospective purchaser of a big block of stock, a Third Market

[1] The organized stock exchanges constitute the first market, where stocks listed on such exchanges are traded. The second market is the "over-the-counter" market, where "unlisted" stocks are traded.

dealer will ordinarily quote a price higher than the current market price on the exchange. Yet the Third Market price would be the total price and ordinarily would be less than the total cost to acquire the stock in an exchange transaction. If the purchaser were to buy the block on the exchange, he would be charged brokerage commissions at the regular rate, with no discount for volume.

Another attraction for a Third Market utilizer is that he is guaranteed the total amount he will pay for the stock, whereas, if purchasing the block of stock on the exchange, the investor could not be sure whether all of his large order could be exercised at the original market price. Before the order could be filled, the market price might be driven up.

By offering the discount to investors of large dollar amounts, the Third Market dealers have been able to make significant inroads into the volume of transactions in certain stocks occurring on the New York Stock Exchange. As a result of this Third Market competition (and the growth of regional stock exchanges), the NYSE may revise its schedule of minimum commissions. A proposed schedule would reduce the brokerage commission on a one-day transaction involving more than 3,000 shares of the same stock. For example, on a purchase of 4,000 shares, the buyer would no longer be required to pay forty times the brokerage commission applicable to a 100-share purchase. Instead, the 4,000-share purchaser would pay a commission of only twenty-eight times the commission on the 100-share purchase. This would amount to a 30% discount.

All of this has very little to do with the small investor, except to point out by negative implication that on a $100 purchase he will continue to pay the 6% commission—unless he takes independent action.

In fact, members of the NYSE may increase brokerage costs by $1 per transaction, an increase ranging from 1.3% to 16.7% of the present dollar cost. You guessed it. The 16.7% increase would be paid by the $100 investor.

As if that were not enough, the NYSE may require its members to charge their customers a service fee, ordinarily amounting to an annual *minimum* of $12 for small investors. Watch out for the word "minimum." It frequently indicates a poor trap. An investor having only $1,000 worth of stock would pay a 1.2% service fee, in contrast to an investor having $10,000 worth of stock, who may pay a percentage equal to only one tenth as much.

The mandatory service fee, running from $1 to $5 per month, would be computed on the basis of 25 cents per month for each stock held by the broker in the customer's account (with a $1 monthly minimum). The proposed fee, highly controversial in nature, would reimburse the broker for certain of his costs in rendering advisory services, providing price quotations, compiling and delivering research material, taking custody of the customer's securities, collecting dividends and paying them over to the customer.

If these proposals to increase brokerage commissions and impose a mandatory service fee are adopted, small investors will be paying substantially more than they are forced to now. This is in spite of the fact that the present cost to small investors, when compared to the rates paid by the substantial investors, seems high enough.

At present, an investor purchasing 100 shares of stock at $80 per share pays a brokerage commission of $47, or a little more than $\frac{1}{2}$ of 1% on his $8,000 stock purchase. Small investors, however, do not fare as well. Someone purchasing only $100 worth of stock is charged a commission which, as a percentage of the amount he is actually investing, amounts to more than eleven times as much (assuming a 100-share purchase).

The practical necessity of buying stocks in odd lots increases the small investor's cost. He will be charged an additional $12\frac{1}{2}$ cents or 25 cents per share, plus brokerage commissions thereon. Although there is a $2 reduction in commissions on an odd-lot purchase, it does not apply to the small investor who makes a $100 purchase. He is required to pay the *minimum* brokerage commission of $6.

PRICING PROBLEMS

The problems of a small investor never seem to end. He is now faced with the difficulty of selecting his stocks. He realizes that he usually must stick to the lowest price range (up to $5 or $10 per share) if he is to invest substantially all of his savings each month. Ordinarily stocks cannot be purchased by dollar amount but must be bought by the share.

If our investor has no more than $100 to invest in a $51 stock, he could purchase only one full share. The remaining $49 could not be invested in this stock until the following month, when he had accumulated additional savings.

The usual unit of stock purchase—the share—forces our investor into an awkward position, presenting him with unhappy alternatives. On one hand, he could invest the full amount of his savings each month, but only if he buys lower-priced, possibly more speculative stocks. As a conservative investor, however, he knows that he is supposed to restrict his investments to high-quality, fundamentally sound stocks, which ordinarily sell for higher amounts.

If, however, he chooses to bank his savings until he can afford to purchase a full share of a more expensive stock (AT&T, for example), the regularity of his savings program will be destroyed; also, he will probably suffer a loss in rate of return. The rate of return, if any, on the savings kept temporarily in a savings bank, will be substantially lower, on the average, than the rate of return (including capital appreciation) on most investments in common stocks.

ENTER MUTUAL FUNDS

The difficulties faced by the small investor were known to the mutual fund industry, which offered him a solution to some of his problems.

Mutual funds are a means by which small-time investors can pool their investment funds. This obtains for them, among other things, the advantages of reduced brokerage commissions; diversification; and investment-unit prices within their budgets. It is not difficult to see why mutual funds became quite popular with the small investor.

Perhaps an equally important reason, it should be noted, is that mutual funds are sold, not purchased. Always eager to expand their sales force, mutual funds advertise in newspapers to attract new sales personnel. And who responds? You may be surprised. Teachers, students, cab drivers, and many others, who are told to begin their new careers by selling shares of mutual funds to associates, friends, and relatives—in something less than an arm's-length transaction.

Regardless of the pressure, investors of modest resources may be attracted to mutual funds by the feature of flexibility, which permits a small investor to purchase an interest in many high-quality and high-priced stocks. He obtains his investment at a cost per investment unit well within his budget. Mutual fund shares are sold at extremely low prices, averaging about $12 per share. Thus, a person having only a small amount of savings can invest all or almost all of the amount without having to settle for low-cost, low-quality stocks.

An additional need of the comparatively poor investor is met by the mutual fund industry: immediate reinvestment of dividends. In lieu of cash-dividend payments, a mutual fund shareholder usually can elect to receive full and fractional mutual fund shares, thereby compounding his investment return.

To clinch a sale to a prospective purchaser, the salesman explains that a mutual fund offers a small investor the advantages of professional management and constant supervision of his investments.

By an all-out effort to sell their services to small investors, mutual funds kept growing—at the expense of members of another investment industry.

III. COMES THE MONTHLY INVESTMENT PLAN

PREPARING FOR WAR

Members of the New York Stock Exchange saw an ever-increasing portion of their business (actual and potential) siphoned off by the mutual fund industry.

True, mutual funds are purchasers of stocks. But a $10,000 stock purchase by a mutual fund produces $49 in brokerage commissions, which is far less than the $600 in commissions on a $100 purchase by each of one hundred small investors. Thus, a mutual fund may pay only one twelfth of the commissions paid by the one hundred small investors to invest the same amount.

The loss of the small investor was a loss in turnover brokerage business to many exchange members. Outright purchasers of stocks can be expected to switch their investments, generating additional brokerage commissions. Mutual fund investors, however, infrequently switch their savings from one fund to another; and switches ordinarily would not result in additional net commissions to stockbrokers for mutual funds.

A brokerage house could choose not to sell shares of mutual funds, but it would lose some profitable business to houses which were willing. Furthermore, after committing itself to a policy of antagonism toward mutual funds, it could hardly expect to be given much brokerage business by the mutual fund industry.

Mutual fund business presents other problems. Even when mutual fund purchases are made through a particular brokerage house, managers of the fund may instruct the brokerage house to "give up" a portion, say 60%, of the commission to some other brokerage house, as a bonus or additional compensation for selling shares of the fund to the investing public.

Needless to say, some members of the New York Stock Exchange felt the competition, especially those who sold few or no mutual funds. Something had to be done to prepare for the battle over the small investor. And so it came about that the problems of the small investor became the problems of the NYSE and some of its members. In response to the challenge presented by the mutual fund industry and to induce fixed-dollar investors to adopt a new way of life, the NYSE established, in January of 1954, its Monthly Investment Plan (the MIP).

A NEW PRODUCT: DOLLAR STOCKS

Underlying the MIP is an accommodation to the small investor, permitting him to make direct purchases of stock by the dollar instead of by the share. By reason of the MIP, an investor with limited means can now say to his broker, "I'll take $40 worth of General Motors." Upon completion of the stock purchase, a fractional share of stock will be credited to the purchaser's account (the fraction being computed to the fourth decimal).

In this way, the New York Stock Exchange and certain anxious members were able to overcome the problems of the investor having only a limited amount to invest. Fractional shares are important because they promote regularity of saving and investment. Also, they allow the purchase of fundamentally sound stocks having a cost per share substantially in excess of the amount which the investor has available to invest each saving period.

Now that dollars have become the unit of investment for the small investor using the MIP, he is able to immediately invest 100% of the amount he periodically sets aside for investment. This prevents any part of his funds from remaining uninvested and, perhaps, from being diverted to non-investment expenditures.

COMPOUNDING WITHOUT DELAY

Small investors had problems extending beyond the making of their original investments: They needed an effective way to reinvest (compound) their cash dividends. Without effective compounding, their investment returns would be unnecessarily and substantially diminished.

Mutual funds knew this and capitalized on the inability of the small investor to obtain immediate reinvestment of the cash dividends on his stock investments. Mutual funds attracted the small investor by permitting him to reinvest his dividends automatically and effortlessly. The mutual fund managers take care of all bookkeeping details for him.

The importance of compounding was a major selling point. Mutual fund salesmen could point out the savings attributable to an immediate compounding of investment dividends. Uninvested assets, on the average, will result in major losses. Routine delays in reinvestment, to give the investor time to accumulate dividends in an amount not embarrassing to reinvest, can be very costly. The longer the delay, the more the loss.

Losses resulting from delays in reinvestment of dividends should not be treated lightly, although this may not be too apparent to most small investors. Over a 35-year period, the losses caused by typical reinvestment delays can add up to $15,300 for a person who saves and invests $1,000 per year. This estimate depends on certain assumptions:

1. The saving and investment program will involve $1,000 per year for 35 years; and that with *no* delay in reinvestment it would return 12% per year, compounded annually, after payment of the 15% Compromise Tax;

2. Cash dividends each year will average, after payment of the assumed 20% ordinary income tax, 3.5% of the value of the investment fund computed as of the beginning of each investment year;

3. The dividends will be reinvested, in a lump sum at the *end* of each investment year, by purchase of additional stock, and that

this delay in reinvestment after receipt of the cash dividends will average 6 months; and

4. The dividends will be deposited in a savings account, to earn a true annual interest of 3.4%, after payment of the 20% ordinary income tax. As a result of delays in deposit and the necessity of keeping the money on deposit for full quarters or until the end of a quarter, we assume the deposited dividends will earn the true annual return for only three fourths of the 6-month average delay. Thus, the dividends would earn a 1.275% actual return (that is, three eighths—$4\frac{1}{2}$ months' worth—of the 3.4% net true annual return) on the 3.5% of net cash dividends in the year of their receipt.

On these assumptions, the delay in reinvestment will cause a net loss in return of 4.725% (one half of 12%, minus 1.275%), during the year of reinvestment, on the annual cash dividends. When 3.5%, representing the annual cash dividends, is multiplied by the 4.725% loss in return on the annual cash dividends, the reinvestment losses, as a percentage of the cash dividends, are translated into a loss of return on the *total* investment fund, which loss amounts to almost $\frac{17}{100}$ of 1% (3.5% times 4.725%). This reduces the 12% annual return on the year-to-year value of the investment fund to about 11.83%. At the end of the 35-year saving and investment program, the total dollar loss caused by the delay in reinvestment will amount to about $15,300, based on the foregoing assumptions.

Prior to establishment of the MIP, small investors experienced great difficulty obtaining reinvestment of dividends without time lag. After all, how could they be expected to immediately reinvest only a few dollars of dividends? Even when an investor accumulated $10,-000 worth of stock, so that his quarterly dividends amounted to about $100, he still had reinvestment problems. It took many more years before it would be practical for him to reinvest 100% of his dividends immediately. And until he could reinvest immediately, he would suffer substantial losses.

Diversification of his investments only made his problems more complex. He received his dividends in smaller dollar amounts, infrequently on the same day. Thus, periods of non-investment seemed unavoidable. Reinvestment, it was believed, could occur only when the small investor accumulated enough dividends (and savings) to purchase a minimum of one full share of stock.

The MIP was designed in part to remedy this problem of immediate reinvestment. A small investor is offered the unique opportunity of automatic reinvestment of dividends, *regardless of the amount,* as soon as they are received by the broker.

The cost of automatic reinvestment is no more than 6%, the MIP rate applicable to any stock purchase amounting to $100 or less. As a result, a $2 dividend paid with respect to an MIP stock can be reinvested at a cost of only 12 cents. Frequently, the cost of postage in notifying the customer of the reinvestment will exceed the brokerage commission applicable to the transaction. The privilege of automatic reinvestment is not a money-maker for the broker, in many instances, but an inducement (or loss leader) for a small investor to open an MIP account.

The MIP affords investors a slight degree of "compulsory" saving. This compulsion is increased substantially by use of automatic reinvestment, because the investor then has no opportunity to touch the dividends.

To some investors, the 6% maximum cost of reinvestment under the MIP appears reasonable, considering the services required to produce the convenience and speed of reinvestment of small sums of money. No longer need he receive, then cash, his dividend checks; nor need he accumulate the dividend proceeds until the purchase of one more share can be afforded. Instead, his MIP broker makes all the arrangements, keeps all the records, and collects the dividends, reinvesting them by purchase of additional MIP stock.

Automatic reinvestment is quite popular among MIP investors—more than 96% of them take advantage of it. This is an excellent commentary on their attitude. Somehow, they know or sense that compounding of their return is the only way for them to reach the 10th Multiple.

For the average small investor, the alternative to automatic reinvestment under the MIP has appeared to be keeping the dividends uninvested (or comparatively uninvested, by deposit of the dividend proceeds in a bank account) until he is ready to make another stock purchase out of his combined savings and accumulated dividends. Some investors, through reasonably delayed reinvestment, pay a commission sufficiently lower than 6% to more than offset the loss resulting from the temporary period of little or no return. Other investors, who cannot make this saving by reasonably delayed reinvestment, will reduce their losses by reinvesting immediately, under the MIP, where the cost is 6% regardless of how little is being reinvested.

Assuming there is a time at which a particular small investor could make a delayed reinvestment on a profitable basis, would he be able to compute this point, and, if so, would he wish to be bothered, at least when the 6% cost of immediate reinvestment appears to be so insignificant?

He could reasonably conclude, therefore, that the automatic reinvestment feature of the MIP is suitable for him, even though his reinvestment will involve a brokerage commission of 6%.

THE $40 QUARTER

For each plan in effect, the MIP investor should consider himself required to make at least one purchase every three months, of not less than $40. (Additional MIP purchases cannot involve less than $40, except by reason of a reinvestment transaction.) At $40 per quarter, the MIP contemplates total annual purchases amounting to no less than $160.

Requirement of one MIP purchase every three months is considered by many proponents of the plan to be a plus factor, a semblance of forced saving. Requirement of *monthly* purchases, however, would have been a more compelling way to save.

Once a payment is made by an MIP investor, his broker makes a purchase of the MIP stock previously selected by the investor (often with the broker's advice). Actually, a $40 payment will not buy full or fractional shares of stock having a total market value of $40. The odd-lot differential and 6% brokerage commission on the odd-lot price of the stock must be subtracted from the $40. The residual amount is the (round-lot) market value of the purchased stock. Subtracting the 6% commission on the odd-lot price of the stock, the MIP investor finds that his $40 will purchase $37.74 worth of stock (at the odd-lot price). A commission of $2.26 will be retained by the broker.

The commission rate of 6%, as applied to stock purchases in amounts of $100 and less, is only an extension of the New York Stock Exchange minimum commission of $6, applicable to a $100 purchase, whether odd-lot or round-lot. For NYSE transactions occurring outside of the MIP, a stock purchase involving less than $100 would be at a price as mutually agreed upon between broker and investor, but probably 6% or more.

After the transaction is completed, the investor's MIP account is credited with the appropriate number of full and fractional shares which the $37.74 will purchase.

Thus, if the odd-lot price of a stock is $45\frac{1}{4}$, the investor will be able to purchase a fractional interest equal to $\frac{37.74}{45.25}$ or .8340 of one share of stock. If the odd-lot price is $20\frac{1}{8}$ per share, the MIP investor will be able to purchase one and $\frac{17.615}{20.125}$ shares of stock.

The 6% brokerage commission on the odd-lot price (involving $100 or less) is the only cost to the MIP investor. There are no penalties and no initial fees, and no service charges for investment advice or custodianship of the stock certificates. It is possible, however, that a mandatory custodial charge will be levied against MIP users and other investors who utilize a broker's services to hold stock certificates and collect dividends.

Many MIP investors may be pleased that the plan involves no binding obligation to purchase stock. At any time, an investor can discontinue his investment program without penalty, unlike many mutual fund and life insurance investment programs. Losses resulting from cancellation of certain mutual fund and life insurance contracts can be substantial. Nor does the MIP involve any borrowing to finance the stock purchases. As a consequence, the investor incurs no interest charges.

For many people the MIP is an attractive way to invest, disregarding for present purposes the cost factor. Also, purchases are easy to make. Whenever the MIP investor decides to make a purchase, he merely sends to his broker a check or money order in the amount of $40 or more (up to $1,000).

The price at which the investor makes his purchase is set by the first odd-lot sale on the day after the payment is credited to his account. After any purchase is made, the broker sends the buyer a confirmation slip indicating the number of full and fractional shares he has just bought, together with a statement of the total number of shares held by the broker in the MIP account.

Upon termination of the plan, the investor will be given a stock certificate covering all of the full shares of stock held in his MIP account. Any fractional shares will be sold at the market price, and the cash proceeds (after commissions and transfer taxes have been deducted) will be paid over to the investor.

It is possible, nevertheless, for an MIP investor to obtain a stock certificate before termination of his plan. When his purchases total 50 shares or more, he can request and obtain free of charge a stock certificate for no fewer than 50 shares. Also, by payment of $1 per certificate, he can acquire a stock certificate covering *any* number of full shares in his account.

An investor is discouraged from taking possession of stock certificates, however. Dividends will be sent directly to the MIP investor to the extent that stock certificates are registered in his name. As a result, automatic reinvestment of such dividends cannot be accomplished.

Some investors, fearful of loss, do not leave their stock certificates with their brokers. Be assured, however, that the possibility of loss is minimal, at least when the broker is a member firm of the New York Stock Exchange. The NYSE has taken steps nevertheless to reduce substantially any possibility of loss.

In 1964, the NYSE set up a trust fund having a potential value of $10,000,000. Out of this trust fund discretionary payments may (but do not have to) be made to customers of any NYSE member, member firm or member corporation who have suffered loss of money or securities as a result of the insolvency of any NYSE member, member firm, or member corporation.

Provided an MIP investor selects a reputable stockbroker having a sound financial condition, there is little possibility of loss even if the stock certificates are held by and in the name of the broker. There is actually a greater possibility of loss if the investor taking possession of the stock certificates does not exercise a high standard of care.

The MIP is simple in practice and effective in results, as we will soon see. But can the MIP be employed by the small investor seeking to protect his investment fund by diversification of his investments?

CONCENTRATED DIVERSIFICATION

Although only one stock can be purchased under a single Monthly Investment Plan, more than one plan can be employed at the same time by a single investor.

If an investor wishes to diversify his investments by purchasing six stocks, for example, he could set up six plans, alternating payment so that purchases under two plans would be made each month. In this way the investor would be able to limit his investment to $1,000 per year and still be able to carry out a program of diversification.

At the minimum rate of $40 per quarter, each plan would require an investment of $160 per year. A $1,000 investment spread over a year would allow maintenance of as many as six plans.

Maintenance of four, five, or six Monthly Investment Plans sounds attractive, setting aside the cost factor for the time being. Nothing is done by the MIP investor; his broker does all the work, collecting dividends and reinvesting them immediately in the stock distributing the dividend. Also, each of the plans would benefit from dollar-cost averaging, a protective device of great importance to the small, periodic investor.

Another protection afforded is the diversification of his investments. By using four, five, or six plans, the investor obtains "concentrated diversification," giving him protection against loss without preventing his well-chosen investments from performing better than the market averages.

We see, therefore, that MIP investors make use of an investment procedure which is simple to understand, easy to carry out, and effective in results (setting aside costs, once again). This accounts for the widespread acceptance of the MIP.

141,990 POTENTIAL SAVE-BY-BORROWERS

As of June 1965, more than eleven years after commencement of the MIP, there were 141,990 active MIP accounts. Since January 1964, there has been a net increase of 45,181 plans.

This substantial growth may be attributable in part to the apparent fact that investors of insubstantial sums (as measured by the volume of odd-lot purchases) come into the market when prices are reaching their peak. When the market is topping off and, supposedly, getting set for a substantial reversal, the professional investor (who may be relying on the popular belief that the public is always wrong) is starting to ease himself out of his cyclical investments and into defensive issues or fixed-dollar investments.

Although these new MIP investors may have been entering the

market when prices were relatively high, they were not necessarily doing themselves a disservice. This is so especially if, pursuant to a regular program of investment, they are going to keep up their investment program for the long run. If this happens, they will derive the twin benefits of

1. higher stock prices, on the average; and
2. profits (irrespective of higher ultimate prices) resulting from dollar-cost averaging.

All that matters is that the MIP investor (and others for that matter) hold onto fundamentally sound stocks for an indefinite period.

Thus, increased popularity of the MIP, even at higher price levels, is not necessarily a bad sign, when the investors are going to hold their stocks for the long run.

A possible reason for increased MIP popularity may have been the reduction in federal withholding taxes, in 1964, which put extra, uncommitted dollars into the pockets of these small investors. Thus, prudence (instead of public foolishness) may have prompted this sudden increase in popularity of the MIP.

A better reason, however, may be that the MIP has been widely promoted as perhaps the best means by which a small, periodic investor can buy his share of American business. New MIP customers were actively being sought. In 1962, Merrill Lynch, Pierce, Fenner & Smith established a stock-purchase program permitting an MIP investor to make his periodic payment through a payroll deduction by his employer. Companies participating in this MIP plan include American Motors, Canada Dry, Rexall Drug & Chemical, Royal Crown Cola, and Wm. Wrigley Jr. Co.

Adoption of the MIP and its extension by the payroll deduction process reflects the public's apparent desire for an easy, effective way to save and invest in equity securities.

If such desire truly exists, the 141,990 MIP investors and the rest of the small investing public should appreciate the Save-by-Borrowing technique. Following it, anyone can reasonably expect savings and profits in excess of what is offered to him by the MIP and these extras can amount to a huge sum of money—$46,900—over the lifetime of his savings and investment program.

Until the public becomes acquainted with the technique, the MIP should keep growing. It does fill a need for the small investor who is unaware of the Save-by-Borrowing alternative. In filling the need for some kind of regular investment program, MIP brokerage houses are aiding the small investor (at a profit, of course), with the hope and belief that he will become a more important investor, and a more desirable customer.

The MIP is not a charitable feature of the brokerage business, not by a long shot. By use of computers, administrative costs of the MIP have been cut, reportedly, to a point somewhat lower than the cost of servicing a regular cash customer.

One might wonder, then, why it is that all brokers do not make the MIP available to their customers. For one thing, a participating broker is assessed by the New York Stock Exchange to pay a portion of the Exchange's expense in running and promoting the MIP. Also, sale of mutual funds may offer greater profits for a brokerage house willing to sell them, especially when it would have to administer the MIP without the cost-cutting efficiency of a computer.

It seems, not surprisingly, that the prospects for greater profits elsewhere may be the factor which makes a brokerage house decide not to recommend or offer the MIP to its customers. It seems doubtful that the decision would be made on the basis of relative costs to the investor, inasmuch as the total cost to make mutual fund investments may be substantially higher.

Whether a customer will be advised to buy mutual funds or adopt an MIP program of stock purchase may have been determined before the customer comes into the office. This sounds like a "daddy always knows best" approach to investment advice. It is submitted, however, that the small investor should know the pros and cons concerning direct and indirect stock ownership. Unless he understands why he selects the MIP or mutual funds one over the other, he may not be making a sound investment decision.

Irrespective of why investors may have chosen the MIP route, there are many MIP regulars who have good reason to be pleased with their direct ownership of stocks. For them the MIP has been an outstanding method of saving and investment.

20 MIP FAVORITES AND PERFORMANCE

Although there are about 1,200 stocks from which to choose (the common and preferred stocks selling in trading units of 100 shares),

MIP investors have narrowed their purchases to a few leading stocks (through their brokers' advice, at least to some extent).

Recently ten stocks accounted for more than 35% of all Monthly Investment Plans. The order of their popularity was:

1. General Motors
2. American Telephone & Telegraph
3. General Telephone & Electronics
4. International Business Machines
5. Tri-Continental (a closed-end investment company)
6. Minnesota Mining & Manufacturing
7. General Electric
8. Standard Oil (of New Jersey)
9. Dow Chemical
10. Radio Corporation of America

The top twenty stocks purchased by MIP customers of Merrill Lynch have produced excellent results. In addition to the ten stocks listed above (in order of popularity), the top twenty stocks included (in alphabetical order) the following ten stocks:

11. American Cyanamid
12. Eastman Kodak
13. Gulf Oil
14. Monsanto Chemical
15. Chas. Pfizer & Co.
16. Phillips Petroleum
17. Safeway
18. Sears, Roebuck
19. Sperry Rand
20. Standard Oil (of California)

The average rate of return on these twenty stocks over the first ten years of the MIP, ending in January 1964, was 16.1% per year (before payment of taxes) or 13.7% (after payment of the 15% Compromise Tax), compounded annually.

Over a period of 39 years, a $1,000 annual investment in a cross-selection of the twenty stocks would amount to the 10th Multiple, on the average. This assumes, of course, maintenance of the 13.7% return.

The value of holding onto fundamentally sound, high-quality stocks cannot be overemphasized. Of the twenty stocks, the least successful produced an annual return, after taxes, of only 3.9%, compounded annually. But the best performer during the 10-year period—IBM—produced an annual return, after taxes, of 24.9%, compounded annually.

Compare the results with life insurance savings and other types of fixed-dollar investments commonly paying 3% to 4% per annum after taxes. Five stocks chosen at random from among the top twenty MIP stocks would have produced a return averaging from 19.5% to 6.0% per year after taxes, compounded annually. This is proof of how successful concentrated diversification can be.

Readers should be advised, however, that I make no recommendation, one way or the other, concerning any specific stock named in this chapter or elsewhere in this book, or whether you should buy securities at all, for that matter. Investments which may have been sound up to the present will not necessarily remain so. My purpose in this book is to provide you with practical information to help you plan your savings and investment program and to give you encouragement to seek competent investment advice about the full details of your program.

From the results above, we see that the Monthly Investment Plan has done well for its followers. But the MIP is not without its fair share of problems, some of which may prove insuperable.

MIP OR MUTUAL FUNDS?

Although concentrated diversification is desirable for investors of comparatively small amounts and can be obtained by simultaneous maintenance of four, five, or six MIP programs, there are some extra-cautious small investors who believe adequate diversification requires no fewer than fifteen or twenty stocks, even though the opportunity for above-average performance is diminished.

These investors can forget about direct stock ownership, whether by MIP or other type of purchase. Diversification costs, resulting from higher commissions, would be excessively high; the problems of administration would be too cumbersome. Instead, they could look to mutual funds, where diversification to the desired extent can be easily obtained.

Most plans of direct stock purchase, including the MIP, which extend over an indefinite period have the disadvantage (some investors say advantage) resulting from lack of professional management. No professional (unless the investor happens to be one himself) is overseeing the decision-making process. This makes the investment fund vulnerable to poor investment judgment, or so it is argued.

A person contemplating direct ownership should remember, however, that even a professional in investments is not immune from making serious mistakes. Poor investment decisions may be largely responsible for certain mutual funds falling into the bottom half or quarter of the list of performance of mutual funds of the same type.

Conversely, direct ownership of stock by a non-professional does not necessarily imply absence of sound professional advice. Capable registered representatives are able and willing to recommend fundamentally sound stocks. After all, these salesmen are hoping to keep their customers satisfied.

Over the course of many years, the direct owner of stocks can keep tabs on his investments by keeping informed. He should read the financial pages of newspapers, study stock analyses published by two or more brokerage houses, and seek advice from his registered representative and other informed persons.

If his original stock purchases were of high quality, the chances are slight that a change will be required. Yet, stocks can and do change in quality, and by keeping in touch with the market the direct owner of stocks can help protect himself against loss, even though he is not a professional investor. His own financial interest in his investments should give him the incentive to be a near-professional investor of his own investment fund.

Inasmuch as good stocks can be selected by a non-professional investor, he need not purchase mutual funds solely for the reason of obtaining professional management of his investment fund.

Even if he *desired* to avoid making investment decisions, he would not achieve his objective through mutual funds. A crucial investment decision is being made when the potential purchaser of mutual fund shares decides which shares to buy. Of course, purchase into several funds would lessen the risk entailed in the investment decision—but which funds?

Then, there is the continuous investment decision occurring as long as a mutual fund investor allows his savings to remain in the same fund or funds. Sound investment judgment may call for a change in mutual funds. Obviously, he still must watch his investments if he expects to maximize his Multiples.

We see, therefore, that the non-professional investor cannot avoid making investment decisions. He keeps his fund invested either in good stocks or in good mutual funds, making changes whenever necessary. The decision-making process is never easy, but when properly done can be highly rewarding.

An investor wondering whether he should go the direct or indirect path should ask himself: How could a periodic purchaser of stocks for the long run have gone wrong if he had bought and held onto four, five, or six of the top twenty MIP favorites?

As we have seen, any five of these stocks produced an average annual return of not less than 6.0% and not more than 19.5%, compounded annually, after payment of the 15% Compromise Tax. (This return, based upon regular investment of equal amounts of money, reflects in part the profits of dollar-cost averaging.)

The lowest average rate of return, applicable if the five stocks were the poorest performers, produced a rate of return twice as high as the return on an investment in a life insurance contract. The highest average rate of return for five stocks would produce the 10th Multiple in only 30 years, for the person saving and investing $1,000 per year, assuming a continuation of the same rate of return.

Concentrated diversification can be highly profitable. An investor should not disregard the Multiple-achieving effect which can be obtained by this method of stock ownership. All he needs, on the average, is diversified investments limited to four, five, or six high-quality, fundamentally sound stocks.

The market price for such stocks can be expected to move higher and higher over a long period of time, but even if the particular stocks purchased by a periodic investor merely return to their original price after equal fluctuations above and below, the periodic investors of equal dollar amounts will show a capital profit, thanks to dollar-cost averaging. (This benefit, of course, is also inherent in the periodic purchase of mutual fund shares.)

Many investors are able to conclude, therefore, that they are not forced to invest in mutual funds merely to obtain diversification or professional management. With adequate attention to their investments and advice from a competent registered representative, they can feel perfectly safe when investing their savings through maintenance of four, five, or six Monthly Investment Plans.

WHY IS THE MIP UNACCEPTABLE?

A real problem exists for MIP investors. Although the MIP has the outward appearance of a forced-savings program, in truth the element of force is minimal, at least when no payroll deduction is used to make the MIP payments. Regular (non-deduction) MIP investors have very little compulsion to save and invest. Expulsion from a plan entails no penalties or losses and occurs, if at all, only after several or more payments have been missed. This major weakness alone may make the MIP unsuitable for persons who need a regimented way to save.

Some investors are more fortunate: Maintaining their plans through the payroll deduction process seems to afford a high degree of compulsion to carry out a regular program of saving and investment. Seldom will an employee request his employer to eliminate the deduction for a month or two; it is simply human nature that 100% voluntary payments are often and easily skipped.

"Permanent" life insurance seems to offer a greater compulsion to save, although the rate of return is quite inferior to an average MIP investment. But there are many people willing, apparently, to sacrifice the possibility of attaining the 7th through 10th Multiples, in order to obtain a virtual guarantee that they will obtain, let us say, the first six Multiples ($64,000).

This sacrifice is unnecessary, at least when based on the argument that life insurance involves the *greatest* amount of compulsion. A more effective system of forced savings does exist. The Save-by-Borrowing technique is such a system, ensuring an individual that he will steadily increase his investments, in securities with a high Multiple-achieving potential. A person never need forfeit the 10th Multiple to force himself to save.

It is quite possible for you to accumulate a million dollars. Do not be fooled by the pessimism of well-meaning middle-of-the-roaders, expressing a suppressed optimism not exceeding the supposed credulity of the average, uninformed saver. The 10th Multiple, as an investment goal, is *not* beyond the reasonable expectations of many millions of potential Save-by-Borrowers. Admittedly, however, everybody cannot be a millionaire at the same time. The only saving grace is that most people do not try to reach the goal.

If you are an individualist, willing to go after your goal, you would do well to remember that YOU CAN ACCUMULATE ONE MILLION DOLLARS—BUT ONLY BY EQUITY INVESTMENTS, as a practical matter. Remember this and you will have made an important step toward accomplishing this desirable lifetime aim. Adopt the Save-by-Borrowing method of involuntary saving and you have an excellent opportunity to force yourself to become wealthy.

But when seeking to accumulate a great amount of wealth, you cannot disregard unnecessary expenses. You should strive to eliminate them.

MIP investors are faced with an insuperable problem—one of inefficiency. A 6% brokerage cost seems small, but it can add up.

By investing once every three months, a person investing an aggregate of $1,000 each year in *one* stock would reduce his brokerage costs to about 2.4% ($6 on each $250 quarterly odd-lot purchase). During the accumulation of each $250, however, it is unlikely that any return would be earned. Thus, there would be 1.5 months of no return during the 6-month period, on the average, his $1,000 in savings could have been invested in stocks at the assumed rate of 12% per year (1% per month). To reflect the real cost of quarterly purchase, we should add 1.5% (representing the loss of return) to the 2.4% brokerage cost; the true cost, therefore, would be 3.9%. This is about $\frac{2}{3}$ of the 6% commission paid by a monthly investor, a difference of 2.1%. The monthly investor may pay more, but he may reasonably conclude it is worth the added cost. Perhaps he could not stick to his saving and investment program any other way.

If *two* stocks are purchased under the MIP, the difference in cost would narrow. The commission on each of the two quarterly (but staggered) purchases of $125 would be $6, or 4%. Adding to this an assumed .75% loss due to non-investment (for $\frac{3}{4}$ of one month), the cost would total 4.75%. But maintenance of *three* stock-purchase plans, to achieve a greater degree of diversification, would involve the full 6% commission; by making one quarterly purchase (of $83.33) each month, the investor could avoid non-investment and would be investing with more beneficial regularity. In this light, it seems proper to compare the Save-by-Borrowing technique with the MIP on the basis of the 6% maximum MIP commission.

Our comparison will vividly indicate why the MIP can be rejected as the medium by which a person invests his $1,000 of annual savings in stocks. The reason is readily given. MIP purchases cost too much, and our 10-Multiple program does not tolerate leakage. The only way to reach the savings goal is to put all your money to work— for *your* benefit, not someone else's.

Disapproval is not limited to monthly stock purchases made pursuant to the MIP. We reject any plan of monthly stock purchase. We do so because of the high cost of brokerage commissions applicable to any insubstantial purchases of stock. An investor purchasing $1,000 worth of stock per year by twelve equal monthly (odd-lot) purchases, of $83.33 each, pays a commission of 6%, a total of $60 per year.

On the other hand, an investor who borrows $1,000 each year, to make a single stock purchase amounting to $1,000, pays only $15 in brokerage commissions (also assuming an odd-lot purchase). Even if he buys two stocks in two separate $500 purchases, he would pay a total brokerage commission of only $20. As a result of the borrowing, the small purchaser is able to save $45 or $40 per year.

Forty dollars per year can add up to a significant sum of money. If a Save-by-Borrower sets aside each year his $40 saving and invests it in a stock or stocks producing an average annual compound return, after taxes, of 12%, the $40 annual investment will be worth $17,300 at the end of 35 years. Thus, $17,300 may be the real cost to persons making monthly stock purchases in small dollar amounts.

Do not be fooled by the seemingly insignificant out-of-pocket expense of an additional $40 each year. Making monthly purchases of stocks in small dollar amounts is a trap which can and should be avoided by small investors, and avoidance is possible by adoption of the Save-by-Borrowing technique.

It is true that to save the $17,300 an interest expense will be incurred by the Save-by-Borrower. On the average, however, the cost of interest will be more than offset by the return on the anticipatory investment of savings before they are actually withdrawn from earnings. The $40 or $45 reduction in commissions, therefore, is a true saving for the Save-by-Borrower.

Just think—the over-all saving in commissions alone is more than many people save in a lifetime through fixed-dollar investments. This supplemental saving can be yours, if you follow the Save-by-Borrowing plan, but would be lost to you if you made your $1,000 stock purchase by means of twelve equal monthly purchases.

A monthly purchase program is so costly, as we have seen, that it must be rejected by Save-by-Borrowers, without any regrets.

MIP FOR REINVESTMENT ONLY?

We have rejected the MIP as the means by which we should make our annual stock purchases of $1,000. Yet, is it possible to utilize the MIP *for reinvestment only,* without being required to make our annual $1,000 purchases pursuant to the MIP?

If this is possible, the immense saving attributable to the Save-by-Borrowing technique would not have to be sacrificed, and the investor could use the MIP to obtain the advantage of immediate reinvestment of all dividends as soon as they were distributed by the companies.

Disregarding reinvestment costs for the time being, a combination program of

1. borrowing to make each annual stock purchase; and
2. automatic reinvestment of all cash dividends pursuant to a Monthly Investment Plan

would seem to be a workable solution to the problems besetting small investors.

Under the MIP, it *is* permissible to reinvest dividends paid on stocks not purchased through the MIP. The investor is required to turn over to his broker the stock certificates (to be held in the broker's name) and instructs the broker to reinvest the dividends as they are paid. One broker, at least, has set a minimum value of $500 for the stock before permitting this arrangement.

For the investor in a single stock, the hybrid program of annual purchase (with borrowed money) and MIP reinvestment would involve maintenance of a single MIP stock-purchase plan, amounting to a total annual purchase of $160 (and involving a 6% commission). The other half of this combination program would call for annual borrowing of $840, using this sum to purchase one or two additional stocks (which would involve commissions of only 1.6%

or 2.2% instead of 6%). The broker would be instructed to reinvest the dividends on all shares as they were paid to him, by purchasing additional MIP stock.

By use of this combination program of investment in only one (MIP) stock, the average commission would be only 2.3% or 2.8% ($13.40 or $18.40 on the $840 non-MIP purchase, and $9.60 on the $160 MIP purchase). For about eight years, commissions on all reinvestments would amount to 6%.

By adoption of the Save-by-Borrowing technique, an investor's payment of commissions on his annual $1,000 stock purchase would be reduced by $37 or $32 per year. The saving would amount to much more, however, over the course of many years. If $37 is saved and invested each year for 35 years to produce an average annual compound return of 12%, after taxes, the accumulation would total about $16,000.

There is, however, a major obstacle for one type of investor; the plan suggested above is of no use to anyone seeking diversification. The MIP does not permit automatic reinvestment of dividends paid on a stock unless the investor is maintaining an MIP plan covering the same stock. Even though Stock X can be bought outside of the MIP and the dividends thereon reinvested automatically under an MIP plan covering the same Stock X, dividends from any other stock cannot be reinvested in Stock X under the present rules.

An investor desiring diversification to the extent of six stocks, let us say, would be able to obtain immediate reinvestment *only* if he maintained a total of six MIP programs. Each of the six plans would require the purchase of $40 or more worth of stock every three months, for a minimum annual purchase of $160. Maintenance of six plans, therefore, would involve $960 of the $1,000 available for investment each year. Thus, there would be no possibility of obtaining any Save-by-Borrowing profits.

A five-stock diversification would free only $200 for Save-by-Borrowing benefits, not enough to make the technique worthwhile to employ. And four-stock diversification, the possible minimum for purposes of safety, would free only $360 for Save-by-Borrowing benefits; the 6% cost of commissions on the $640 of MIP purchases still would amount to a substantial loss of Save-by-Borrowing benefits.

No workable arrangement is offered by the MIP to Save-by-Borrowers seeking diversification. As a result, the Save-by-Borrower is faced with the choices of losing his benefits or seeking automatic reinvestment in some other way.

Would he be pleased to obtain

1. Save-by-Borrowing benefits on the full $1,000;
2. Progressive, concentrated diversification;
3. Forced saving; and
4. Instantaneous reinvestment of dividends at a commission of only 1% (which is one sixth the rate customarily charged under the MIP)?

All this and much more can be accomplished by going all the way with the Save-by-Borrowing system—to the complete exclusion of the MIP.

IV. SAVE THE SAVE-BY-BORROWING WAY

ANTICIPATORY INVESTMENT —
$25,900 SAVING AND PROFIT

A small, periodic investor can avoid the poor trap of paying a 6% brokerage commission on his $1,000 annual investments. All he need do is adopt the Save-by-Borrowing technique. In this way he can reduce his investment costs to a minimum amount, consistent with a savings and diversified investment program involving $1,000 per year.

The small investor, who cannot afford to spread each annual investment over a well-diversified list of stocks, obtains protection by "progressive diversification" instead, where his purchases for several years will add up to the requisite diversification.

Each year the Save-by-Borrower will borrow $1,000, then purchase $500 worth of each of two stocks in two separate transactions. Until diversity to the desired extent of, say, six stocks is obtained, he will continue to add new stocks to his investment portfolio.

During the first several years of his stock-purchasing program, before his total investment is adequately split among the desired number of stocks, his invested savings at risk (the risk of inadequate diversification) will not be too substantial. Therefore, until several years' worth of the $1,000 annual savings have been invested, full diversity does not seem to be essential.

Several years after the start of the Save-by-Borrowing program, full diversity finally will be achieved (which means, let us say, substantially equal investment in each of six different stocks). Thereafter, the annual purchases will not upset, to a significant extent, the previously established diversification.

By diversifying progressively, a Save-by-Borrower puts himself in the enviable position of having an investment program which will outperform, on the average, simultaneous monthly investment programs involving the same stocks. Difference in investment results will amount to a sizable sum of money.

All he need do, for example, is purchase two stocks each year, at a total cost of $500 for each purchase. Commissions would amount to only 2% ($20) per year (on the odd-lot price). In only three years, diversity of six stocks would be achieved, with little risk.

By purchasing two stocks in lieu of a single stock, he will experience a slightly higher cost—$5 per year. This extra cost is the fixed-fee brokerage commission applicable to the purchase of the second stock.

The Save-by-Borrowing technique for making the annual $1,000 investment is quite simple to understand and put into effect. A Save-by-Borrower's $20 annual brokerage cost is $40 less than the cost of investing on a monthly basis (assuming odd-lot purchases in each case). As we've seen, a $40 annual investment producing a 12% net annual return would amount to $17,300 in 35 years. This amount need not be sacrificed—but often is, by inefficiency of investment technique.

The advantages of borrowing do not cease with the $17,300 saving. As a result of the borrowing, the investor enables himself to avoid *investment delays* he would otherwise experience.

Let's look at an investor who accumulates his savings in a savings account until the end of each year, then makes his annual stock purchases. We'll refer to him as a "year-end investor." The return from the savings account (due to delays in deposit and failure to have the savings on deposit for full interest-paying periods) is about $13 (actually, $12.75). This is about ⅜ (37.5%) of an assumed 3.4% net return.

The Save-by-Borrower suffers no delay in investing his annual $1,000 in savings, being able to obtain half ($60) of the 12% ($120) net return on his $1,000. The $1,000 saved through twelve equal monthly installments is invested at 12% for an average of 6 months, amounting to a 6% ($60) return on the $1,000. In comparison to the Save-by-Borrower, *the year-end investor suffers a net loss in return of $47* ($60 return of the Save-by-Borrower minus the $13 received by the year-end investor). Over 35 years, at a 12% net return per annum, this would involve a *total loss of $20,300* for the year-end investor.

Save-by-Borrowers, as well as investors using the Monthly Investment Plan, avoid this substantial loss. The cost to the monthly investor, however, is the $17,300 relating to increased brokerage commissions.

In addition, the Save-by-Borrower is able to obtain, on the average, a certain profit. Deduct $40 (the after-tax cost of interest to borrow the annual $1,000) from $60 (the other 6 months' worth of the 12% return on the $1,000—that is, the extent to which the $1,000 is anticipatorily invested). We find an anticipatory investment profit averaging $20 per year.

When $20 per year for 35 years is invested at 12%, the accumulation will total $8,600. The monthly investor does not derive this borrowing profit, however. Of course, if the average net rate of return is only 10%—or 11% if he fails to itemize his interest deduction —there will be no such profit for the Save-by-Borrower. But there are other profits remaining, making it worthwhile to borrow if you can maintain an average return in excess of 5.3% (or 6.3%) after taxes.

By immediate investment of savings, the Save-by-Borrower and monthly investor each prevent a total loss of $20,300. The monthly investor, however, derives no further benefit, in comparison to the Save-by-Borrower. As we have just discovered, a further saving of $17,300 and a profit of $8,600 belong to the Save-by-Borrower alone—a potential combined saving and profit of $25,900. This is reason enough to adopt a Save-by-Borrowing program. But this is not all.

Surprisingly enough, *reinvestment* is much easier to accomplish, is also brought about by an anticipatory procedure, and costs only 1%.

ANTICIPATORY REINVESTMENT —
$21,000 SAVING AND PROFIT

It may be difficult for the small, periodic investor to believe that the effect of immediate reinvestment can be achieved at a cost of only 1%, but it is possible. This cost is 50% less than the low 2% cost of making the annual purchase of two stocks, and $83\frac{1}{3}$% less than the 6% (maximum) cost of immediate reinvestment within or without the MIP.

Both monthly investors and Save-by-Borrowers benefit from the immediate reinvestment of dividends. We saw on pages 130–31 how the benefit can amount to $15,300, for a person who saves and invests $1,000 per year. But to benefit from this saving, the monthly investor is required to pay a high price—more than $10,000. This represents the 6% cost of reinvestment paid by MIP investors, which should not be overlooked. Six per cent is very high and will be paid over a period of many years.

Assuming a monthly investor diversifies his stock ownership to the extent of six stocks, it will take him about twenty years of saving and investment of $1,000 each year to accumulate an investment fund valued at about $70,300 (assuming a 12% net return). At this point, assuming that the value of each stock holding is equal and that each stock is paying a net cash dividend of 3.4%, each stock would be paying an annual dividend of $400, or $100 every three months. Thus, nearing the end of twenty years, the monthly investor will still be paying 6% to reinvest his cash dividends.

In comparison to a reinvestment cost of only 1% (offered by the Save-by-Borrowing technique) the monthly investor pays an *added* cost of 5% of the net value of the dividends, which, in comparison, reduces his 3.4% net dividend to approximately 3.23%. This reduces his over-all return by $\frac{1}{6}$ of 1% per year. In twenty years, this loss would total $1,310. At the end of 35 years, however, the twenty-year loss would grow to about $7,200.

Also, losses attributable to reinvestment *after* the end of the 20 years—when reinvestment costs drop below 6%—should be added to the $7,200 loss, which, we will assume, would make the total loss about $10,000. This $10,000 loss is paid unnecessarily by monthly investors to obtain the $15,300 advantage of immediate reinvestment.

The Save-by-Borrower can benefit from the effect of immediate reinvestment *without* having to pay the monthly investor's extra cost of $10,000. He obtains this combined saving by a process we will call *anticipatory reinvestment*. This automatic reinvestment of dividends is accomplished by an extension of the Save-by-Borrowing process. Two steps are involved in the reinvestment process.

FIRST: The investor should estimate (before making his annual two-stock purchase) how much in cash dividends he expects to receive during the forthcoming year. This estimate should include the dividends on the stock he is getting ready to purchase for the next year.

Let us assume he expects to obtain dividends aggregating $50 on his $1,000 two-stock purchase. To this $50 purchase of additional stock should be added an amount equal to the dividends expected to be paid on the $50 worth of additional stock; such dividends would amount to $2.50. Theoretically, computations could continue, but the point of diminishing returns has been reached, at least in year one of the saving and investment program.

We find, after making the above computations, that the Save-by-Borrower should invest approximately $1,052.50 when he makes his first annual purchase of two stocks.

SECOND: A stock-purchase order must be given to the stockbroker. But before this can be done, the $1,052.50 to be invested must be allocated between the two stocks.

Assume the odd-lot prices of the two stocks are $40 and $60 per share. How can an investor allocate the $1,052.50 between the two stocks to invest the full amount *and,* at the same time, invest equal amounts in the two stocks? Precision is impossible to attain, in most instances; anyway, an approximation of the two goals will be entirely suitable.

Knowing that the total brokerage commissions would approximate 2%, he should subtract $21 from the $1,052.50, leaving $1,031.50 to be allocated between the two stocks. Therefore, about $516 worth of each stock (at the odd-lot price) should be bought.

If the (odd-lot) price for each share to be purchased averaged $50, twenty full shares of stock would be bought with the $1,031.50. A greater number of shares, however, will be bought when the same amount of money is used to purchase shares at a price equally above and below the $50 price. This is the "magic" underlying dollar-cost averaging, which will show a capital profit if equal amounts are invested periodically regardless of the price level. Assuming continuation of the buying program, and that the purchases are made at prices which, on the average, are equally above and below the price of the original purchase, the investor will have a dollar-cost averaging profit if the price goes back to the original level.

Although the purchase of an aggregate of $1,031.50 worth of the $40 and $60 stocks does *not* produce a dollar-cost averaging profit, it can be used to point out how dollar-cost averaging works. Half of the $1,031.50 (that is, $516) will purchase 12.9 shares of the $40 stock; and the other $516 will purchase 8.6 shares of the $60 stock; for a total of 21.5 shares of stock. Thus, one share, the number of shares in excess of 20.5 (the number which would have been purchased at an average price of $50 per share), would be the dollar-cost averaging profit.

We return to anticipatory reinvestment, to allocate the $1,031.50, on a roughly equal basis, between the $40 and $60 stocks.

A possible solution would be to purchase 9 shares of the $60 stock (having a $540 market value, in total) and 12 shares of the $40 stock (having a $480 aggregate market value), which totals $1,020 in market value.

Commissions would amount to $10 plus 1% for the two-stock purchase, or a total of $20.20. Thus, the total cost of the two stocks would amount to $1,040.20.

Out of the original $1,052.50 available for investment, $1,040.20 would be spent to acquire the nine shares of the $60 stock and the twelve shares of the $40 stock. It makes no practical difference whether the final purchase price is more or less than the $1,052.50 available for investment, as long as the final figure reasonably approximates the amount available.

Even though you understand the two steps, you may still be uncertain as to the procedure by which the additional $40.20 is to be acquired to pay for the stock. You may remember that only $1,000 is to be borrowed from the bank, by a signature (unsecured) loan.

Anticipatory reinvestment requires that the $40.20 be *borrowed* from your stockbroker and that dividend payments be made to him, automatically reducing the $40.20 anticipatory reinvestment loan. At the end of the year, when all the dividends will have been paid, the loan will have been fully paid and the anticipatory reinvestment process will have been completed for the year. The full amount (or an approximation thereof) of the yearly dividends paid on your investments will have been used to buy additional stock, without any time lag whatsoever. In fact, reinvestment is better than immediate; it occurs in advance, working to obtain substantial profits for the Save-by-Borrower.

The 1% cost of reinvestment results from the fact that the aggregate $10 fixed fee (on two odd-lot purchases, each involving from $400 to $2,400) has been paid on the annual $1,000 investment. Simultaneous reinvestment of the anticipated annual dividends involves no additional $10 fee; only the 1% commission increases the total commission payable on the two-stock purchasing involving $40.20 in excess of $1,000.

When the $40.20 is borrowed from your broker, the borrowing will take the form of a margin transaction. To obtain the loan, the investor must pledge some of his stock with his broker, to ensure that the lender will be repaid. The minimum initial margin requirement set by Rule 431 (a) of the New York Stock Exchange demands that no less than $2,000 in equity, consisting of cash or securities, be deposited with the broker. The pledged stock can be used by the broker, if he desires, as collateral to secure any loans *he* may have to obtain. The initial margin requirement of the American Stock Exchange is $2,000 also. But a member firm of the NYSE or ASE is allowed to set initial margin requirements higher than the established minimum.

In the first few years of your program, cash dividends on *all* investments will not exceed 30% of the value of the pledged stock; and you will be able to make the annual margin transactions in increasing dollar amounts without being required to pledge additional stock with your broker, to meet the initial margin requirements (of 70%, presently) fixed by Regulation T of the Federal Reserve Board. Therefore, you will be able to request and obtain delivery of all stock purchases, except for the stock certificates originally pledged with your broker and, later, any additional stock required by Regulation T to be pledged when dividends exceed 30% of the value of the original pledge (as of the time each additional margin transaction is being made). You would have, therefore, the security of knowing that the certificates are under your own possession and control.

Perhaps, though, you sense a problem. How can the dividends

be paid to the broker if the certificates are registered in your name? Would you have to go through the trouble of endorsing the dividend checks and sending them to the broker, assuming he would be willing to let you reduce your margin loan this way?

If you are willing to leave the certificates with him, as many investors are, the problem is purely academic. The certificate would be registered in the name of the broker (called *street name*), and the dividends would be automatically paid to him. Upon receipt of the dividends, the broker would credit them to your margin account, reducing the outstanding balance of the margin loan as of their receipt.

However, you may not wish to leave the certificates with your broker, except for the minimum amount necessary to facilitate the dividend reinvestment process. What, then, should you do? Here is the answer. Ask your broker for the name and address of the bank acting as *dividend disbursing agent* for each dividend-paying corporation in which you own stock. Then, execute a *dividend order* in favor of the broker and mail it to the agent. A dividend order form can be obtained through your broker or directly from the agent. The dividend order will direct the agent to pay all cash dividends to the broker for your account. This allows you to retain possession of the certificates even though the dividends will be paid to the broker. Also, it enables you to obtain an *immediate* reduction of the outstanding balance of the margin loan and, therefore, the effect of immediate, automatic reinvestment of all cash dividends, no matter how small the amount.

Margin purchases, when used primarily as a speculative tool, should be shunned by conservative investors. However, our use of margin to effect anticipatory reinvestment is *not* for the speculative purpose of obtaining "leverage," where profits are attempted to be made on borrowed funds at the risk of losing equity in excess of any decline in value. Leverage exists, for example, where a person buys $10,000 worth of stock with only $1,000 of his own money and $9,000 of borrowed money. If the value of the stock increases by only 10%, he will have a 100% increase in the original $1,000 value of his equity investment (the benefit of leverage); whereas, if the market price drops only 10%, he will suffer a 100% loss of his equity interest (the risk connected with leverage transactions).

Borrowing of $40.20 (in the first year) is employed only to facilitate reinvestment, to make reinvestment as immediate, automatic, convenient, inexpensive, and profitable as possible. At no time would the amount borrowed to facilitate reinvestment exceed (by anything more than a minimal amount) the total anticipated dividends for the forthcoming year. This would seldom be more than 6% or 7% of the value of the Save-by-Borrower's investment fund; and by the end of each year the borrowed funds would be repaid by the broker's receipt of the dividend distributions. Use of margin for anticipatory reinvestment is perfectly consistent with conservative principles of investment. There would be no more than a minimal speculative value, as a by-product of the reinvestment process, producing a tidy profit over the course of many years.

Even if you choose to keep all of your stocks with your broker, only 5% or so of the total value of your stocks at the beginning of the investment year would have been purchased on margin. The 95% equity position is not speculative, but safe.

An average return of 12% on the portion of the dividends which is anticipatorily reinvested (100% of the dividends for an average of six months, minus about 4.8% representing the cost of interest on the margin loan after taking a tax deduction) produces a net annual return of 7.2% on the dividends for half a year—or a 3.6% return on a full-year basis. When 3.6% is multiplied by the 3.4% net rate of dividends, it produces $\frac{1}{8}$ of 1% return on the investment fund. This $\frac{1}{8}$ of 1% return represents the profit to be expected from anticipatory reinvestment, a profit which is in addition to the $10,000 saving resulting from the lower cost of commissions and the $15,300 advantage of immediate reinvestment. Over 35 years, the $\frac{1}{8}$ of 1% will amount to about $11,000.

Save-by-Borrowers, therefore, can derive the $21,000 combined advantage of the $10,000 saving on commissions and $11,000 profit on anticipatory reinvestment, which is in addition to the $15,300 resulting from immediate reinvestment. Monthly investors are not as fortunate. They lose the $21,000 combined advantage, to obtain the $15,300 effect.

Anticipatory *reinvestment* is a new application of well-known market devices, but at this writing it appears to be unknown to investors or to the 650 or so member organizations of the NYSE. After becoming acquainted with the technique, some of the member organizations, on an individual basis, may decide not to permit the periodic reduction, in small amounts, of the outstanding balance of the margin loan. This is their privilege. After all, the technique does reduce substantially a broker's commissions, while adding slightly to his bookkeeping costs. On the other hand, a broker would be more favorably disposed if:

1. comparatively large dollar amounts—especially for dividends—were involved;
2. the investor practiced concentrated diversification, minimizing the total number of dividend payments; and
3. all stock certificates were left with the broker, and he would be given the power to lend them to short-sellers (at his profit, of course).

A large, aggressive organization, making full use of electronic computers and seeking to retain and increase its customers, would probably be more likely to permit anticipatory reinvestment. This would make good business sense because Save-by-Borrowers stand an excellent chance of becoming favored customers, and the broker would be ill advised to turn them away.

REVIEWING THE BALANCE SHEET

The combination of anticipatory investment and anticipatory reinvestment can be of substantial advantage to a small investor.

In reviewing the balance sheet, we find that the following savings and profits can be achieved by the Save-by-Borrower:

ON HIS $1,000 ANNUAL BORROWING:

(a)	Reduced Commissions	$17,300	
(b)	Anticipatory Investment	8,600	
(c)	Immediate Investment	20,300	
			$46,200

ON HIS BORROWING TO REINVEST DIVIDENDS:

(a)	Reduced Commissions	$10,000	
(b)	Anticipatory Reinvestment	11,000	
(c)	Immediate Reinvestment	15,300	
			36,300
			$82,500

Thus, the Save-by-Borrower can expect savings and profits approximating $46,900 more than can be expected by the monthly investor ($82,500 minus the $35,600 savings resulting from immediate investment and reinvestment, which are obtained by the monthly investor too). Of course, this assumes a 12% compound annual return, after taxes, including dividends and capital appreciation.

This $46,900 will be small in comparison to the $431,700 value of your investments at the end of 35 years, but would exceed 10% of such amount, affording a soft cushion of protection to the conservative investor, who needs to insure against losses in his long-range investment program.

So, if you save by borrowing, you will achieve the 10th Multiple in the quickest possible time, consistent with fundamentally sound equity investments, with a 10% cushion of protection, assuming maintenance of the assumed rate of return.

We have talked about mutual funds, having compared them with the Monthly Investment Plan. Now we are going to examine them more closely, to see what they are and why they are so popular. Maybe they are not for you—or maybe they are.

Chapter Nine

WHAT TO TELL A MUTUAL FUND SALESMAN

THE END OF INVESTMENT COMPANIES

Mary and Fred, fully convinced of the long-run advantage of investment in equity securities, had to decide whether to invest their savings by direct or indirect purchase of common stocks. Recalling what he had learned from sales literature and several encounters with mutual fund salesmen, Fred was able to present to his wife Mary an understandable explanation of how they could invest in common stocks indirectly. All they needed to do was purchase investment company shares, particularly the shares of one or more mutual funds.

"A mutual fund," Fred explained, "is a corporation or trust primarily engaged in the investment, reinvestment, or trading of securities, such as stocks and bonds. Mutual fund shares, representing part ownership of the trust or corporation, are sold to investors at a price based on 'net asset value' per share, which is the value of all assets held by the mutual fund, minus liabilities, divided by the total number of mutual fund shares outstanding. This price ensures that already outstanding shares will not be diluted in value upon issuance of additional shares."

Deciding that Mary could use additional basic information about mutual funds, Fred continued by saying that moneys raised by a mutual fund through the sale of fund shares are invested in accordance with the policy and objectives of the fund. For example, a fund's objectives may be to obtain income, protection of capital or long-range capital growth or any combination thereof. To achieve its objectives a fund's policy may be to invest in common or preferred stocks only, or fixed-dollar securities or a combination. Specialty funds limit their investments, for example, to life insurance or science stocks. A prospective purchaser must be careful to select a fund or funds having the desired policy and objectives.

A shareholder in a mutual fund has a fractional interest in each and every investment held by the fund, affording the small investor a greater degree of diversity than he could obtain by direct purchase of stocks. Some mutual funds hold stocks issued by more than one hundred different corporations.

If an investor decides to take his money out of the fund, he cannot expect the fund to distribute his fractional interest in each investment held by the fund. Instead, the mutual fund is obligated to pay him a redemption price equivalent to the net asset value, minus an appropriate redemption fee, if any.

Except in extraordinary situations, this redemption price will be paid to the redeeming shareholder in no more than seven days after tender of the shares for redemption, and usually much sooner. This feature of ready convertibility to cash makes mutual fund investment attractive to many people. An investor is warned, however, "that the value of the shares on redemption may be more or less than the investor's cost, depending upon the market value of the portfolio securities at the time of redemption." (SEC, Statement of Policy.)

The mandatory redemption privilege is considered justification for the continuous offering of shares, by most mutual funds, to raise money to meet redemptions without having to sell any investments held by the fund. In this way, the fund can avoid payment of brokerage commissions, to the extent redemptions are offset by sale of new shares. Net proceeds from any excess of sales of new mutual fund shares over share redemptions are available for investment by the fund in additional securities.

To reflect the ever changing number of outstanding shares of a mutual fund, the Investment Company Act of 1940 gives it the official name of *open-end investment company*. This distinguishes a mutual fund from a *closed-end investment company*, which ordinarily does not and is not required to offer a continuous redemption privilege and ordinarily does not offer new stock to the public.

Shares of a closed-end investment company, available on a securities exchange or in the over-the-counter market, may be selling for more or less than net asset value, unlike the shares of a mutual fund. This is one reason why closed-end investment companies are not as popular as mutual funds. Yet, if closed-end investment companies made a similar sales effort to sell additional shares, their popularity would increase, undoubtedly.

Examples of a closed-end investment company are Tri-Continental Corporation, Madison Fund, and Lehman Corporation, the common stock of which are listed on the New York Stock Exchange. This stock is purchased in the same way as shares of corporations such as General Motors and American Telephone & Telegraph, by placement of an order with a stockbroker and payment of the regular brokerage commissions.

The brokerage commission to buy shares of a closed-end investment company is less than the usual sales charge to purchase shares of a mutual fund. Persons making small monthly purchases may find, however, that the total brokerage cost of purchasing *and selling* closed-end investment company shares will equal or exceed the sales cost of purchasing and redeeming mutual fund shares.

For Save-by-Borrowers, the preceding comparison of costs is irrelevant. Closed-end investment company shares can be purchased on an annual Save-by-Borrowing basis as other stocks can be purchased, with the same advantages. The brokerage cost (on the odd-lot price) would be only 1.5% to purchase, no more than 1.5% to sell, and only 1% to reinvest—assuming a $1,000 annual investment in one company.

Fred recalled that his father's stockbroker had mentioned several closed-end investment companies which seemed to be attractive investments. But Mary had heard mutual funds mentioned at the bridge table many times and was anxious for Fred to elaborate further upon mutual funds.

INVESTING THE EASY WAY

Fred learned much from his father, an owner of stock in about sixteen different corporations. With no difficulty, Fred could recite a few good reasons for refusing to invest by direct purchase of common stocks, reasons which were equally convincing to Mary.

Four times each year Fred's father receives a dividend check from each of the sixteen corporations, a total of sixty-four checks in the course of each year. Meticulously, whenever a check arrives, he makes a notation in his records, to ensure that he receives all payments and to prepare the way for annual computation of income taxes. Within several days after receipt, he fills out a bank deposit slip and deposits the check in his savings or checking account.

Fred estimates his father spends fifty hours per year keeping records on his investments and depositing his dividend checks, not including the endless hours spent reading investment letters and the financial pages of newspapers and the innumerable telephone conversations with his stockbroker. Some hours could be eliminated if he would execute a dividend order to have all dividends sent to his bank or broker; or if he would entrust his stockbroker with the stock certificates, to be held in street name, so all dividend checks would be sent to and cashed by the stockbroker. Yet, the gentleman likes this arrangement better and seems to enjoy complaining about the dividend-check nuisance as he carries his dividend checks to the bank. Mary, on the other hand, had no desire to study or keep current in stock market affairs, nor did she lend much encouragement to Fred in this regard, making it unbearable for him to be caught reading the financial pages instead of the book section of the Sunday newspaper.

Fred's father is fortunate in having enough money to purchase one hundred shares or more of each of sixteen stocks. On the other hand, Fred and Mary were just getting started in life, with much hope but no capital to speak of. To buy as much as one hundred shares of just one good stock would be impossible for them now.

After thinking things over, Fred decided to invest in several mutual funds. By such a purchase Fred would be acquiring a fractional interest in all of the underlying investments in each of the mutual funds, a diversification he believed was necessary. Over-diversification is considered an evil by some investors, preventing them from doing better than the market averages. Fred was not too worried, however. He would be satisfied (and justifiably so) if he could select several mutual funds which, on the average, would perform as well as the market averages.

By his decision to make indirect stock investments, Fred eliminated perhaps hundreds of hours each year of investment analysis and supervision and record-keeping. The funds would take care of all the details and make computations for tax purposes. Distributions from each fund unless reinvested would be made only four times each year, as if he owned only several stocks instead of hundreds.

Diversification and convenience are attractive features of mutual fund investments, but not as attractive to Fred as the managerial ability he is purchasing, the expertise of competent professional investors who will make all investment decisions and exercise continuing supervision over the fund's investments.

Yes, Fred is happy with his decision. Mary is neutral, not really caring one way or the other, or so she says. She is in a hurry to leave for a bridge tournament.

There would be a cost, of course, for having somebody else do the work—a cost amounting each year to only 1% or so of the net asset value of the investment, a sum small in comparison to the anticipated benefits, or so Fred believed. After all, why shouldn't he chip in to pay for the professional advice, services, office expenses, legitimate profits, etc.? If he selected satisfactory mutual funds, a 1% reduction from the over-all rate of return would give him nevertheless a net profit in excess of what he probably would have been able to do for himself, assuming he was not devoted to the market.

Several subsidiary reasons for purchasing mutual fund shares had been considered by Fred. He knew that many funds offered accumulation plans whereby a small investor could buy a few shares of a fund each month over a long period, to take advantage of dollar-cost averaging. Also, most funds permit automatic reinvestment of distributions, to facilitate the compound process.

In addition, many funds afford special services, such as completion life insurance, which provides money to pay for the unpurchased shares under an accumulation program terminated prematurely by the death of the investor. Or, if an investor reaches retirement and has accumulated shares valued at no less than $10,000 (usually), he can adopt a withdrawal plan, similar in some respects to an annuity. Under a withdrawal plan, the fund would pay him $150 per month, for example, and any deficiency in ordinary dividends from the fund would be made up by sale of some of his mutual fund shares. To the extent that shares are sold, there is a withdrawal of capital. Unlike a life annuity, the investor takes a chance that his withdrawals will exhaust his capital prior to his death, in which case he may suffer deprivation in the remaining years of his life. Also, some funds offer plans for the self-employed to establish pension funds qualified to take advantage of favorable federal tax treatment.

With the numerous bases for differentiation of mutual funds, Fred will have a difficult time trying to select the funds most suitable for him. Many funds can be eliminated from further consideration, however, once Fred determines his investment objectives. Probably, he would not want an income fund, because he would be reinvesting the income anyway. He probably would reduce his over-all liability for income taxes by investing in growth mutual funds, which invest in companies often using most of their earnings for research and development and to finance expansion.

A balanced fund, consisting of various types and proportions of stocks and fixed-dollar investments may be appropriate. Fred decided to the contrary. He thought it best to invest in a growth fund, the type of fund which should produce the highest return over the course of his savings and investment program.

TRICKS OF THE TRADE

Fred was not quite certain how to go about purchasing mutual fund shares, so he called upon his father's stockbroker for advice. The stockbroker was exceedingly helpful, reviewing Fred's investment objectives, then recommending a particular growth mutual fund.

The stockbroker explained that, customarily, $8\frac{1}{2}\%$ of the purchase price constitutes a sales charge, most of which he would retain as a concession from the fund. After all, he was not in business to lose money and he needed some reimbursement for the present and future loss of brokerage commissions which Fred otherwise might pay to him in direct purchases and sales of stock.

A sales charge of $8\frac{1}{2}\%$, the most typical sales charge, amounts to $85 on a $1,000 purchase, the remainder, $915, being applied to the purchase of mutual fund shares. The $85 sales charge would be split up among several levels of distribution, including the underwriter and mutual fund salesman, broker-dealer, or registered representative making the sale.

Persons investing in mutual funds should be on guard, especially when dealing with a mutual fund salesman. Failure to exercise a proper degree of caution can involve the loss of many thousands of dollars, by investment in a poorly managed mutual fund. The sales-man, receiving a commission for each sale, has a natural tendency to promote his own interests, at the expense of the fund purchaser. A salesman selling only one fund or one group of funds obviously is biased toward sale of the recommended fund. One can easily arm himself against a salesman's natural predisposition of this type.

More difficult, however, is the situation where an apparently dis-interested investment counselor, a broker-dealer, or a registered rep-resentative, appears to be making his selection from the entire list of mutual funds. A prospective purchaser of mutual funds can easily understand why the counselor is apt to recommend investment in a fund selling its shares at the customary sales charge of $8\frac{1}{2}\%$, instead of some lesser percentage. You would think, however, that the counselor would choose the most suitable fund from among the many funds with an $8\frac{1}{2}\%$ sales charge.

Unfortunately, this is not necessarily so. There may be other con-siderations, completely unknown to the investor. No disclosure is made to the investor that sale of the recommended fund would earn the counselor a higher percentage of the $8\frac{1}{2}\%$ sales charge than if he sold to the investor shares of another, more suitable fund. The prospective purchaser is not informed when the counselor would receive additional compensation—a kickback on related brokerage commissions which have been paid by the fund; nor does he find out the size of the kickback.

Sale of mutual fund shares is wholly unlike the sale of other kinds of stock, where the counselor's commission for execution of the cus-tomer's order does *not* increase without the knowledge of the in-vestor. A higher rate of commission will be earned upon an order involving lower-priced stocks, but the purchaser should be aware of this higher cost and have a fighting chance to counteract any abuses.

Other abuses are present in the sale of mutual fund shares. New mutual fund salesmen are given a short orientation course, then turned loose on the public as "financial consultants" or some other designation equally misrepresentative of their education and expe-rience. Most of the salesmen are recruited from unrelated fields and have little or no prior training or background to qualify them as financial planners—nor does the short orientation course change the situation more than a minimal amount. Accordingly, one who deals with mutual fund salesmen should seldom place 100% reliance upon their statements. Instead, he should seek independent verification. It is unfortunate for the ethical qualified salesmen that his position is deprecated by the low caliber of many mutual fund salesmen.

Some of the blame should be placed on the industry, which advocates use of the hard sell, a technique by which investors become such only by reason of a massive sales effort and not because the investors had originally decided to purchase the fund shares. A very high percentage of the 3,300,000 mutual fund shareholders have become such only by reason of the hard sell.

Hundreds of thousands if not millions of people have experienced the sales technique of being shocked into listening to a mutual fund salesman who asks his prospect whether he would like to have $50,-000, or some other sizable amount. The question needs no answer. What should be asked is whether the particular fund shares offered by the salesman can be expected to do all that the salesman suggests they will. Funds run from good to bad, and the fund first brought to a person's attention probably will not be the best for him. Through the hard sell, however, the first fund is frequently the one purchased by the unsophisticated investor.

In furtherance of the hard sell, new salesmen are told to compile a list including all neighborhood, business, and church acquaintances, then make the rounds, trying to sell them mutual fund shares. By the time the new salesman has exhausted his list of prospects, he has become discouraged and leaves the field. Acquaintances are not the only prospects on the new salesman's list. He is told to call upon a friend or relative for a "favor," to listen to and comment upon the sales talk he has been practicing. Finally, nearing the end of the "practice session," the salesman becomes "serious," telling his unsuspecting friend that he really does need to purchase the mutual fund shares. How low can you go?

Those who have been tricked into purchasing mutual fund shares from purported friends can derive a small measure of revenge in knowing that the salesman himself may have been duped into purchasing fund shares on the same terms, particularly under a contractual plan. A technique frequently employed by members of the mutual fund industry is to urge the new salesman himself to purchase shares before he sells any; otherwise, he is told, he will not be able to sell with any conviction to others. He must first be sold himself.

As a practical matter, the turnover rate of mutual fund salesmen is so high that many funds seem to be engaged in the profitable business of selling shares to their new salesmen. In some cases the salesmen are to make no further sales.

Perhaps the lack of an elementary education in financial matters explains the use of one particularly reprehensible technique, grounds for suspending or otherwise penalizing the salesman: the sale of dividends. A prospective investor is told that he should buy shares right away, to get in on a forthcoming distribution of dividends. It sounds good to many unknowledgeable investors. But what are the consequences?

If a $1 distribution is to be made with respect to a share selling for $12, does the share remain at the $12 value after the $1 has been distributed? Of course not. The value of a share is determined by adding up all the assets, subtracting the liabilities, then dividing by the number of mutual fund shares outstanding. When $1 is distributed to each share, there will be an equivalent reduction of the assets allocable to each share; hence, the market value for the share will fall to $11.

What is so bad about this? He paid $12, and, after distribution of the $1 dividend, he has a share valued at $11 and has $1 in cash, for a total of $12. Plenty is wrong! In some instances there will be a sales charge payable to reinvest the distribution. What is much worse, he has purchased a needless tax liability. The $1 may be taxed as ordinary income (20% rate, we assume), as long-term capital gain (10%), or as a combination of both (15%, our Compromise Tax), a needless reduction in value of the dollar to 80 cents, 90 cents, or 85 cents. The salesman pulling this stunt should be reported immediately to the National Association of Securities Dealers, which is the semi-governmental body exercising regulatory control over many mutual fund salesmen, or to the Securities and Exchange Commission, which supervises the remaining salesmen.

Another hard sell occurs by convincing an older person to sign up for a long-range (say ten-year) accumulation plan. Although the person has a statistically limited opportunity to complete his program, the salesman does not care, obtaining from the purchaser in the first year of the program a substantial portion of the sales charge for the entire duration of the plan.

The foregoing abuses—and others—are well chronicled in the Report of Special Study of Securities Markets of the Securities and Exchange Commission, available at the United States Government Printing Office, at a cost of $3.75 (88th Congress, 1st Session, House Document No. 95, Part 4). Mutual fund investors should take the time to read this report.

Suffice it to say that an individual who purchases mutual funds from a salesman should be on constant alert, to detect and report any unethical sales practices.

More important, however, is the need for an investor to learn about mutual funds before purchasing any; he should learn how to separate the good from the bad. Particularly, he should look at the prospectus (containing a description of the fund, which the salesman is obligated to deliver to him) to determine such factors as sales charges and fund issuance and redemption fees; fund policy, objectives and performance; operating expenses and the management fee as a percentage of the net asset value of the fund; and the percentage of unrealized capital gains, which is a measure of the potential income tax liability unrelated to any increase in value of a new purchaser's investment.

Fred cannot afford to delegate his investment decisions to somebody else. Thus, he must not purchase shares of the first mutual fund brought to his attention. Instead, he must make his decision on the basis of anticipated performance and select from those mutual funds most suitable for him. Sales charges are of utmost importance, and unless there is good reason for selection of a mutual fund with a high sales charge, the reader may wish to narrow his search down to the forty-seven funds the names and addresses of which are set forth in Appendix A to this book.

To choose the proper fund or funds, an investor should do a considerable amount of research. But substantial effort can be avoided if he refers to published statistics on comparative performances of mutual funds over various periods. The investor can find useful statistics in the annual mutual fund edition of *Forbes,* a financial and business magazine published biweekly. Also, performances are compared in the annual mutual fund guide and other issues of *Fund-Scope,* an independent magazine published monthly for mutual fund investors. Inquiries should be addressed to FundScope, 5455 Wilshire Boulevard, Los Angeles, California 90036. Most elaborate of all is each annual edition of *Investment Companies*. This is a book of about 400 pages, selling for $30, published by Arthur Wiesenberger & Company, 61 Broadway, New York, New York 10006.

Wanting to learn more about mutual funds, Fred rejected, temporarily at least, the recommendation by the stockbroker.

1,123,000 SAVE-BY-BORROWING CANDIDATES

Remember these terms, Fred: *"Contractual plan," "penalty plan," "systematic accumulation plan," "front-end load."* They refer to a monthly accumulation plan which 1,123,000 investors have adopted, only to line the pockets of mutual fund salesmen.

If the reader gets nothing more out of this chapter, he would be greatly benefited if he made an everlasting mental note, as follows:

I should never buy mutual fund shares through a contractual plan.

For persons already purchasing shares pursuant to a contractual plan, the following may be in order, depending on relative costs:

Make no more payments. Request the custodian to send to you the underlying mutual fund shares already purchased under the plan.

Some contractual plan investors will be able to recover 100% of their initial payments. If the plan sponsor is a member of the Association of Mutual Fund Plan Sponsors, Inc., one can obtain a full refund by filing a written request within thirty days after making the first payment. In actual practice, the thirty-day refund privilege is used as a selling point by salesmen, who are well aware that only a very small percentage ever use the escape hatch, even though many investors do terminate the plan during the first few months.

What is so wrong with a contractual plan? It calls for nothing more than monthly payments in equal dollar amounts, over a stipulated period, to purchase (indirectly) shares of a mutual fund. The answer: prepayment of a substantial portion of the total sales charge. Under a "contractual" plan the investor promises (but does not legally obligate) himself to purchase mutual fund shares, by paying, say, $50 per month for a ten-year period.

Persons entering into a contractual plan do so under the impres-

sion (given to them by a fast-talking salesman) that they will be forcing themselves to save. Pressure to save, it is said, results from
substantial prepayment of the customary 8–8½% sales charge for
the total purchases to be made under the plan (say, $6,000). The
prepayment is made by deduction of a sales charge not in excess of
50% from each of the first thirteen monthly payments or their
equivalent. Thereafter, the sales charge for each monthly purchase
is reduced, ordinarily varying from 1.6% to 6.0%, to be deducted
from each of the remaining 107 monthly payments under the plan,
an expense not charged by the mutual funds listed in Appendix A.

Under a $50 plan, an investor intends to make payments totaling
$600 each year, or a total of $6,000 over a ten-year period. Of the
$6,000, 8% (or $480) is payable in sales charges, assuming completion of the plan. In the first thirteen months of the plan (actually,
the first year, the first payment being equal to two monthly installments), $650 is paid by the investor, but 50% of this amount ($325)
is deducted as a sales charge, leaving the contractual plan purchaser
with an investment of $325, *before* deduction of the 2% ($13)
custodial fee.

Although the sales charge in the first year of the contractual plan is
extraordinarily high, the Special Study reported that "40 percent of
contractual plan purchasers could make no estimate of the first year's
sales charge. . . ."

Also, the Special Study said that more than 75% "of investors
in contractual plans were unaware that fund shares could be purchased with sales charges different from those of the plans they
bought or that no-load funds [entailing no sales charge] were
available."

These quotations support the belief that the average contractual
plan purchaser has no greater pressure to save than purchasers of
fund shares under voluntary accumulation plans, where the sales
charge, if any, is paid on a "level-load" basis—the same percentage
on each purchase.

The major disadvantage of the contractual plan is that if an investor terminates his purchasing program when no more than the
first thirteen monthly payments or their equivalent have been made,
he will receive cash amounting to about 48% of his payments to date
(assuming no change in value of the underlying mutual fund shares).

On the other hand, if he had followed a voluntary accumulation plan, about 92% of his total payment would be returned.

For each of the first thirteen installments of $50 paid under the contractual plan, the investor receives an investment valued at $24. The sales charge (including the 2% custodial fee) amounts to about 108% of the amount actually invested. Thereafter, the *effective* sales charge steadily decreases until, at the end of the ten years, it equals about 10.8% of the money actually invested (including the 2% custodial fee).

A voluntary plan is a more reasonable way to purchase mutual fund shares, as termination at any time during its indefinite duration entails no forfeiture by the investor. The effective sales charge for purchases will at all times be equivalent to the nominal sales charge of, say, 8%, amounting to 8.8% of the amount actually invested.

Small investors frequently invest some of their emergency funds in mutual funds and, as a result, may need to redeem their mutual fund investments, to raise cash to meet an emergency. Voluntary plans, the availability of which is unknown by many contractual plan purchasers, afford small investors a way to avoid the loss of more than one half of their first year savings.

Salesmen may argue that an investor completing a contractual plan will reduce his cost to the nominal rate, say 8%. This is not true for two reasons: (1) There is the additional 2% charge by the custodian of the investor's shares; and (2) the investor has lost the return on his capital during the period of prepayment of sales charges. The difference in final values between accumulation under a voluntary plan as compared with an accumulation under a contractual plan, *assuming completion of the plans,* approximates 5% of the value of the voluntary plan accumulation (for a plan covering shares of a balanced mutual fund during a rising market). This is a loss which can never be recovered by the contractual plan purchaser.

Recognition of the unfairness of the contractual plan has occurred in about ten states, which have either prohibited or curtailed the practice. Self-regulation by the investor is much more effective, however. He need do no more than refuse to buy mutual fund shares under a contractual plan.

By now you should know "what to tell a mutual fund salesman" who tries to sell you a contractual plan.

BE YOUR OWN SALESMAN AND SAVE $23,000

The customary sales charge (commonly called a sales "load") of $8\frac{1}{2}\%$ of the offering price (9.3% of the money actually invested) is justified by some industry spokesmen as an expense properly borne by the investor to compensate persons selling mutual funds for their time spent in bringing investor and mutual fund together. No doubt can exist about the over-all effectiveness of the industry-wide sales force. Mutual funds sold with a sales charge experience a substantially higher rate of share sales than funds not charging any sales load (commonly called "no-load" mutual funds).

No-load mutual funds can result from a change of mind, where a load fund eliminates its sales charge. In 1964, the One William Street Fund, previously selling its shares at a maximum sales charge of $8\frac{1}{2}\%$, turned into a no-load fund. Ordinarily, however, no-load mutual funds are established by investment counselors, to pool investment accounts too small to be handled economically by the counselor on an individual basis; or, a no-load fund may be established by a broker-dealer organization, to benefit from the brokerage commissions to be paid by the mutual fund. These commissions can amount to a sum far in excess of the customary $\frac{1}{2}\%$ annual management fee.

In 1962, no-load mutual funds owned little more than 3% of the total assets held by the mutual fund industry, indicating how little known they are among the investing public and how ineffective they have been in selling their shares to the public. Even a one-third increase in size, resulting from the quarter-billion-dollar One William Street's switch to a no-load status, does very little to increase the relative importance of no-load funds.

Could it be that no-load mutual funds have not performed as well as load funds? In other words, can an investor expect better performance on the average from a mutual fund investment for which he has paid a sales charge, in comparison to the average no-load fund? The answer is found in the Wharton School study, prepared in 1962 for the Securities and Exchange Commission, which concluded: "no relation was observed during the period of study between the investment funds' sales charges and their cumulative performance results. This finding indicates that a higher sales charge is not indicative of superior performance."

"Cumulative performance," as used in this quotation, does not take sales charges into account. Therefore, everything else being equal, an investor will experience better over-all investment results if he purchases shares of a no-load mutual fund. And the Wharton School study informs us that some no-loads have a cumulative performance record comparable to the best of the load funds.

Fred, upon learning that there are some excellent no-load funds as well as some excellent funds charging a sales load, sat down with pencil and paper to make certain computations. He assumed that someone invested $1,000 per year in a no-load fund over a 35-year period, and Fred compared this with the situation where one purchased shares of a load mutual fund with an $8\frac{1}{2}\%$ sales charge. Each year, the no-load investor received mutual fund shares having a value $85 in excess of the share value received by the load-fund investor.

Quickly, Fred computed that if this $85 were set aside and invested each year in mutual funds to produce an average compound return of 10% per year, after taxes, the accumulation would amount to $23,000 at the end of 35 years. This is the high cost of purchasing mutual fund shares from a salesman, broker-dealer, or registered representative. By making your own careful selection of good no-load funds, and purchasing the shares directly from the fund, you can be your own mutual fund salesman and save $23,000.

Avoidance of unnecessary expenses is not the only reason for buying shares of a no-load mutual fund. Another reason is to prevent the investor from being locked into his investment, feeling unable to redeem his shares once he has paid a substantial sales commission, even though he may have changed his investment objectives. Or, he may have lost faith in management of the fund or may need money to meet an emergency.

Most no-loads permit an investor to purchase and redeem shares almost as if the investor were depositing and withdrawing money from a bank—without deduction of any fees. Of course, mutual fund investors cannot be guaranteed that the value of their investment will be at least equal to the amount originally invested.

"If no-load funds are so good," asks Fred, "why is it that only a wee percentage of mutual fund shares have been sold pursuant to a no-load arrangement?" Of course Fred was only kidding. He was well aware that no-loads, the shares of which are sold without a sales charge, do not employ salesmen to push sales. About the only way for no-loads to attract investors is to advertise in newspapers and magazines, but they are unable to say little more than: "We have no salesmen. You pay no loading charge or commission. 100% of your money is invested—none goes to pay salesmen." The extent to which mutual funds can sell their shares through advertising of this nature is limited. This is so particularly where a fund has no salesmen to follow up leads resulting from responses to an advertisement. Unless an investor desiring to purchase no-load shares initiates the communication with no-load funds, they will never learn of his interest. Initiation is not enough, however; he must follow through until he has made his investment.

At this point, Fred breaks in to ask: "How can I identify a no-load mutual fund?" Turn to the financial pages of your daily newspaper and find the price quotations for mutual funds. You will see *"bid"* and *"asked"* prices. A bid is the amount offered by a mutual fund in redemption of one of its shares, whereas an asked price is the amount an investor must pay to purchase one share. The difference between the two prices (the *"spread"*), expressed as a percentage, represents the sales charge.

Assume XYZ Mutual Fund is quoted at 19 bid, 20 asked. The difference of one, when divided by 20, represents a sales charge (or "load") of 5% of the offering price for the mutual fund shares, or about $5\frac{1}{4}\%$ of the bid price, the amount actually invested.

When the bid and asked quotations are equal, there is no sales charge; hence, the quoted fund is a no-load, and an investor can redeem his shares for the same amount he would be required to pay if he purchased additional shares. The advantage, of course, is the "friction-free" nature of the transaction, by which the investor is able to invest 100% of his money. And, assuming no change in values, he can liquidate his investment for cash in the same amount. No money will be deducted either at issuance or redemption to pay sales commissions.

Several no-loads, however, charge or reserve the right to charge an issuance or redemption fee of 1%. This fee, when charged, is retained by the no-load fund, for the benefit of all mutual fund shareholders, to defray expenses incurred by the fund upon the issuance or redemption of mutual fund shares. Even though the investor's transaction in such a case is not friction-free, the charge may be fair and reasonable. When a mutual fund has a current excess of sales over redemptions of mutual fund shares, resulting in an increase in uninvested assets beyond the desired level, additional investment securities will have to be purchased by the fund, entailing brokerage costs averaging about 1%. Or, when redemptions exceed purchases of mutual fund shares, investment securities held by the mutual fund will have to be sold at a brokerage expense of about 1%.

When a fund does purchase or sell investments because of a redemption or issuance of fund shares, it seems equitable to charge this expense to the particular mutual fund shareholder. It is less equitable to charge the issuance or redemption fee when no additional brokerage costs are incurred by the fund. Yet, as long as the overcharge is retained by the fund to increase ever so slightly the value of each mutual fund share, I believe it is justified to include these funds in my list of no-load funds, set forth in Appendix A. Although I believe the list is complete, as of this writing, including all no-load funds (funds investing in foreign securities excepted) currently offering their shares to the general public, it is possible that other no-load mutual funds meeting the foregoing qualifications were inadvertently excluded from the list. Undoubtedly, some of the listed funds make highly desirable investments, while others afford little reason for an investor to part with his money. This is true as well for a complete list of mutual funds with a sales charge. Also, a fund may be quite suitable for one investor but totally unsuitable to an individual having different investment objectives.

Selection of a suitable fund requires a great deal of time and study. Most if not all of the information needed is set forth in the prospectus for each fund, which will be sent to a person upon his request. A postcard to each fund will do. Response by all but a few of the funds will be surprisingly prompt—within a week, most likely. After receiving the prospectuses you can study them to make your own comparisons and investment analyses, in the privacy of your home and away from the potentially destructive pressure of a mutual fund salesman. If possible, discuss your selections with a friend or relative competent in the field of mutual fund investment.

SAVE-BY-BORROWING AND MUTUAL FUNDS

After consultations with a knowledgeable friend, Fred decides to purchase shares of three particular no-load funds.

On the average, the shares are selling for about $12 each. This does not mean, however, that Fred will be allowed to purchase as little as one share from each fund. Minimum requirements for initial and subsequent purchases of shares vary from fund to fund. More than three fourths of all mutual funds offering a voluntary plan for purchase of fund shares require an initial subscription ranging from $100 to $500; frequently, subsequent purchases are required to be $50 or higher.

These minimum requirements pose some problems for the periodic investor. If he accumulates, say, $20 per week until he saves enough money to meet an initial subscription requirement, he may never start his mutual fund investment program, or he may begin belatedly. After all, how does he know what his feelings toward savings and investment will be three or four months from now? By that time he may have his heart set on a second car or some other luxury.

By adoption of the Save-by-Borrowing technique, the investor could virtually ensure that his savings goal will be realized. Once the money has been borrowed, then tucked away in mutual fund shares, the saving process is well underway toward completion. All the saver need do is continue making his monthly installments to the lending institution. In making these payments, he can exercise no discretion. He is obligated to repay the loan, to fulfill his savings aspirations.

Borrowing has the added advantage of immediacy. Instead of waiting for several months or longer, the investor can purchase the mutual fund shares right away and see the results of his savings effort for the next year. Psychologically, the Save-by-Borrowing procedure is of great value.

After Fred has made his initial purchases of shares in the three funds and has paid off his initial loan, he will be faced with another decision: Should he continue with his Save-by-Borrowing program or, because of the substantial decrease in subsequent purchase requirements of the fund, switch to a voluntary accumulation program in which he borrows no money, but purchases the shares each month out of current income?

With outright purchases of stock (such as General Motors or AT&T) the percentage cost of commissions depends upon the amount involved. Therefore, it is less expensive to make one annual purchase instead of twelve monthly purchases. Shares of load mutual funds, however, can be bought in equal dollar amounts each month for twelve months without the investor incurring any increased sales charges. A single lump-sum purchase each year would produce no savings. The "breakpoint" at which sales charges are reduced averages about $25,000, far in excess of the means of a small investor; however, by use of a "letter of intention," the monthly investor would be allowed to treat his purchases over a thirteen-month period as if they had been made at one time, to take advantage of a lower sales charge applicable to the $25,000 lump-sum purchase. For Fred, the problem of reducing sales charges does not exist. He has decided to purchase shares of no-load funds.

Borrowing to make subsequent mutual fund purchases does afford a saving for small investors. When purchases of shares are made in a dollar amount less than $100, some funds charge a service fee of, say, 60 cents. On a $30 monthly investment, this amounts to a charge slightly above 2% on the $29.40 actually invested. By borrowing, the small investor avoids this service fee.

Borrowing to make subsequent mutual-fund purchases may eliminate investment delays, thereby producing a higher rate of return for the investor. Inefficiencies cannot be tolerated by one seriously working to reach the 10th Multiple. Also, the Save-by-Borrower avoids the annoyance of allocating his savings among funds having different purchase requirements. He avoids the inconvenience of making frequent payments to the several mutual funds, each time the necessary purchase price has been accumulated. A sound program for saving and investment requires constancy. This is afforded by the Save-by-Borrowing process.

The main advantage of using the Save-by-Borrowing technique to make subsequent purchases is compulsion, to eliminate the risk of savings loss caused by diversion to consumer purchases. Borrowing enforces an investor's promise to save regularly, unlike other plans for purchase of mutual fund shares. Even the "contractual" plan is ineffectual, the investor being under no contract or obligation to continue making his monthly purchases.

More than 1,123,000 mutual fund investors buy shares under a contractual plan, according to statistics recently published by the industry. Most popular of the plans is the one calling for monthly payments of $25. The average plan, however, involves a higher amount. Contractual-plan investors reading this book may be investing, on the average, $50 or more per month. Over a ten-year period, payments under a $50-per-month plan would total $6,000, but $614 would be deducted to pay an assumed 8% sales charge, 2% custodial fee and $1.50 annual service charge. In contrast, after ten years, a voluntary plan follower, paying the 8% sales charge (but no custodial or service fee), would have an investment more than 5% greater in value than the contractual-plan investor.

Save-by-Borrowers purchasing shares of load mutual funds other than by a contractual plan would derive two additional benefits: greater compulsion and the elimination of overhanging penalties.

Assume a purchaser of shares in a common stock fund may realize an average return (including capital appreciation) of about 9% per year, after taxes. On the basis of a $600 borrowing and investment, there would be a gross return of $54, out of which must be paid the $23 after-tax cost of borrowing (a nominal pre-tax rate of $4\frac{3}{4}$%, but a true annual rate of 9.2%). The $31 remaining return for the Save-by-Borrower slightly exceeds the 9% ($27) return the monthly investor would receive (since his investment averages about $300 during the year). Thus, the Save-by-Borrower can obtain his forced savings program with a slight profit. This assumes, of course, maintenance of the 9% return.

If, however, the Save-by-Borrower cannot utilize the interest payment as a tax deduction, he will show a $2 loss in comparison to the monthly investor, also assuming the 9% return.

Clearly, therefore, there are savings *and* profits to be made, on the average, by adoption of a Save-by-Borrowing program. What is most important, however, is the avoidance of the infamous contractual plan and the losses and penalties which inevitably accompany it.

Contractual plans purport to have an element of force, quite a lure to unsophisticated investors; however, this forced-savings feature, if any exists, is still not as helpful as the mandatory savings feature of the Save-by-Borrowing technique, a profitable, non-penalty method.

We have discussed load and no-load funds. What about the third type of fund—the Reform Fund, which, although not now in existence, should be, for excellent reasons. At this point we shall look at its benefits, most of which are designed for the small investor who wants nothing more than a fair share of the economic pie.

Chapter Ten

A LOOK AT THE FUTURE—
THE REFORM MUTUAL FUND

ELIMINATION OF RISK OF POOR PERFORMANCE

The impressive growth record of the mutual fund industry is not difficult to explain, realizing that almost all mutual fund shares have been sold with a sales charge added to the price. With the incentive of a high sales commission, the "hard sell" is bound to be employed, to add to the earnings of mutual fund salesmen. Little investigation into the quality of a fund is made by a prospective mutual fund purchaser, who probably is more influenced by the smoothness of the salesman than the logic behind investing in the offered fund.

A comparatively unsophisticated investor may be easily convinced that a particular mutual fund investment would be the best bargain of his life. A sales load of 8.5% of the total payments (a markup of 9.3%) sounds surprisingly minimal to a person who thinks in terms of the markup on vegetables or soft goods. But has he compared the cost of a no-load mutual fund?

The annual operating cost of about 1% of the value of his investment seems well-spent. It pays for the convenience, professional management, and diversification available to him, a small investor, through purchase of mutual fund shares. Whatever the cost of mutual fund investment (which cost is reasonable, the average investor believes, because everybody seems to be paying it) he will be able to derive benefit from the superior knowledge and full-time attention of the professional investor entrusted with management of the investment fund.

Before passing judgment upon mutual funds, the reader must give recognition to the fulfillment of dreams of many mutual fund shareholders who have experienced a doubling, then another doubling of the market value of their holdings. Professional management can produce excellent results, according to these shareholders. Acquisition and management costs may be high, but investment results should more than offset such costs, leaving the investor with profits greatly in excess of what he could have obtained by himself—or so the rationale goes.

With small investors so fully convinced of the benefits of professional management, would anyone be taken seriously if he suggested that the average professional investor choosing investments for a mutual fund can achieve investment results no better than a non-professional *who selected at random* a portfolio of securities having the same ratio of common stocks, preferred stocks, bonds, etc.? Yet the suggestion has been made by the "Study of Mutual Funds," prepared in 1962 for the Securities and Exchange Commission by the Wharton School of Finance and Commerce of the University of Pennsylvania. In what appears to be implicit condemnation of the value of professional management, the study reported:

> The more appropriate comparison of the common stock funds with the Standard & Poor's Index reveals that these funds had an average cumulative increase of 123.6 percent, higher than that of any other fund, but still lower than the increase achieved by the market index [139.53 percent].

The Wharton Study went on to note that *only 25%* of the common stock funds (made up of growth, income, and mixed common stock funds) had been able to achieve investment results superior to that of an unmanaged portfolio of securities consisting of appropriately weighted investments in the 425 industrial common stocks constituting the Standard & Poor's industrial index. (The S&P 425 stocks are used in an index instead of an average; thus each stock is assigned a percentage of importance—that is, it is *weighted*—to reflect the total market value of all its outstanding shares as compared with the value of all outstanding shares for the 425 stocks.) Such an investment would be "unmanaged" because the funds could remain in such investments indefinitely.

Always on the lookout to make fair comparisons, we must take into account certain mitigating factors. The S&P fund (the "unmanaged fund") referred to by the Wharton Study was 100% invested at all times, whereas in actual practice mutual funds (that is, "managed funds") ordinarily will maintain a certain percentage of cash or near-cash items in their portfolios. The study did not charge the unmanaged S&P fund with brokerage commissions that would have been necessary to make the original investment purchases of the S&P stock. This criticism is equally applicable, however, to the managed funds. However, managed funds *were* charged with brokerage commissions arising subsequent to the beginning of the study period, but the unmanaged fund probably would not have incurred any such expense.

Operating costs (including the management fee) amounting to about 1% of net asset value were deducted annually from the performance of the managed funds; however, no such charge was deducted from the performance of the hypothetical S&P fund, a factor which operates in favor of the mutual funds.

In the Wharton Study, capital-gains distributions by the managed funds were assumedly reinvested not at the date of distribution but at the end of each year, such time lag putting mutual funds at a disadvantage in comparison to the hypothetical S&P fund, in a rising market.

Based on these factors alone, it is not completely fair to mutual funds to state that 75% of the common stock funds were not able to equal the performance of Standard & Poor's 425 industrial common stock index. It may be more appropriate to make no more than the following, conservative assumption: more than 50% of the managed common stock funds did not exceed the S&P Index.

Mutual fund shareholders pay each year many millions of dollars in management fees to the professional investors in charge of the funds. But, if our assumption is reasonably accurate (and it appears to be), investors in an average mutual fund may not have received what they expected.

Critics of the Wharton Study argue that a mutual fund performs well if it can merely equal the averages. Others do not find this argument convincing. They expect common stock mutual funds to perform better than the market average, considering the expensive expertise employed by the mutual fund shareholders to purchase the good investments and weed out the bad. As we have seen, the Wharton Study seemed to be critical of the performance record of the average common stock mutual fund. And maybe such a position would be justified. Based on our conservative assumption, it would have been better, on the average, if one had invested in Standard & Poor's 425 industrial common stock index, instead of the average common stock mutual fund.

Millions of investors, large and small, naturally would be delighted to be able to invest in a market average or index, knowing that they could not be hurt by poor management. They then could expect a return almost equivalent to the return of the average or index (any deviation being attributable to mechanical imperfections regarding precise apportionment and investment timing), minus operating expenses of about 1%. Professional management, hence possible mismanagement, would be eliminated.

If an investor has faith that the stock market averages and indices will always go up, in the long run—and they have so far—he would do well to invest in them. Although his investment would not be able to outperform the market, he would be able to eliminate the substantial risk and constant fear that his investments were being handled by poor professional management. (Actually, dollar-cost averaging benefits would boost the unmanaged fund return, perhaps to a point equal to the "return" of the market average or index. These benefits also apply to systematic investment in a managed mutual fund.)

No longer would an investor have to worry about the quality of performance of his professional manager. No longer would he need to undergo the expense or inconvenience of shifting his investments from one mutual fund to another. Instead of devoting innumerable and irreplaceable hours of his lifetime to obtain his financial objective, he could spend these hours in more pleasurable activities—far removed from what may be to him the tedious field of finance. No longer would he need to follow the market to maximize his investment success. If he could invest in the market average he would be able to assure his participation in what he must believe to be an ever increasing growth of the economy, eliminating all risks that poor management may rob him of his legitimate share. Of course, if the market average should fall in the long run, he would suffer a corresponding loss.

As a practical matter, it is quite cumbersome to invest in all 1200 to 1300 common stocks listed on the New York Stock Exchange; therefore, an investor must think in terms of investing in a group of stocks which are representative of all the NYSE-listed stocks.

It is true that an individual with only limited funds cannot invest in the averages. To invest in a 100-stock average, for example, would be to buy an equal number of shares of each stock. Brokerage costs (including odd-lot differential) probably would exceed 6%. Even then, the investor would find it next to impossible to apportion his investment fund so as to obtain substantial compliance with his objective. A mutual fund, on the other hand, would experience little difficulty investing in an average, if it chose an investment policy of this type. Consideration would be given immediately to investing in the 30 Dow Jones industrial stocks, constituting the most popular market average.

Several problems would arise, however, for investors in the Dow Jones (DJ) Market Average. These 30 stocks are "blue chips," generally high-priced, non-speculative stocks of large, leading corporations such as General Motors and AT&T, and hardly representative of all stocks listed on the New York Stock Exchange (even though they represent about 37% of total stock values). If an investor purchases the Dow Jones stocks, he may be purchasing a class of stock with less growth potential than average, especially when blue-chip prices have reached new highs, as a result of institutional and pension-fund demand for these stocks. Yet, who is to say that the demand will soon cease?

Perhaps a greater risk is in the fact that these 30 stocks do not afford the degree of numerical diversity sought by many mutual fund investors. All too often a significant change in the DJ industrial average is directly traceable to the price movement of a single stock. This indicates that 30-stock diversity may be insufficient to protect the DJ investor from the effects of a radical price decrease in two or three of his stocks.

There could be a bonus, however, to an investor in the DJ Average. His own DJ investments could outperform the published average.[1] Stock splits (usually occurring with the stocks of the more prosper-

[1] On the other hand, they may not do as well. Thus, we will assume no variation between performance of the DJ Average and the actual investment results which would have been achieved by an investor.

ous companies) tend to reduce the influence of these companies upon the DJ Average, which tends to make the DJ Average trail behind the actual investment results of an investor in the average. Thus, a stock included in the DJ Average at $100, after undergoing a 2-for-1 split, would be included in the average at its new price of $50. Continuity of the DJ Average immediately following a split is maintained by adjustment of the divisor which produces the average, to eliminate the immediate effect of the split upon the average price of all stocks included in the average.

Consider the $100 average value of three stocks, each valued at $100. When one of these stocks splits 2-for-1, each of the two resulting stocks has a $50 value; therefore, the total value of the three stocks constituting the average is reduced to $250, for a new average of $83.33, unless something is done. In order to prevent this decline from the $100 average, the divisor of 3 is reduced to 2.5. Thus, the average price of $100 for the three stocks is continued.

By reason of this adjustment, however, the stock of the successful company has been reduced in influence from $33\frac{1}{3}$% to only 20%. Henceforth, increases in value of the $100 worth of stock (two shares now) will be counted in the total market value of the three stocks to the extent of only 50%.

After weighing the pros and cons, some persons undoubtedly do invest in the Dow Jones 30 industrial stocks. Admittedly, it is more convenient and less costly than investing in 425 stocks. They may wonder, however, how the Dow Jones Average has performed in comparison to Standard & Poor's 425 industrial common stock index (which is weighted to reflect total market values of all outstanding stocks).

For the 15-year period starting in June 1949 (the beginning of an extended bull market), Standard & Poor's Index increased at the annual compound rate (exclusive of dividends) of almost $12\frac{1}{2}$% before taxes, whereas the Dow Jones 30 industrial common stocks experienced an annual compound increase (also exclusive of dividends) of almost 12% (before taxes) during the same period.

In spite of this surface equality, the DJ 30 stocks cannot be relied upon, it seems, to continue to reflect the performance of all NYSE-listed common stocks. Instead, it would appear advisable to purchase Standard & Poor's Index of 425 industrial common stocks to obtain a return representative of all the listed common stocks.

From year-end 1954 to year-end 1964, a total of ten years, Standard & Poor's Index (using 10 as a base, for the years 1941–43) moved from 36 to 89.6, a gain of about 150%. Although this is a 15% gain per year, the annual compound rate of capital appreciation (before taxes) is only 10%, approximately. During this period dividends averaged about 4.26%, making the over-all annual compound rate of return (before taxes) about 14.26%.

If the Wharton findings have relevance beyond the 5¾-year period of coverage, only 20% or so of all mutual funds (after adding 7% to adjust, roughly, for the unequal comparison) exceeded this rate of return. The full membership of the 20%, we can surmise, consisted of fewer than one half of the common stock funds and several specialty funds.

Based upon the limited success of mutual funds over Standard & Poor's 425 Index, investors may wonder whether it is possible for them to buy shares in a managed mutual fund which is guaranteed to do merely as well as the average. Unfortunately, there is now no such guarantee. There will always be a risk of sub-standard selection when quality of management is a determinant in investment results.

Ideals are seldom attainable, but in the mutual fund business the adage "you cannot invest in an average" should no longer be applicable. From a practical standpoint, it should be possible for an investor to prevent error in investment selection and be guaranteed a close approximation of the average rate of return (before taxes), less annual operating expenses of 1% of investment value. This estimated return on S&P's Index has been surprisingly high—13.26% per year, before taxes, compounded annually for the ten-year period beginning January 1, 1955. All the investor need do is purchase shares of a mutual fund which invests in Standard & Poor's 425 industrial common stocks, the investments being appropriately weighted to reflect total market value of each of the stocks. Let's call this fund the Reform Fund, for reasons that will soon become apparent.

An advantage of investing in the S&P Index is that management discretion is minimal: The "managers" of the Reform Fund would invest in the index and hold onto the stocks indefinitely. Stocks would be sold only if S&P removed a stock from the index, or in certain circumstances such as a company's becoming bankrupt. Seldom, however, should the manager's power of sale be exercised. Management should avoid straying away from the investment objective of investing in Standard & Poor's 425 industrial common stock index.

The fund necessarily would sell some of the S&P stocks when current redemptions by fund shareholders exceeded sales of new mutual fund shares. Even then the fund manager could liquidate fund investments on a random (unmanaged) basis (even when balancing capital gains and losses, the importance of which will become apparent later), to avoid the risk of poor judgment. Later, when sales of mutual fund shares exceeded redemptions, the fund manager would reinvest in the stocks previously sold, then continue investing in accordance with the normal policy of the fund, to purchase a close approximation of S&P's Index.

WHAT'S THE CATCH?

The catch to the practicability of investing in Standard & Poor's 425 stocks involves the cost of brokerage commissions (including odd-lot differential) and the weighting of stock purchases.

A mutual fund having many millions of dollars available could restrict all of its purchases to 100-share lots, thereby reducing the cost of commissions to about 1% (assuming purchases were made on the New York Stock Exchange, and not on a regional exchange or in the Third Market). One hundred shares of each of 425 stocks would cost more than $2,000,000. The necessity of weighting purchases, however, would require many more millions of dollars, in order that the least-weighted purchase be made in round lots.

Realistically, a new mutual fund could have as little as $100,000 to invest, so 425 odd-lot purchases in small dollar amounts would necessarily result in higher initial brokerage costs than experienced by the managed common stock mutual funds.

Before estimating the percentage cost of commissions, we must examine a related problem: allocation of the available assets among the 425 stocks.

To obtain a performance substantially identical to Standard & Poor's Index, it would be necessary to purchase each of the 425 stocks with a percentage of the available assets equivalent to the total market value of all outstanding shares of such stock, divided by the total market value of all outstanding shares of all 425 stocks. Four elements are found in the allocation formula, as follows:

I = Investment in stock #1
V = Value of all outstanding shares of stock #1
T = Total value of all outstanding shares of stocks ##1-425
A = Assets to be allocated among the 425 stocks

The formula, accordingly, looks like this:

$$I = \frac{V}{T} \text{ (times) A.}$$

Theoretically, the formula works. In actual practice, precision would be impossible to obtain. Unless the Reform Fund were able to establish 425 Monthly Investment Plans (maintenance of which probably could not be guaranteed), fractional shares of stock (as a means of achieving almost perfect allocation) could not be purchased. Therefore, apportionment would have to take place on a rough but workable basis. The fund manager would have to establish guidelines—for example, purchases of no less than $100 worth of stock. To equalize the situation where apportionment required an investment of only $50, let us say, the manager would make a $100 purchase every other time this particular stock would otherwise be scheduled for purchase. Diversity is not disrupted by this random approach toward purchase.

The average market value of the 425 stock purchases would equal about $250 (for an average of a little more than 5 shares per purchase). Total market value of the 425 purchases would be $106,250, a little bit more than the $100,000 minimum requirement for the establishment of a mutual fund registered with the Securities and Exchange Commission.

A purchase involving a $251 odd-lot price would entail costs of about $7, as follows:

Fixed fee	$1
Odd-lot differential for 5 shares	1
2% of $251	5
	$7

It was assumed, in the above computation, that the average odd-lot charge would be 20 cents per share. The 12½-cent charge for stocks selling at less than $55, and the 25-cent charge for stocks selling at $55 and above, could well average out to about 20 cents per share for the 425 different stocks, the average market value of which exceeds $50 per share. This amounts to an odd-lot cost of about $\frac{2}{5}$ of 1% of the market value of the fund's investments as they are acquired.

A cost of $7 to make a $250 stock purchase equals a percentage cost of 2.8%. Actually, as a result of the weighting requirement, few purchases would be made at $250. Although purchases exceeding $250 would decrease the 2.8% cost, they would not offset entirely the higher costs resulting from purchases involving less than $250. Therefore, the fund could expect to pay initial brokerage commissions running as high as an estimated 4%.

Critics of the proposed Reform Fund could argue that mutual funds of the ordinary type, not diversifying to the extent of 425 stocks, are able to purchase stocks in 100-share lots, at a cost of about 1%. This is about 3% less than the estimated average cost of investing in 425 stocks. The critics would be technically correct, but they would be shortsighted, overlooking certain compensating factors, which we will explore.

Having the Reform Fund invest in Standard & Poor's 425 industrial common stock index certainly constitutes a change from present practices of mutual fund investment. But does it constitute a reform? What advantage is there in paying the 4% cost when an ordinary common stock mutual fund pays only 1%?

The announced purpose of the Reform Fund is to purchase S&P's Index, then hold onto the stock purchases for the long run. No investments would be sold by the fund, except under highly unusual circumstances. Thus, the Reform Fund would be able to eliminate in one fell swoop the practice of turning over the fund assets every so many years (in some cases amounting to the abuse known as "churning").

In terms of cost analysis, turning over of the investments can be much more costly than the initial 4% cost of acquisition for the Reform Fund. In the Wharton Study it was reported that the average common stock fund (including growth, income, and mixed common stock funds, thus comparable in composition to the Reform Fund) had an investment turnover of approximately 18.6% per year from 1953 to 1958. Moreover, the current turnover rate is about 25%.

Thus, the average comparable mutual fund sells all of its stock and repurchases other stock every 4 years, necessitating payment of an additional (round-trip) commission of 2%, bringing the total cost of brokerage commissions for the first 4 years to 3%. In another 2 years, the total cost would amount to 4%, the rate paid by the Reform Fund. Furthermore, an additional 2% would be incurred every additional 4 years. But these supplemental expenses are not chargeable to the Reform Fund.

It is true that managed funds would not have to pay the full 4% at the outset, and, therefore, assets representing the delayed payment of commissions would be earning a return before the commissions were actually paid. However, when the managed funds finally pay the aggregate commission of 4%, the commission is applied to funds having an *increased dollar value*. We assume this increase in dollar cost of commissions equals the return lost by the Reform Fund by its prepayment of commissions. We can reasonably conclude, therefore, that brokerage costs are about the same by the end of the six-year period for the Reform Fund and the average managed common stock fund.

In comparison to the Reform Fund, therefore, the cost of commissions for managed common stock mutual funds is higher in the long run. We can conclude, accordingly, that the cost to the Reform Fund of acquiring 425 stocks becomes comparable to the average of all managed common stock funds after passage of about six years. After that, the Reform Fund takes an ever increasing lead. The Reform Fund's 4% cost of brokerage commissions is a one-shot cost, but managed common stock funds, on the average, incur round-trip commissions on the entire investment fund, as increased in value, every 4 years.

Once the Reform Fund has been established, new money would be coming in, to be added to the original $106,250. This new money would not be sufficient to permit purchase of 425 stocks at one time (even in purchases averaging only 5 shares or so). Investment of the new money would have to be on a progressive basis, starting with stock number 1 and ending with stock number 425. For each $106,-250 coming into the fund, a new cycle of purchases would be made.

Brokerage commissions for the Reform Fund could be reduced substantially if the 425-stock investment cycle were spread over a larger amount of money, such as $425,000, so the average stock purchase would involve $1,000. (The odd-lot differential would still be a cost, however.) A successful Reform Fund would probably attract enough investors to base its cycle on this larger amount. Nevertheless, we will assume that the 4% cost would still apply.

Although the first few cycles of new money would, when used to make progressive purchases, cause an imbalance of diversification, the extent of the imbalance would be temporary only, and would lessen with each succeeding cycle. Only a minimal deviation from the investment objective would be experienced as a result of the practice of progressive diversification. This would be so especially where the purchases were made on a random, unmanaged basis. In other words, to rephrase a certain political theory, "he who manages least manages best."

Do not be fooled by anyone who says it is not practical to invest in market indices or averages (insofar as a mutual fund is concerned, at least). It would be of high demonstrable advantage for a person to purchase shares of the hypothetical Reform Fund, which invests in Standard & Poor's industrial common stock index.

The cost of acquisition would be an assumed 4%, but this cost would be paid only once, unlike managed funds, which start off at 1% and incur additional 2% charges (on increasing net asset values, it should be remembered) every 4 years. Also, there is the possibility that even the initial 4% cost of the Reform Fund would be reduced, either by odd-lot differential reforms or by the use of an over-the-counter dealer who would be willing to undercut members of the New York Stock Exchange in order to acquire the heavy volume of business expected from the Reform Fund.

We have discussed costs and allocation only to show that the problems are of minimal importance. In fact, we have turned a 4% liability into an asset, after 6 years, resulting thereafter in the 2% saving every 4 years.

There is a much greater saving, however, for the investor in the Reform Fund, a saving which no managed common stock fund offers. This special feature is reason in itself for a person to invest in an acceptable market average or index.

ELIMINATION OF THE CAPITAL-GAINS TAX

When first glancing at the promise above, the reader may be suspicious. Yet, it's true. According to present federal tax law it appears that the Reform Fund would enable its shareholders to postpone in-definitely, perhaps even eliminate, the long-term capital-gains tax.

Elimination of the capital-gains tax has an obvious value to the investor. The value of tax postponement has been mentioned earlier in this book, but is worthy of repetition. The long-term capital-gains tax is paid on any profit made upon the sale of most capital assets held for longer than six months. If an investor buys 100 shares of ABC stock at $10 per share, he has spent $1,000 for his stock (we'll disregard commissions and transfer taxes). If he sells these shares several years later for $3,000, he would have to pay a long-term capital-gains tax (up to 25%) on the $2,000 profit, leaving him with a minimum profit of only $1,500.

Although he had 100 shares of stock (valued at $30 per share) immediately before his sale, he wound up with only $2,500 in cash after the sale and payment of the capital-gains tax at the maximum rate of 25%. Later, if he decided to reinvest in the same stock, he could purchase only $83\frac{1}{3}$ shares. As a result of the sale, therefore, he suffered a $16\frac{2}{3}\%$ loss of his capital, a loss which could never be re-stored.

True, if he sold the 100 shares 35 years from now, he would have to pay the same tax on the $2,000 (and more) of capital apprecia-tion; in the meantime, though, he would have had the $500 working for him to produce additional profits.

An investor in the Reform Fund would have to pay a capital-gains tax if he redeemed some or all of his shares. Minimization of the tax could be achieved, however, by redemption of the shares which cost the most (hence have the highest tax basis).

The investor who purchased outright shares of ABC and XYZ stock could minimize the capital-gains tax impact by selling the shares (ABC or XYZ) having the lesser capital-gains potential. The only difference between the outright purchase of stock and the Reform Fund investor is that as to the latter all of his investments are identi-cal. It makes no difference from an investment standpoint which of his mutual fund shares he redeems. But, the owner of ABC and XYZ shares of stock might have to sell the comparatively better investment in order to minimize his capital-gains tax liability.

When a managed mutual fund sells an appreciated stock and dis-tributes a capital-gains dividend, the investor must pay a capital-gains tax. Even when the distribution is not made, the fund must pay a 25% capital-gains tax in behalf of its shareholders. A portion of the tax paid by the fund will be credited or refunded by the government to investors having an applicable ordinary income tax bracket of less than 50%.

Managed mutual funds, turning over their assets every 4 years, necessarily realize capital gains, assuming successful management of the fund. After offsetting capital losses, the mutual fund shareholder must pay the capital-gains tax. Managed mutual funds cannot shelter their shareholders from payment of the tax.

In the Reform Fund, however, there is no reason to sell the underlying investments. The fund would have as its objective the long-range investment in the 425 Standard & Poor industrial common stock index, except in the rare instance when one or more stocks would have to be sold. Even if the Reform Fund were forced to sell some of its assets, the manager of the fund could prevent payment of capital-gains taxes, under other than extraordinary circumstances, by random (or, perhaps, managed) sale of stocks to balance capital gains with capital losses.

As soon as new stock purchases could be made, the fund manager would repurchase these stocks, bringing the investment portfolio back into Standard & Poor's balance. Thus, payment of the capital-gains tax could be avoided easily—and this is how it should be. In all other mutual funds, when the investment objective of a particular stock has been reached or, perhaps, when the managers feel it would be good public relations to distribute some capital gains, shareholders will be required to pay a tax on the realized gains, directly or through the mutual fund.

COMPARATIVE PERFORMANCE:
REFORM VERSUS MANAGED FUNDS

The difference in tax consequences to investors in the Reform Fund requires a recomputation of performance of managed mutual funds. In the Wharton Study, performance was computed as if 100% of the net capital gains had been reinvested in the mutual funds. This is misleading when comparing the performance of the average common stock mutual fund with that of the Reform Fund invested in S&P's Index. We must take the capital-gains tax into account, to arrive at a meaningful comparison.

When reinvestment of 100% of the net capital gains does occur, it is being subsidized by the shareholder, who had to pay the capital-gains tax out of another pocket.[2] Capital-gains tax payments by a shareholder should be treated, therefore, as additional capital added to his original mutual fund investment, a hidden contribution which necessarily lowers the over-all rate of return on his original investment.

The Reform Fund, however, would not cause the shareholder to lose any of his capital. Capital gains are not intended to be realized by the fund; instead, all capital gains are to keep increasing, hopefully, to have the greatest amount of capital working for the benefit of each shareholder of the Reform Fund. To him the advantage can be seen if we make certain reasonable assumptions.

If the average managed common stock mutual fund were able to equal the Reform Fund's net rate of return of 13.26%, before taxes, compounded annually, payment by the managed fund of the Compromise Tax of 15% would reduce the average managed fund's return to 11.27%.

On the other hand, assuming no payment of any capital-gains taxes, the Reform Fund investors would be paying a tax of 20%, but only on the net dividends, which average only 3.26% per year, after deduction of the assumed 1% in operating expenses. Thus, dividends would be reduced to 2.61%, after taxes, and the total compound annual return for the S&P investors would be about 12.61%, a difference in annual compound return of about $1\frac{1}{3}$%. This difference is attributable only to the postponement of the long-term capital-gains tax.

Although the Wharton Study concluded that the average common stock mutual fund did not perform as well as an unmanaged investment in S&P's 425 Index, we have made the reasonable assumption that performance was about the same. The Wharton Study did not charge S&P's fund with operating expenses. Nor did it charge the fund with cash holdings, to facilitate payment of various expenses, including redemptions. However, the Reform Fund probably would not have as high a percentage of cash as the average common stock fund holds in fixed-dollar securities and cash.

[2] The Wharton Report *may* have taken capital-gains tax payments *by the funds* into account to the extent this did occur, when determining investment performance, and if so, the necessary subsidy would be correspondingly reduced.

Another factor is the cost of brokerage commissions, higher for Reform Fund investors for the first few years, but beyond the sixth year of operation, the managed mutual fund pays more in brokerage commissions, at the rate of about 2% every 4 years.

In light of the foregoing, it seems fair to assume substantial equality of pre-tax performance between the Reform Fund and the average managed common stock mutual fund (disregarding sales costs).

Now we can proceed with the comparison. At the end of a 35-year period, if an individual invested $1,000 each year in the average common stock mutual fund, which produced an annual compound return of 11.27%, after taxes, he would have investments worth about $322,000. If, however, he invested the same amount in the Reform Fund, having the net rate of return, after taxes, of about 12.61%, his investments would be worth about $500,000. *The difference, about $168,000, results from the postponement of the capital-gains tax.*

If this Reform Fund investor then terminated his relationship with this world still holding onto his mutual fund shares, present tax law would impose no capital-gains tax on his estate or his successors in interest to the shares (although an estate tax probably would be payable). These shares would be received by the beneficiary with a recent fair market value as their tax basis (thus having no potential capital-gains tax liability). The appreciation in value during the decedent's lifetime would be disregarded. Whether this "loophole" will be allowed to continue we cannot predict. But as long as it is there, it is an additional reason for investing in the Reform Fund.

HOW DO THE LOAD FUNDS PERFORM?

Now we will consider the effect of the sales charge, which amounts to about 9.3% of the amount actually invested. To be fair, we will look at the long-run performance of the Reform Fund and the average "load" fund (which charges a sales commission), to amortize the sales charge over a lengthy period of investment. For shorter periods, the results would put the load funds at an unnecessary disadvantage.

Making our customary comparison of a $1,000 investment per year, we find that the Reform Fund investor received investments having a net asset value of $1,000 each year (disregarding brokerage commissions paid by the Reform Fund, for reasons explained above).

The investor in the average load fund, however, received shares having a net asset value of only $915. The other $85 was deducted as a sales charge.

Over the 35-year period, the Reform Fund investor would benefit from a performance $195,000 in excess of the load-fund investor (as compared to $168,000 in excess of the no-load investor), a $27,000 additional cost when mutual fund shares are purchased from a salesman. Load and no-load funds may produce the same rate of return on amounts actually invested, but when the sales charge is taken into account, no-loads are better performers by $27,000.

In spite of the advantage which the no-load fund has over the load fund, even the no-load fund cannot compete with the Reform Fund.

If at the end of the 35-year period a Reform Fund investor decided to redeem his shares, his $168,000 additional profit would be reduced a maximum of $42,000, making him at least $126,000 better off than his counterpart who invested in an average no-load common stock fund.

Although we had assumed equality of performance among load funds, no-load funds, and the Reform Fund, this is so only before taxes. Taking taxes into account, the average no-load fund would have to perform about 11% better, and the average load fund would have to perform about 14% better, than the S&P Reform Fund (or a little less than such percentages, to reflect the ultimate capital-gains liability of S&P's investor).

With the foregoing in mind, selection of a better common stock mutual fund than Standard & Poor's 425 Reform Fund seems quite difficult, if not impossible, to make.

REFORM FUND II, REFORM FUND III, ETC.

Investors in the hypothetical Reform Fund as well as investors in managed common stock mutual funds should pay particular attention to the percentage of unrealized appreciation of the fund's investments. For latecomers buying into a fund having a high percentage of unrealized appreciation, there could be a substantial loss.

If a fund realizes a net capital gain by sale of appreciated assets, each shareholder of the fund, whether he be old or new, will be responsible for his proportionate payment of the capital-gains tax. For the newcomer to the fund, the tax is being imposed on what is, in substance, a partial return of his capital.

For example, if the assets over many years have tripled in value, a newcomer would be paying $300, let us say, for an interest in stock having a tax basis of only $100. In other words, he would be buying a potential tax liability for capital gains totaling $200. If the fund distributed $100 in long-term capital gains immediately after the newcomer purchased his $300 interest, the interest would decline in value to $200 and he would have to pay a long-term capital-gains tax of $25 (or less) on the $100 distribution, reducing his investment capital by as much as $8\frac{1}{3}\%$.

Investors in the Reform Fund are better off than investors in managed funds. The Reform Fund should not be realizing any capital gains except in rare situations. Yet, it contemplates unlimited appreciation, over the course of innumerable years.

Later purchasers should be wary about buying into the fund. The possibility of capital-gains realization may be small, but the danger does exist; and if the gains must be realized, the latecomers would be taxed on what is nothing more than a return of their capital. As protection for the new investor, it would seem to be necessary to cease selling new shares in the Reform Fund and establish Reform Fund II whenever the unrealized capital gain amounts to, say, 25%. (Because of the constant addition of new money to the fund, gains on old assets would be diluted, making it more difficult to reach the 25% cutoff for unrealized capital gains.) By use of a series of Reform Funds this way, newcomers (including earlier investors making additional purchases) would not be saddled with the potentiality of substantial reductions in their investment capital. If one of the older Reform Funds experienced a high rate of redemptions, threatening to leave remaining shareholders holding the capital-gains bag, the fund could liquidate and dissolve, by selling all its assets and distributing the proceeds to its shareholders, who would pay a capital-gains tax based on their own investment costs—not the cost of the stock to the Reform Fund.

CAN A MANAGEMENT FEE BE JUSTIFIED?

Some persons may have wondered why a charitable organization (such as a tax-exempt foundation) does not donate its time and money to establish and operate a Reform Fund by which investors can make an indirect purchase of Standard & Poor's 425 industrial common stock index or some other group of stocks representative of all the stocks listed on the New York Stock Exchange.

Charities are organizations taking care of the poor and unwanted; prospective investors in the Reform Fund would not seem to fit in such a category. There is a way, however, by which necessary goods and services are provided for the nation. This system, being capitalistic, depends on the incentive of possible profits.

Establishment of the Reform Fund would occur only if a group of persons thought they could make a profit on their investment of services and capital. To set up the Reform Fund the promoters would incur substantial expenses, for which the investors in the Reform Fund could not be charged, at least as a practical matter. As listed in the Wharton Study, there would be expenses for office space; secretarial, bookkeeping, accounting and auditing services; officers' salaries and directors' fees; determination of net asset values; stationery, supplies, printing, and postage; registration with the SEC and filing numerous reports therewith; preparing and mailing stockholders' reports; legal fees; holding annual meetings; transfer agent and custodial fees; disbursing dividends, arranging for automatic reinvestment and computation of fractional shares. Furthermore, advertising, to attract the investors needed to make the business profitable, would be a substantial expense.

Although the Reform Fund could legitimately be charged with most of the foregoing expenses, it would be impractical to do so. In the first year of operation, the foregoing expenses could easily add up to 50% of the assets in the fund. Even if the fund were charged with only $5,000 in expenses (to pay a full-time secretary—but not to provide her with a telephone, desk, typewriter or office), the charge would be too much. A $100,000 Reform Fund would show thereby an annual operating expense of 5% of net asset value, a recurrent charge which would deter, unsurprisingly, most prospective investors from buying into the Reform Fund.

Getting the fund started would require the group of promoters to risk some of their own capital, to pay almost all of the initial and operating expenses for the first several years. Promoters would be willing to do this only if they could expect to recover their capital and service outlays and make a fair profit as well.

For this reason, a management fee is clearly justified, even though the managers of the fund would not necessarily be using any special skills in selecting investments for the fund. Merely because no investment advice is needed does not mean that management fees should be substantially lower than in managed funds. To think so is to overlook the important point that fees paid to advisers and managers of managed mutual funds bear no discernible relationship to the amount or quality of the advice they may render. In reality, the payment of an adviser's or manager's fee often constitutes reimbursement and profit for setting up the mutual fund.

The size of the fee paid to the management of the Reform Fund must be competitive with other mutual funds. These funds are charged a fee of approximately $\frac{1}{2}$ of 1% of average net asset value per year. Yet, for several years at least, the managers of the Reform Fund would not be receiving their fee. What is worse, they would be taking out of their own pocket to pay a good portion of the other operating expenses of the Reform Fund.

Payment out of their own pocket is necessary to guarantee to the shareholders of the Reform Fund a total operating cost of no more than 1% (including a maximum management fee of $\frac{1}{2}$ of 1%, let us say). In this way, the Reform Fund would be fully competitive with other mutual funds and, accordingly, would be bound to increase in size, assuming an adequate program of promotion.

As the fund grew, so would the dollar value of the 1% operating charge, paying an ever increasing portion of the operating expenses of the fund and, in due course, a management fee to the promoters. Finally, the managers would be obtaining a return of their capital and then payment for past and present services. At the end of several years, if they are successful, they would realize their first profits.

Economies in size are possible with regular mutual funds but to a lesser extent with the Reform Fund, which must cease selling shares when unrealized capital gains reach too high a percentage of net asset value. To continue the growth of the Reform Fund enterprise, additional expenses would have to be incurred by the Reform Fund promoters to set up Reform Fund II, Reform Fund III, etc. Furthermore, there would be additional expenses resulting from the earlier investors who have split their investments among many if not all of the Reform Funds.

As a reform, the proposed fund would be quite successful, but not to the extent where the reformers offer their services and risk their capital without expectation of reasonable compensation. In short, the management fee is well justified.

NO SALES CHARGE — NO SALESMEN

Without a sales charge to pave the way for tens of thousands of salesmen to seek out, then hard-sell, millions of prospective mutual fund purchasers, the Reform Fund would seem to have the same prospects as most other funds not having salesmen: prospects for no or only limited success. Success could come to the Reform Fund only if a sufficient number of investors could be attracted to the fund.

Anyway, the Reform Fund should not charge investors with any sales expenses (other than issuance and redemption fees paid to the fund and reasonably related to the cost of purchasing or selling underlying investments), at least not if it wanted to keep its name. The sales load is a totally unnecessary expense if the investor knows what he wants and how to obtain it without payment of the sales charge.

Exclusive of charges for special services, and the guaranteed 1% to cover operating expenses (including the management fee), the only cost to an investor in the Reform Fund would be an issuance fee and, possibly, a redemption fee. The issuance fee would be necessary to prevent newcomers to the fund from imposing related brokerage costs on prior mutual fund investors. The redemption fee, to the extent charged, would prevent the same imposition upon shareholders remaining behind in the fund. It prevents a shareholder from taking $100 out of the fund when the cost of commissions to the fund to raise the $100 would be, we assume, $4. Also, it would act as a slight deterrent from pulling money out of the fund. And, when sales exceeded redemptions, the redemption fee would build up for the benefit of the investors remaining behind in the fund.

INVESTORS' CONFIDENCE IN MUTUAL FUNDS RESTORED

Investors in mutual funds (load and no-load), badly shaken by their own investment experience and by revelations in the Wharton Study and Special Study, would find their confidence restored by establishment of the Reform Fund.

Contractual plans, clearly the most egregious of all abuses, would be eliminated as the first reform. As the very next reform we must list the absence of salesmen and related sales charges, thereby ending the notoriously effective hard-sell by salesmen who call themselves "financial planners"; and the churning of fund investments to create additional compensation for the more zealous salesmen.

Elimination of the sales charge would have the advantage of increasing over-all investment performance, of course. But what seems more important, an investor would no longer feel locked into the fund of his original choice. If his investment objectives change, if he needs to raise cash to meet an emergency or if he loses faith in the abilities of the fund manager, he could cancel out without payment of more than the equivalent of a reasonable round-trip brokerage expense.

Reform reaches its quintessence in the guarantee against poor management. Gone forever would be the vagaries of investment performance attributable to differing and changing qualities of management or investment advice. The Reform Fund investor would be guaranteed a performance, less operating expenses of no more than 1%, substantially equivalent to the rate of return achieved by Standard & Poor's 425 industrial common stock index. Actually, for the periodic investor, dollar-cost averaging profits would tend to provide a return nearer to S&P's return (as it would aid any mutual fund investment).

Initial brokerage costs would be higher, admittedly. Asset turnover and the abuse of churning would cease, however, leading to a measure of profit, after passage of six years. Every 4 years thereafter, the Reform Fund investors would save a 2% brokerage charge, as a result of this reform.

More important in connection with elimination of churning is the tax consequence, highly favorable to Reform Fund investors. By holding onto investments "forever," the fund shelters (although imperfectly) an investor from payment of capital-gains taxes, unlike managed mutual funds. This reform is so important that no-load funds equaling the before-tax return of S&P's 425 index would have to exceed S&P's performance by 11% to equal the after-tax performance (assuming no payment of capital-gains taxes by the S&P investor). More realistically, the difference would be less. Tax on some capital gains would probably be paid at infrequent intervals, but the reduction of capital should not be significant, except if a capital-gains tax is paid at the end of the common stock investment program.

REFORM FUND COULD BE FULLY COMPETITIVE

Very few funds (load or no-load) could be expected to outperform the Reform Fund. Unless an investor is a gambler willing to accept long odds or is able to foresee the future, he would be better off investing in the Reform Fund over any other common stock mutual fund.

From a cost point of view, the Reform Fund would be much cheaper than load funds, being reflected in higher investment performance. Also, the Reform Fund would incur no brokerage expenses after the initial purchase (with respect to a given investment). Even though brokerage costs, when incurred, are high, in six years the cost would be equivalent to total brokerage expenses by the average common stock mutual fund. Thereafter, the total brokerage costs paid by the average fund would exceed the one-shot brokerage expense of the Reform Fund.

Competition could be met in areas other than price. Investors in the Reform Fund, who would frequently be seeking to compound their investment, would be able to reinvest all distributions automatically. Also, there could be a variety of voluntary accumulation plans (but no contractual plans).

Save-by-Borrowing could be suggested as a purchasing method, especially for persons who could not afford to meet the minimum requirements under a voluntary accumulation plan or who wanted to enforce their voluntary accumulation program.

The Reform Fund could make available decreasing term life insurance, which, according to the Special Study, would act as an enforcer of the voluntary accumulation program, although not to the extent obtainable by adoption of the Save-by-Borrowing method. The cost of the life insurance, as group insurance, would be comparatively inexpensive. Nevertheless, investors would be cautioned not to let such insurance take the place of a regular life insurance program.

A shareholder nearing retirement may be interested in the offering of a periodic withdrawal program by which he could withdraw a fixed amount of money per month—let's assume $100. For some protection against exhaustion of his capital, he would not be allowed to fix the monthly amount so that it exceeded, say, $\frac{1}{2}\%$ of the original principal value of his Reform Fund investment. (On an annual basis, the limit equals 6%, which seems conservative for a Reform Fund investment.) Thus, to meet this test, he would have to possess shares valued at $20,000 or more. The monthly payment would first be drawn from dividends (and in some cases, where capital gains are being paid to shareholders, this would be sufficient to supply the $100); and any additional amount needed to complete the $100 payment would be obtained by redemption of an appropriate number of Reform Fund shares. To minimize the cost of this service to the fund, the withdrawal option would have to be restricted to investors having shares valued at, say, $10,000.

The Reform Fund could offer more, to effectively meet the competition of other mutual funds, especially funds of the load type. A prospective shareholder could be offered a self-employed qualified pension plan; suggested forms of trust instruments and other estate-planning arrangements, all subject, of course, to review by the attorney for the shareholder.

IN REFLECTION

Mutual funds, as an investment medium, can be advantageous to a small investor, affording him diversity, convenience, and professional management. But, as we have seen, professional management can be of poor quality, far inferior to an investment in an unmanaged portfolio of securities comparable to Standard & Poor's 425 industrial common stock index.

It would be possible for a Reform Fund to operate, investing in each of the 425 stocks, even though the initial cost of brokerage commissions could approximate 4%. Advantages to an investor would be manifold, more than sufficient to make the Reform Fund an attractive medium of investment, without the necessity of paying a 9.3% sales charge (which must be reflected in the performance of load mutual funds when determining to what extent they have performed as well as S&P's Index).

Thrifty-minded investors, seeking a return almost equivalent to the market averages, together with decided tax benefits, would do well to consider the merits of the Reform Fund, if it becomes available (probably under a different name). The 10th Multiple would become a greater possibility for many millions of investors, even though any mutual fund method of investment takes somewhat longer than direct ownership, assuming that direct ownership results in average or better-than-average performance.

Now we turn from equity investments into the field of life insurance, to see what it is and how it can be used by a person who intends to go after the 10th Multiple.

Chapter Eleven

HOW TO COPE WITH A LIFE INSURANCE SALESMAN

DOES EVERY DEATH RESULT IN LOSS?

Don, an intelligent young man of 25, is married and has two children. He has had great difficulty trying to accumulate savings, and so when the Save-by-Borrowing technique was explained to him and his wife, they wholeheartedly agreed it would be the most practical and effective way for them to provide for the future of their family.

Of great importance, they felt, is the element of forced saving found in the Save-by-Borrowing plan. Periodic saving and investment without interruption during the forty-year period preceding Don's anticipated retirement is bound to prove beneficial, especially as they take an interest in stock market matters and will follow their investments quite closely, to eliminate any unsound ones. They do not worry about the long-range success of their savings and investment program.

If he withdraws $1,000 from current earnings to invest each year, Don could accumulate approximately half a million dollars by the time he reaches his anticipated retirement age of 65. This assumes he will be able to maintain a 10% rate of return on his investments, after taxes and compounded annually.

What does worry Don, though, is the risk of non-completion of his savings program resulting from a premature termination of his earnings. If misfortune should strike and he dies early in his Save-by-Borrowing program, he would leave behind only a few thousand dollars, hardly enough to support his wife and children. His insurance needs would be different, he realized, if nobody were dependent upon him. Then, his death prior to completion of the savings and investment program would not deprive anyone of continued support. And, in such circumstances, premature death would result in no loss against which insurance would be necessary to afford protection.

On account of his wife and children, however, Don must face a serious problem. He wishes to invest in equity securities, to afford himself the opportunity of possibly achieving the 10th Multiple. Yet, he wants to ensure that his dependents would not be deprived of sustenance in the event of his untimely death.

Having some knowledge about life insurance, but certainly not enough to be considered an expert, Don decides to talk to a specialist in the field. A life insurance salesman or agent of a company, Don believes, may represent a company not offering the type of policy he needs and, instead, try to sell him an undesirable policy, just to make a sale. On the other hand, a person acting as *his* agent (an "independent agent") would be able to obtain a greater variety of insurance policies, suitability of at least one virtually being guaranteed. Yet, independent agents often form close associations with particular companies, and may not be as specialized as company agents, which tend to narrow the difference between company agents and independent agents.

The appointed day and time arrived and Don found himself sitting across a desk from smiling Bobby Broker, a charming, disarming gentleman of about 50. (Although the public may call Bobby a *broker,* he will be acting as Don's *agent* to procure a suitable life insurance policy.) Without any hesitation, Don proceeded to discuss with frankness his financial affairs, setting forth in detail his net worth and describing his Save-by-Borrowing aspirations. Also discussed, among other topics, was Don's desire to make provision for his wife and children.

Because of the cost, Bobby Broker pointed out realistically, Don must reject the idea of carrying $500,000 of life insurance coverage, no matter what kind.

Don readily agreed with this conclusion and said to himself, "This guy is pretty sharp, starting off by making a recommendation against his own interest. I wonder how long he could stay in business if he kept this up?"

Bobby Broker, leaning back in his swivel chair, volunteered that many people (but not the average, Don surmised) carry life insurance having a death value of approximately five times their annual salary. The coverage may or may not be adequate, depending on such factors as Social Security entitlement, employee pension-plan benefits, mortgage obligations, net worth and earning capacity of the insured, and the ages and number of his children.

Another factor which Don should consider is that the $500,000 Save-by-Borrowing goal may be exceeded—or realized results could fall far short of the goal. It is safe to say that Don cannot rely on having a retirement fund at age 65 substantially equivalent to $500,-000, nor can he expect proportional realization of his goal during each or even any of his saving years. For various reasons, Don agreed, it would be unwise or unrealistic to relate any loss caused by premature death to his $500,000 Save-by-Borrowing goal.

After consideration of the relevant factors, Bobby Broker and Don agreed that Don needed at present $60,000 in life insurance coverage. This amount would be a practical way to insure against premature death, even though the full economic loss resulting to his wife and children if Don died next month probably would not be covered. Nor should it be fully covered in most situations. To provide additional living benefits to the insured and his wife during the years following his retirement—and living in retirement is more probable than death before retirement—it is necessary for Don to reduce the insurance benefits payable upon his death prior to retirement.

Looking at the $60,000 coverage from another point of view and accepting that it is small in comparison to Save-by-Borrowing possibilities, $60,000 is equivalent approximately to the accumulation value of a $1,000 annual investment for 40 years, assuming a 2% annual compound return, after taxes. This return would produce an accumulation value slightly less than the value produced by the return on certain popular fixed-dollar investments. It would be a return which no adequately-diversified Save-by-Borrowing program could fall below, or so it seems, over an extended period.

Thus, $60,000 could be considered the *minimum loss* which would be caused if Don died today, and to protect his family he must obtain insurance covering his own life. By selecting $60,000 as the minimum final value of his long-range savings and investment program, Don will be able to afford insurance to cover the contingency of his death prior to the completion of his working and saving years. The cost of insurance, however, would not deprive him of the benefits of a Save-by-Borrowing program, which he could still afford to maintain.

Once Don retired, his earnings would cease, and his Save-by-Borrowing program would terminate. Furthermore, full compounding would cease too. The investment income (if not some principal too) would be used by Don to supplement Social Security and other pension payments, to support himself and wife during his retirement, and then his wife, if she survived him, during the remainder of her life. Don has not forgotten about his children, but logically expects them to be self-supporting or supported by someone else by the time he retires.

Don's plan, it is seen, contemplates no saving and investment beyond the last of his working years. By the time he retires, therefore, his death would cause no loss of earnings against which insurance coverage should be provided. Any losses resulting from reduced Social Security or other pension payments would not be real losses to the extent such payments would have been used in his own support. Any excess would be a loss to the wife, but more than offset by the availability to her of 100% of the income (and some principal, perhaps) of the estate which Don would have left behind.

Bobby Broker states that he understands Don's Save-by-Borrowing plan and the desire to provide for his wife and children. Then he gives his opinion that Don should purchase $60,000 of *ordinary life insurance* (also known as *whole life,* or *straight life*), which would cost about $777 per year[1] "on a level-premium basis," payable until Don died or reached the age of 100.

"*Level-premium* basis," Bobby explained, "means that the insurance premium will remain the same from year to year, not increasing each year as the risk of your death increases."

Anticipating Don's reaction, Bobby Broker hurriedly went on to explain that ordinary life insurance is the least expensive type of "permanent" insurance, due to the fact that the insured keeps paying until he dies (or reaches 100). The other permanent types of insurance, such as endowment policies, life paid up at 65, 20 pay life and retirement income at 65, have shorter periods for payment of premium, but of course the premiums will be higher, substantially higher in many cases.

---

[1] Non-participating in dividends. Includes coverage for waiver of premium in the event of Don's disability.

"The added advantage of the recommended ordinary life policy is the cash surrender value of $34,210 which will have accumulated by the time you reach 65," continued Bobby, "$3,130 more than you will have paid in premiums—with 'free' life insurance protection all along. Then, too, you should not forget that the insurance company pays a guaranteed interest on your savings (technically, the legal reserve set aside for the policy) and, if you want to buy insurance from a 'mutual' or buy a 'participating' policy from a stock company, you will have the added benefit of dividends."

"But . . ." Don managed to get out before Bobby Broker continued with his well-rehearsed sales pitch.

"Also, ordinary life insurance is 'permanent,' as I have said, in the sense that it pays your estate or beneficiaries the full death value no matter when you die, unlike *term* insurance, which affords coverage for a temporary period only. When you are thinking of your loved ones, you should be having permanent, not temporary, thoughts. And you must remember . . ."

"Now wait a minute," interrupted Don, "you've been talking pretty fast. Slow down so we can discuss this. I have been doing some reading in the field of life insurance and have learned a few things, enough at least to ask some questions."

Bobby Broker thought, "Oh well, I may as well see it through. Maybe I can sell him some theft insurance, at least."

ANOTHER BANK ACCOUNT

Don pulled out a pencil and paper and jotted down the following points made by Bobby Broker concerning ordinary life insurance.

1. $777 per year—least expensive
2. level premium
3. pay until death or 100
4. permanent—not temporary
5. $34, 210 cash value at 65
6. $3,130 in excess of premium payments
7. free life insurance protection
8. guaranteed interest
9. dividends too

"Let's consider the first point on my list," said Don, being careful not to let Bobby see the contents of the list. "I can't afford $777 each year for insurance coverage. Every year I set aside $1,000 of my earnings through my Save-by-Borrowing program. Isn't there some way by which I can insure against premature death without jeopardizing my independent program of saving and investment?"

Before Bobby Broker could answer, Don added, "Besides, I don't need any cash surrender value. I already have an effective savings and investment program. Any cash necessary to meet emergencies can be obtained immediately from my emergency fund, which is safely tucked away in a federally insured account with the savings bank around the corner.

"This permanent insurance you are trying to convince me to buy sounds suspiciously similar to another bank account, am I not correct?

"A level premium, from what I have read," continued Don, "is no more than a device by which the premium in excess of the present cost of my $60,000 face amount of insurance would be put in a separate account, called the 'legal reserve' for the policy, with such reserve being credited with compound interest at the guaranteed rate of 2% to 3% per year.

"The legal reserve pays the excess cost of $60,000 of insurance coverage during my later years, when the risk of my death will be much greater. By overpayment of premium today I can enjoy what you call 'permanent' coverage at no increased cost later. This I know is a very rough description of the legal reserve concept.

"But what is this 'permanent' coverage you seem so proud to offer? Does it mean that no matter what happens, assuming I keep up the payment of premiums, $60,000 of *pure insurance coverage* will be paid as a death benefit? Does it mean that, at the age of 65, I will be permitted to withdraw my $34,210 cash surrender value (by borrowing) without having such amount reduced from the $60,000 'coverage'? Of course not, even I understand that.

"When a life insurance company gets set to pay the death claim on my policy, it will take whatever 'savings' I have built up (in the form of cash surrender value) and add to them a pure insurance payment necessary to bring the total death benefit to the face amount of $60,000. In other words, as I see it, my savings go to reduce the *amount at risk,* so that, at age 65 when I have a cash surrender value of $34,210, the amount of insurance in force will be only $25,790.

"What is so *permanent* about the $60,000 in pure life insurance coverage admittedly applicable to the first one, two or three years of the policy, when there ordinarily is no cash surrender value? Permanent insurance gradually reduces in pure insurance coverage as the 'savings account' grows, so that by the maturity of the policy (death or age 100 for an ordinary life policy), when the savings account (exclusive of any dividends and interest thereon) is equivalent to the face amount of the policy, *no insurance is in force.* My death shortly before maturity would involve almost no benefit for my estate or beneficiaries which I could not have taken by drawing my savings out of the life insurance savings account.[2]

"For many buyers of insurance the term 'permanent insurance' is misleading. In reality, the insurance element in permanent insurance can be just as temporary as it is in term insurance."

Don shifted into high gear.

"You say that ordinary life insurance is less expensive than other kinds of life insurance, such as endowment and paid-up at 65. But why would I wish to carry life insurance after reaching 65 and, more particularly, as to certain policies, why would I wish to add to my cash surrender value, in view of the fact that at 65 I will go into retirement and start drawing on my savings to supplement my retirement income? Certainly you are aware that I will want to maximize my income, to help me enjoy my retirement years. I would hardly wish to use my retirement income to increase a 'life insurance savings account.'

"Furthermore, Mr. Broker, you mentioned 'free' life insurance protection as an advantage and a $3,130 cash surrender value in excess of the total paid in premiums by the time I reach 65. By your statement you seem to assume that I would not be doing anything constructive with the $777 annual premium if I had not purchased the policy. Is this a fair assumption? What if I were taking the portion of the premium allocable to the legal reserve, averaging about $454 per year, and investing it in, say, life insurance company stocks, obtaining a 10% net rate of return, compounded annually? How much more than $34,210 do you think I would have? As I recall, I read somewhere that at age 65 I would have about $171,000 *more*

---

[2] Don disregarded the liability for income taxes, resulting from a surrender of the policy, on the excess of cash surrender value over the total premium payments. He knew that Bobby would not raise the point.

than the cash surrender value of the $60,000 policy. Do you still maintain that the insurance would be at no cost?

"You mentioned dividends and guaranteed interest rates," Don went on to say, "but I trust you did not mean to imply that the guaranteed rates are high or that dividends should be considered as a supplement to the guaranteed rate. Remind me to explore this with you when we talk about which type of insurance is less expensive, the kind that participates in dividend distributions or the kind that does not.

"Now that I have aired my views on your proposal for me to purchase permanent insurance," said Don, "please tell me how I can obtain the desired coverage without having to establish another bank account. Perhaps we should explore the possibility of 'term insurance'—you know, you called it 'temporary' insurance. Is that O.K. with you?" queried the overheated Don, getting set to respond to at least one more devious proposal.

SO WHAT IF IT COSTS MORE?

"Well," said Bobby Broker, unaccustomed to being put on the defensive, "as you've indicated there is a type of life insurance known as term insurance. And, as you know, its cost for the *immediate* future would be much less than permanent insurance, when comparing the total premiums to be paid. A purchaser of term insurance must beware, however. The cost of term insurance increases as he grows older, until the cost far exceeds the cost of permanent life insurance in the same face amount.

"To show you what I mean, $60,000 of term insurance at age 25 would cost about $300 for that year. Yet, at the age of 65, the cost would approximate $5,000 to be insured for one year, if you could find an insurance company willing to accept you for insurance coverage."

"Hold it!" Don demanded. "Why would I need $60,000 of coverage at the age of 65 when the loss of earnings resulting from my death hardly would be more than several thousand dollars? Apparently, you forgot about my Save-by-Borrowing program. Isn't there a type of insurance comparable to the pure insurance element in a 'permanent' insurance policy, a coverage which would decrease constantly until I attain a certain age, when coverage would cease?

"Here, let me show you what I mean," volunteered Don, producing a sketch showing the relationship between the cash surrender value and pure insurance coverage in an ordinary life insurance policy.

$60,000 WHOLE LIFE INSURANCE–RELATIONSHIP BETWEEN CASH SURRENDER VALUE AND PURE INSURANCE ELEMENT

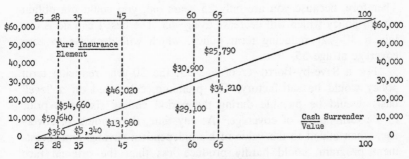

Range of Don's Age and Period
During Which He Would Pay Premiums

Don did not have to explain to the broker how, at any given age, the cash surrender value and pure insurance element, when added together, would always equal the face amount of the policy. Nor did Bobby Broker interrupt to say that the legal reserve of the policy (always greater than the cash surrender value until passage of a specified number of years, sometimes twenty) is used by insurance companies as the basis for determining the amount at risk. He knew that Don was knowledgeable enough to counter with the argument that, insofar as an insured is concerned, the cash surrender value is the amount available to him during his lifetime. The difference between such cash value and the face amount becomes available only upon his death and, accordingly, is the insurance element as far as he is concerned.

Don went on. "Doesn't the life insurance industry offer insurance coverage essentially similar to the pure insurance element on this sketch? Of course, I would like the coverage to reduce to zero by the time I reach age 65, not 100. After all, once I retire, my death would involve no substantial loss in earnings to be insured against."

"You know something?" queried the broker, "I believe I can find just the policy you want . . . and need," Bobby Broker added hastily, sensing that a sale was in the offing, even though it would involve much less in commissions for him than a sale of permanent insurance would have produced.

"The policy is called either 'reducing term' or 'decreasing term.' Often it is sold as mortgage protection in conjunction with a policy of permanent insurance. Reducing term coverage will decrease to zero over a limited number of years, ordinarily 10, 15, 20, 25, or 30. Therefore, because you are only 25 years old, you could not obtain a term policy which will decrease to age 65. The best I can do is obtain a 30-year reducing term policy, which will decrease to zero coverage at age 55.

"For a Save-by-Borrower of age 35, the 30-year reducing term policy would be satisfactory. The premium, calculated on a 'level' basis, would be payable during the period ending six years prior to the termination of coverage.[3] At any time, the amount of coverage, when added to the value of his independent savings and investment program, could hardly produce less than the original face amount of his insurance, say $50,000. In later years, the total should far exceed $50,000, if he chooses his Save-by-Borrowing investments wisely."

Bobby had all the answers!

"As the insured advances in age," Bobby continued, "the cost per thousand dollars of insurance will increase, but the total coverage will decrease. Therefore, the total cost of his insurance will be kept to a low level. By paying a level premium, he will be creating a reserve to offset insurance costs in excess of premium, during the later years of the policy.

"The 30-year decreasing term policy is roughly comparable to the pure insurance element of an endowment-at-65 policy, issued at age 35. At age 65, the endowment policy will mature ("endow") and the "insured" or his beneficiary will be entitled to the accumulated savings, equal to the face amount of the policy (plus any divi-

---

[3] This involves a prepayment of premium. Insurance companies impose this prepayment requirement to discourage policy lapses when coverage is comparatively small in amount.

dends and interest thereon). The pure insurance in force gradually decreases during the life of the policy until, at age 65, coverage will cease to exist altogether.

"Now, Don, if you desire decreasing term insurance, you would probably want to combine it with an underlying base of 5-year *renewable term* coverage. For example, if you wanted $60,000 in total initial coverage, you could obtain $45,000 of 30-year decreasing term insurance and a 5-year $15,000 renewable term policy. At age 55, upon expiration of the decreasing term policy, you would still have $15,000 of insurance in force (assuming you did not fail to renew the policy). Prior to each anniversary date of the renewable term policy during your fifty-sixth through sixty-fourth years you would advise the company to decrease your coverage by $1,000 or $2,000. At age 65, you would fail to renew the remaining $1,000 or $2,000 coverage—but, as you say, you would no longer need coverage.

"The renewable term insurance should have renewability guaranteed, without medical examination or other evidence of insurability; also, the policy should be renewable up to age 65, at least. This is of the utmost importance. Without it the availability of sufficient insurance would depend on the status of your health."

Bobby promised that through his knowledge of the business he would be able to procure the desired policies. All Don would have to do is take and pass a medical examination.

Don was ready to agree with Bobby that a 30-year decreasing term policy combined with a 5-year renewable term policy would be suitable. Before he was willing to accept Bobby's advice, however, Don wanted to be told more about renewable term policies.

Noticeably hurt by Don's continuing distrust, Bobby answered as candidly as he could. "Advocates of term insurance programs are not in complete agreement about which type of term insurance to recommend, reducing or renewable term.

"Per thousand dollars of actual coverage, renewable term insurance is *more expensive:* renewal commissions and administrative expenses are built into the renewal premiums; and there is an added charge for the renewal right. Renewable term insurance is *less convenient:* renewals must take place without fail; a notice to decrease coverage must be sent to the company annually; and premiums will vary in dollar amount from year to year.

"On the other hand, decreasing term involves *higher initial premiums* than renewable term. A reserve must be accumulated to offset the higher mortality cost of later years and to pay the premium during the last 20% of the decreasing term period (6 years for a 30-year policy). The reserve will be larger than the slight reserve for a 5-year renewable term policy.[4] Thus the Save-by-Borrower insured by reducing term has, at the outset, less than the maximum amount working for him in equity securities. If the difference in initial cost between renewable and decreasing term is invested in equities, the higher cost per thousand dollars of coverage should, on the average, be more than offset. This would tend to maximize your Multiples.

"Furthermore, renewable term is *more flexible*. The insured is not required to decrease the insurance; instead, he has the option of carrying his present term coverage to the end of the final renewal period (age 70, frequently). Thus, if his income and investment status warrant, he may choose not to decrease his renewable term coverage any further. Otherwise, he could slow down the rate of decrease. The renewal right can be very valuable indeed."

"How would a program of renewable term insurance work?" queried Don, sensing that he had seen the last of Bobby's tricks.

"Well," Bobby responded, "to make my illustration easy to understand, let me assume you need $40,000 in present insurance coverage. You would take out a 5-year renewable term policy in the face amount of $40,000. Each year before the anniversary date of the policy you would notify the company to decrease coverage by $1,000. The company would inform you of the revised premium payable. Every five years you would renew the policy, until age 65, when you would fail to renew the remaining $1,000 of coverage.

Companies will not let you decrease coverage by other than $1,000 multiples ($1,000, $2,000, $3,000, $4,000, etc.). Therefore, to decrease your $60,000 of coverage over the 40-year period, you would have to decrease alternately by $1,000 and $2,000 amounts. Or, perhaps, you could choose to decrease by $3,000 every two years. You do not have to decide upon this now."

Bobby doubted the wisdom of continuing to talk about permanent insurance of any kind, but decided that Don should be possessed of

---

[4] Decrease of coverage during the middle years of each 5-year period involves a forfeiture of the reserve as to the coverage so decreased.

additional information; therefore, at great risk of alienating Don, Bobby continued, "Let me point out one more way for you to obtain term coverage of the type you seek. If you would permit yourself to take out, for example, $10,000 in whole life coverage, you could add a term rider, decreasing to age 65. Although the maximum permissible term coverage varies according to age, perhaps you would be allowed 3.7 times the amount of permanent insurance coverage (that is, a term rider for $37,000). The advantages are that you start off with a very high percentage of term insurance coverage (about 79%) and, I must emphasize, you obtain your reducing term coverage *at the lowest possible rate."*

Bobby went on. "Now that you have received my comments, which type of term insurance do you favor? Either type will produce a substantial cost difference in comparison to a comparable permanent insurance policy. Assuming you can discipline yourself to save the difference in premiums, your independent savings and investment program should produce a considerable accumulation value, especially when the difference is invested to obtain the net return of 10% which you have been talking so much about."

Don was unsure which insurance plan to adopt. He asked Bobby to give him specific figures for the least expensive reducing and renewable term programs suitable for him. Then he would seek independent advice.

Also, Don would flip through the most recent edition of *Flitcraft Compend,* which provides insurance rates and other information for most of the prominent insurance companies. This useful publication, priced at $6.00, can be ordered from Flitcraft Incorporated, 75 Fulton Street, New York, New York 10038. By comparing the rates for comparable policies of different insurance companies, he can make sure that he pays no more than necessary for his insurance coverage.

Save-by-Borrowers can expect to encounter obstacles substantially similar to those presented in the foregoing hypothetical dealing between a man and his agent. One major reason seems obvious: a salesman's commissions are much less when he sells decreasing or renewable term insurance than when he sells permanent insurance in the same face amount.

An apparent drawback to term insurance is its cost, *higher* than the cost allocable to the term insurance element in a comparable permanent policy. People who believe they have a short life expectancy try (and do succeed frequently) to obtain the greatest amount of coverage per dollar by loading up with term insurance.

If the term insurance has a conversion feature, there will be an additional cost. When in ill health, especially, insureds will exercise their option to convert from term to permanent life insurance, before expiration of the conversion period. By conversion they will obtain coverage after expiration of the reducing term or final 5-year term and, in the case of reducing term, they will slow down the steady decline in pure insurance coverage. This gives them the advantage of insurance rates substantially lower than rates they could obtain elsewhere, in their present state of health.

Also, higher issuing costs are charged to term policies than to the term aspect of similar permanent policies, where part of these costs is charged against the bank account feature.

This higher cost of term insurance is offset to some extent by the fact that term has no savings feature (other than a small prepayment of premium), hence no sales commission is payable on the investment of your savings. Upon purchase of permanent insurance, the sales cost is 100% of your savings (now equating savings with the legal reserve), to the extent a surrender of the policy would produce no cash surrender value. Gradually, however, cash surrender values increase, until the twentieth year of some policies, at which time the value will equal the legal reserve. From then on, a surrender would entail no *visible* sales costs.[5]

Surrender of the policy frequently occurs, and for insureds who turn in their policies prior to the twentieth year (or whatever other year may be applicable), there is an appropriate comparison. Imagine how a depositor would feel if he saw the bank teller legally crediting all of his deposits for three years to an account bearing somebody else's name, to belong to that other person if at the end of the third year he terminated his relationship with the bank. Of course, if his life insurance bank account is maintained, his savings will be fully restored to his account by the twentieth year of regular deposits.

Is this the only offsetting factor? If so, it would seem that term

[5] The *invisible* sales cost is the reduced return on your savings.

insurance really does cost more, as insurance salesmen and agents are so quick to make prospects believe. When the insured puts the difference in premiums in equity investments, the higher rate of return, on the average, will completely overwhelm the slightly higher cost of term insurance.

WHICH COSTS LESS: PAR OR NON-PAR?

The most important factor to be considered is the rate of return which could be obtained on an alternative investment—other than the investment in the life insurance savings account, which pays a guaranteed return ranging from 2% to 3%. We will assume that the guaranteed rate is 3%, compounded annually, after taxes (as a practical matter).

Non-mutual life insurance companies (called *"stock companies"*) are run for the profit of their stockholders. They customarily guarantee this 3% rate to their insureds who purchase *"non-participating"* life insurance contracts. Some of the stock companies, in addition, issue policies on a *"participating basis"* (called "par" in contrast to "non-par" policies), but the insured must take a reduction of the guaranteed rate from 3% to about $2\frac{1}{4}$%. "Participation" means the right to receive *"dividends"* from the company, assuming the company has a divisible surplus allocable to policies of his class.

Mutual life insurance companies (run for the benefit of the policyholders) issue participating policies, employing a $2\frac{1}{4}$% or $2\frac{1}{2}$% guaranteed interest rate. The policyholder participates by receipt of dividends from the company. When dividends are taken into consideration, the rate of return is brought back into competition with stock companies, which guarantee 3% but pay no dividends on their non-par policies.

Debate between salesmen of par and salesmen of non-par insurance rages on, as to which type provides the less expensive coverage. Stock companies, issuing non-par insurance, afford the same insurance coverage at *less initial cost* than the par policies of mutual companies. With less initial cost and a higher guaranteed interest rate (3%), how could stock companies be the loser?

Mutuals do charge more, but they ordinarily return the overcharge *and then some*—by distribution of *dividends*. These dividends should not be thought of as supplemental to the guaranteed rate of $2\frac{1}{4}\%$ or $2\frac{1}{2}\%$, however. They are for the most part nothing more than a return of the *premium overcharge*.

Out of caution at least the mutual company will assume a lower interest rate, a greater administrative expense, and a greater death rate than actually anticipated. Based on such assumptions, it will charge a higher premium than charged by stock companies for their non-par policies. When fewer deaths occur and less money is spent for administration than assumed, and a higher interest is earned on investments than assumed, a surplus is created, some of which is returned to the insured in the form of dividends. The rest remains in surplus, to add to the margin of safety for present and future policyholders.

To the extent that earnings on investments exceed the guaranteed rate of $2\frac{1}{4}\%$ or $2\frac{1}{2}\%$, dividends are more than a return of premium; they are, in a technical sense, an increase in the rate of return. Thus, a portion of the dividends reduce the cost of par insurance, and the remaining portion is a practical increase in the rate of interest, to let the mutual policies (and par policies of stock companies) compete against non-par insurance.

When dividends are taken into consideration, the net dollar outlay for *par* insurance will usually be *less* than the guaranteed cost of non-par insurance. Here is another "trap," set for the unwary. Which is less costly, then, par or non-par insurance? You have fallen in the trap of the "net-cost" sales pitch if you answered "par" insurance.

You may not have realized that dividends are not returned each year in the same amount. A certain level-premium ordinary life insurance policy issued in 1944 by a leading mutual company paid the following dividends from 1945 to 1964:

$3.93
4.32
4.48
4.64
4.78

4.93
5.09
5.24
5.38
5.53

5.75
6.30
6.44
6.89
7.02

7.14
7.26
7.36
8.24
8.36

Dividends averaged about $6 per year per thousand dollars of coverage. But notice how they increased from year to year. There was no *level reduction* of the level insurance premium. Part of the reduction in cost was postponed for many years. If the dividends had been received in equal amounts each year, the insured in earlier years could have invested the excess amount ($6 less the actual dividend). Instead, the insured lost the return which the excess amounts would have produced. No wonder, then, that dividends reduce, in many instances, the net cost of par insurance below the cost of non-par insurance. The delay in returning part of the premium overcharge *should* result in some additional payment, representing interest earned by the company during the period of retention.

Although the dividends, when finally received, could be invested, substantially better results will be produced by investing the difference in premiums as early as possible, to take full advantage of the sizable anticipated difference in rates of return. Why should the overpayment be sitting around in a life insurance company, doing nothing more than drawing interest? It would be better, therefore, for Don to purchase non-par insurance, thereby cutting his insurance costs to a minimum.

A possible exception is savings bank life insurance (even though it is participating), which normally costs less than similar policies issued by mutual and stock companies. Savings bank life insurance is available to persons residing or working in Connecticut, Massachusetts, or New York, and is worthy of their consideration. One drawback, however, is the "do-it-yourself" nature of the business, where the buyer often fails to obtain any effective professional counseling.

Another good reason for purchasing non-par insurance is that the insured need not speculate on the probability that a company will maintain its dividend schedules. Thus, one factor adding to the complexity of purchasing life insurance can be eliminated—without any regrets.

WORDS THAT MAKE INSURANCE SALESMEN SHUDDER

Don decides to purchase the non-par, renewable term policy. He makes sure it does not require any medical examinations for renewal. Then he invests the difference between its cost and what would have been the cost of purchasing comparable permanent life insurance in the same face amount.

COMPARISON OF INVESTMENT PERFORMANCE ASSUMING
$1,000 ANNUAL INVESTMENT FOR 40 YEARS
IN LIFE INSURANCE RESERVE PAYING 3% NET RETURN
OR IN EQUITY SECURITIES PAYING 3% TO 15%
NET RETURN

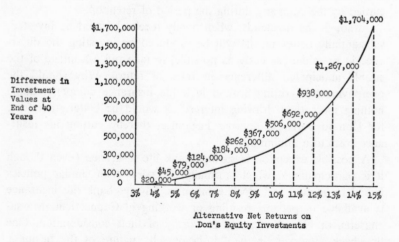

Difference in Investment Values at End of 40 Years

Alternative Net Returns on
Don's Equity Investments

To make calculations comparatively simple, let us assume the difference in cost is $1,000 per year. By the graph above, we can see an approximation of the *difference* in value to Don at age 65, assuming a 3% net return on ordinary insurance (which he did not buy) and a range of 3% to 15% on his $1,000 annual investment.[6]

Looking at this chart, you can see approximations of the real cost of carrying ordinary life insurance. Although the pure insurance coverage will cost a little more (and one should deduct such excess from the accumulation value), Don is able to avoid a much higher cost: the loss of equity investment opportunity.

Any term insurance program would require additional insurance—disability income protection—to assure that the difference in insurance premium would continue to be available for investment in the event of disability of the insured. The cost equivalent may be about $50 per year. Thus, the accumulation value difference on this and other charts should be reduced by the value of $50 per year for the appropriate number of years invested at the indicated rate. Assuming 40 years, the deduction would range from $3,770 at 3% to $88,955 at 15%.

Even if the investor selected a savings and loan association as the medium of investment, which may net, after taxes, about 3.6% per year, compounded annually, he would have an additional $11,000 at the end of the 40-year period (before deduction of disability income coverage and higher term insurance costs). Furthermore, when investing in certain savings and loan associations, he would have the advantage of federal insurance covering his deposits, not obtainable for the savings held by a life insurance company.

When the rate of return for equity securities is 10%, the difference between the two alternatives—term and permanent insurance—amounts to about one third of a million dollars. This should be more than sufficient to pay the additional costs.

Forty years may be appropriate for some readers but not for most. Perhaps you wish to fulfill a Save-by-Borrowing program in less time than that. Refer, then, to the following chart, which is based on the assumption of a 7% *difference* in rates of return.

As can be easily seen, the 7% spread in return does make a difference, ranging from $800 to $367,200 over the period of 5 to 40 years. This is the true cost of buying permanent life insurance. Term insurance may be "more costly," but one must admit that it is worth the price.

---

[6] The renewable term premium includes the features of convertibility, before age 70, and waiver of premium.

DIFFERENCE IN VALUES BETWEEN LIFE INSURANCE RESERVE (3%) AND EQUITY INVESTMENT (ASSUMED 10%) FOR ANNUAL $1,000 INVESTMENT FROM 0–40 YEARS

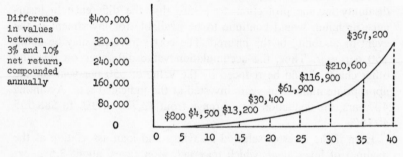

Years of $1,000 Annual Investment

Recently, the author received a letter from a life insurance salesman apparently on the lookout for new business. In his letter he took the bull by the horns by quoting the words which make lesser insurance salesmen shudder:

"'Buy term—and invest the difference?' Sure you're not kidding yourself? Most people never get around to 'investing the difference.'"

If this is the only reason to buy permanent life insurance, forget about it, Bobby Broker. Save-by-Borrowing has even greater compulsion to save. The Save-by-Borrowers are legally bound to make repayment of their (unsecured) loan, unlike the purchaser of permanent life insurance. He can always fall back on the cash surrender value of his policy, if any, to keep the policy in force, which results in a "withdrawal" of savings.

With these thoughts in mind, you are ready to face an insurance broker or agent, to inform him of your intentions; you will not be diverted.

You cannot afford the high cost of investment inevitably resulting from maintenance of a permanent life insurance policy. You need life insurance, yes—but not necessarily another bank account.

FOR THOSE WHO HAVE BOUGHT
PERMANENT LIFE INSURANCE

Unlike younger readers desiring to get started on their savings and investment programs, older readers already may have made substantial life insurance commitments, probably by purchase of "permanent" life insurance protection.

Over the years, the cash surrender values of such permanent insurance have been increasing steadily, after the first one, two or three years of the policy, depending on the age at which the policy was purchased. For younger insureds, it may take until the end of the third year before some policies will have any cash surrender value; whereas, with older insureds, cash surrender values commence earlier in the life of the policy, even by the end of the first year.

We now consider an insured, age 45, whose life insurance policy has a cash surrender value amounting to about $12,000. Desiring to invest this sum in specific equity securities, he asks what he can do to convert to a Save-by-Borrowing program—or is it too late for him?

Explaining that he desires to leave at least $50,000 to his wife, the face amount of his permanent life insurance policy, he asks what he can do to fulfill his objectives. If he surrendered his policy, took the $12,000 surrender value in cash, and then invested the money in equity securities (gradually, at least when market prices are high), he would be $38,000 short of his goal if he died right away. Also, unless he continued to save, his savings would not reach the $50,000 goal fast enough to satisfy him, assuming a rate of return less than spectacular. To avoid these problems he should follow these instructions:

FIRST: Do not surrender the policy; instead, borrow against 100% of the cash surrender value (in several stages, when prices for equities seem vulnerable). Immediately after each borrowing, invest the loan proceeds (in truth, your own money) in the equity securities.

SECOND: Maintain the policy by paying your premiums as they become due. Each year, as the cash surrender value increases, you borrow against such increase, investing the amount (the "difference") in the equities.

By this method of borrowing your own money (which, you should note, does not obligate you to repay) you obtain reducing term coverage. The amount of pure insurance in force (the difference between the cash surrender value—as if no borrowings have occurred —and the face amount of the policy) would not be reduced by the initial and annual borrowings so much as 1 cent. And you would obtain reducing term protection beyond the age of 65, the age by which many companies terminate their term insurance coverage. Also, you will be taking advantage of pure insurance coverage less expensive than a similar term insurance policy. *"Minimum deposit"* insurance is based on this approach.

To borrow your own money you will be required to pay interest, usually 5% or 6% per annum, true annual interest. Consult your policy for the interest rate and the maximum amount of the loan. Ordinarily, the loan on older policies will be at 6% interest, but newer policies have included a more favorable rate—5% interest per year on the outstanding balance of the loan. For many persons, this interest will be a tax deduction (if interest payments are made in cash), even though there is in effect a *tax-free build-up* partially offsetting the interest payments. (Be careful, though, about relying on the availability of the tax deduction. The tax law is getting tough in this area, denying the deduction in certain situations. For policies purchased after August 6, 1963, systematic borrowing of increases in cash values to pay the insurance premiums will cause disallowance of a tax deduction for the interest payments on the indebtedness, with certain exceptions.)

This tax-free build-up is the guaranteed interest rate of 3% (we assume) which continues to be paid on the legal reserve of your policy, even though you have borrowed against its cash surrender value. As the legal reserve increases, so will the cash value, only to be withdrawn again when the next annual borrowing takes place. Nor does borrowing diminish the rate of dividends, if any, payable on a policy.

Taxpayers in higher income tax brackets can derive a profit by converting their permanent insurance program into a Save-by-Borrowing program. This occurs when, as to the borrowed sums, the annual cost of interest, after taking a tax deduction, is less than the annual addition to policy reserves, hence cash value (which we assume goes tax-free). *Caution:* Before borrowing against your policy *for tax reasons,* seek competent professional advice. You may avoid great disappointment.

Another factor to be concerned with is the ever-increasing amount of interest you will be obliged to pay, in order to keep the pure insurance element of your policy in force. On paper the offsetting 3% reserve addition and the presumably favorable tax status look fine, but in actual practice will you be able to get up the cash when the interest payments are due? A negative answer would mean termination of your insurance coverage (which is steadily declining anyway), there being no cash surrender value to fall back on.

If the equity investor decides that he should switch back to his original insurance investment, he could sell his equities and pay off his policy loans to the desired extent. But if he could invest the borrowed funds to produce a return substantially higher than 3% —say 10% to 12%—why would he want to switch back? The 2% net cost of borrowing his own money would be comparatively insignificant.

An insured under a new permanent policy, one having little or no cash surrender value yet, may decide—after thorough consideration of taxes and comparable costs—to surrender the policy or let it lapse. Before doing this, however, he would obtain a renewable or decreasing term policy. Then he could invest the difference in premiums plus any other available sums through utilization of the Save-by-Borrowing technique. He would not convert to a Save-by-Borrowing program in this manner if he believed there were any reasonable possibility that the insurance company would succeed if it were to contest, on the ground of misrepresentation or fraud, its liability for payment in the event of his death. After one or two years, depending on the policy, payment would be incontestable.

This has not been a complete discussion of life insurance but a basic explanation of the difference between permanent and temporary insurance. Temporary insurance is *pure* insurance, any reserves being small and of temporary duration only, to pay the slightly higher cost of the reducing coverage in later years. On the other hand, all permanent insurance is temporary insurance *plus* a "bank account," used to pay some or all of the face amount of the policy, in the event of the insured's death. When the bank account equals the face amount of the policy, the "permanent" insurance becomes nonexistent.

Suitability of permanent insurance may be found for individuals desiring another bank account. For other reasons, too, permanent insurance can be useful. Persons in *high* income tax brackets can obtain the equivalent of, say, a 9% return *before taxes,* when compared with a program of buying term and investing the difference. (Brokerage commissions and the higher cost per thousand dollars of insurance, for the person investing the difference, are taken into account.) Yet, when you look at the *net* (assumedly after-tax) return, it still amounts to only 3%. As a rough guess, it would require a *net* return of 3½% to 4% on the invested "difference" to produce an accumulation equal to the cash value after taxes of an ordinary life policy. The higher cost of term is offset, therefore, by a slightly higher net return.

Save-by-Borrowers may see some usefulness in having an underlying base of permanent insurance (say $5,000 or $10,000 coverage) as a means of avoiding delays of will probate or estate administration. Such permanent insurance would be particularly valuable for one's later years, especially after age 65. Within a few days after the insured's death, the policy beneficiary will receive the insurance proceeds, to assure continued support during the delay and provide for burial expenses. With forethought and preparation, however, the insured could see to it that adequate cash would be available to his dependents, to tide them over during the delay. In later years, when his insurance was running out, he could establish for each dependent an emergency bank account.

Readers, after giving consideration to the merits of permanent insurance, may wish to invest their savings in equity securities. They will insist therefore upon renewable or decreasing term insurance, to cover the contingency of premature death, prior to the completion of their accumulation objective.

The whole issue of (1) buying term and investing the difference, or (2) buying permanent insurance, relates to our prior discussion of fixed-dollar versus equity investments. You must determine for yourself whether it would be worthwhile for you to invest in equities and, if so, to what extent.

Even if you choose not to invest in equities, you can still buy term and invest the difference more profitably in certain fixed-dollar obligations than by investing your savings in permanent insurance; this is especially true for persons in lower income tax brackets.

What is more important, you would not be "locked in," unlike the purchaser of permanent life insurance, who must wait as long as twenty years (in some cases) before the full reserve of his policy is made available to him as savings.

Admittedly, a life insurance savings program has certain minimal effectiveness—it forces some people to save. But have these persons tried the Save-by-Borrowing technique?

"Buying term and investing the difference," especially by the Save-by-Borrowing method, has certain advantages:

- The average rate of return from equity investments will take many persons to the 10th Multiple by the end of their long-range savings and investment programs—life insurance cannot.
- Investing the difference the Save-by-Borrowing way avoids the high cost of saving—life insurance does not, at least during the years the cash value is less than the legal reserve for the policy.
- Save-by-Borrowing has the law as an enforcer of regular saving —life insurance does not.

MAKING YOUR BROKER LIKE YOU

Non-completion of the savings and investment program may result from lack of necessary life insurance. It can occur also from accident or illness, causing a loss of income and, possibly, a severe drain upon accumulated savings, unless other insurance is carried in addition to life insurance.

It would be advisable, therefore, for you to talk over with Bobby Broker (and usually he really is a nice fellow) your need for "waiver of premium" waiving the insurance premium in the event of your disability; and your need for "disability income" to support you and allow continuation of your Save-by-Borrowing program, in the event of an extended period of absence from employment caused by the disability.

Medical expenses of the ordinary type can be covered by programs such as Blue Cross (covering certain hospital expenses) and Blue Shield (covering certain doctors' bills). This may not be sufficient, however. If catastrophe strikes, you would be protected only if you had major medical insurance. Preferably, an individual should have a comprehensive major medical insurance policy, usually issued to a group of insureds, which affords perhaps the greatest amount of protection (outside of socialized medicine) against losses resulting from the high cost of adequate medical attention.

By bringing these additional profit possibilities to the attention of your insurance broker, he will be more kindly disposed to you—perhaps even come to like you.

Finally, we arrive at the last chapter, required reading before starting out on our course. Let us see what order can be made out of this far-reaching Save-by-Borrowing concept.

Chapter Twelve

LOOKING BACKWARD AND FORWARD

SAVE-BY-BORROWING AND INTEGRATION

To plan a sound program of saving and investment, an individual must consider and choose intelligently from many alternatives. For example, he must ask himself about life insurance. What kind? How much coverage? Also, what part, if any, of his capital should be invested in equity securities? If he selects real estate for any part, should his investments be made by direct ownership, or by purchase of syndicate shares? He may desire stocks instead. If so, should he buy them directly, or indirectly, by purchase of mutual fund shares? If mutual funds, should he buy into load or no-load funds?

These are only a few of the questions. You should be or become equipped to supply the answers to these questions and others. You can achieve an effective accumulation program only if you have a fundamental knowledge of the possible alternatives.

Throughout this book there has been a discussion of basic alternatives, the author hoping that he has not eliminated too much, or dwelled upon fundamentals too long. With so much discussion of the several component parts, however, the reader may be unable to relate the basics to the over-all purpose of this book: to point out how an individual can force himself to save—by borrowing—and how he can avoid payment of unnecessary sales and brokerage commissions, with success being measured in terms of the 10th Multiple.

To develop the whole Save-by-Borrowing concept completely and clearly, it has been necessary to present its parts in depth but in isolation. Now, though, let's devote this final chapter to an integration of the preceding chapters, staying away as much as possible from a mere restatement of what has gone before.

A fighting chance to reach the 10th Multiple requires protection of investment capital, economies in investment, effective compounding, and additional profits whenever available. But this is not enough.

Save-by-Borrowers must put their savings in equity investments. Nothing else will do the job. Equities are desirable as a hedge against inevitable inflation, to prevent the gradual loss in purchasing power of the dollar resulting from the inflationary policies of our country. There is perhaps no other practicable means available for protection of savings against this destructive force. Going further, however, than protection of capital, the Save-by-Borrowing method of periodic saving and investment over the course of many years should produce substantial wealth for the faithful.

It is true that even sound stock investments may for some months or years show nothing but losses, especially for the person who made his stock purchases at the peak of prices. To make matters worse, he may retain his fundamentally sound investments during a decline, only to sell them when prices reach all-time lows. He fails to recall the past, when stock prices have, on the average, always recovered from their lows and have gone on to new highs.

Dollar-cost averaging, if understood by an investor, should indicate to him the long-run desirability of retaining sound investments, even during a decline. Not only should he keep his sound investments, he should continue his periodic purchase program, picking up additional stocks at "bargain" prices. Dollar-cost averaging, to be successful, requires periodic investment in equal dollar amounts, *no matter what price level*.

For those who practice Save-by-Borrowing, the goal of the 10th Multiple cannot be guaranteed—not by a long shot. But the point is, it is quite *possible* for it to be realized, as many investors in equity securities can testify. Some persons who have the capacity to reach the 10th Multiple are not as fortunate, however. Ineffectual savings and investment plans plague them when what they should do, to give themselves a chance, is undertake a Save-by-Borrowing program.

The program this book outlines and explains has numerous advantages, not the least of which is that it absolutely forces you to save, more so than any other practical method of saving. One could join the Peace Corps, of course, and in essence be forced to set aside a certain number of dollars each month. This would be an example, however, of an impractical way to force himself to save. Join the Peace Corps out of patriotism, for adventure, to learn a foreign language, or for any other motive you desire, but not to save. The cost in these and in too many other circumstances would be high, the years irreplaceable.

Forced saving is the only way for many if not most people to accumulate capital. There are many mandatory methods, but doesn't it seem that the *best* is establishing a Save-by-Borrowing program? There are many sound reasons why the program should be immensely successful, beyond the immediate advantage of mandatory saving.

DOLLAR COMPARISON OF THREE ALTERNATIVE PROGRAMS

Followers of the technique are able to avoid the high cost of saving, a cost usually not discernible to the average investor. He merely follows the crowd, paying little attention to the well-being of his personal finances. Because others before him have done what he is doing, how can he go wrong? What fallacious thinking! Little does the average investor know about the poor traps set for him. Less yet does he know about the simple ways to avoid them.

The high cost of saving and investment has been pointed out and means of avoidance have been thoroughly analyzed. To estimate the cost, we assumed that an individual saves $1,000 each year and invests this amount in stocks producing an average annual return of 12%, after taxes, compounded annually. At the end of 35 years, he would have an investment fund valued at about $431,700.

These calculations, based upon annual compounding, assume that dividends paid during a year will be reinvested in a lump sum at the *end* of the year.

Also, we have supposed that, during the twelve months of repayment of a $1,000 loan, no return will be earned on the $1,000. (The 35-year calculation presumed that each $1,000 was added to the investment fund at the *end* of the borrowing year.) Thus, any "profits" during the borrowing year (the "first-year profits") are in excess of $431,700, the accumulation value. In addition, all other profits should be added to this 35-year accumulation value.

We have made a further assumption—that 100% of the $1,000 in annual savings is invested in stocks *without deduction* for brokerage commissions or odd-lot differential. Therefore, to the extent these costs are reduced or eliminated, there will be "savings." These savings do not increase the 35-year accumulation value, but would cause a loss to the $431,700 accumulation value to the extent they were *not* achieved by the Save-by-Borrower.

Based on these assumptions, we can compare the Save-by-Borrowing technique with the alternatives of

1. The Monthly Investment Plan; and
2. Regular deposit of savings in a savings account until the year's end (a "year-end" purchase program), when the $1,000 of accumulated savings for the year (with interest of $13 net, after taxes) would be withdrawn to purchase the same stocks purchased one year earlier by the Save-by-Borrower, and monthly throughout the past year by the monthly investor.

As you will see, the Save-by-Borrower participates in *all* the savings and profits. But how do utilizers of the alternative methods of saving and investment fare?

COMPARISON OF $1,000 ANNUAL SAVE-BY-BORROWING PROGRAM (SBB) WITH THE MONTHLY INVESTMENT PLAN (MIP) AND A YEAR'S END PURCHASE PROGRAM (YEPP), ASSUMING A 12% ANNUAL RETURN, AFTER TAXES, COMPOUNDED ANNUALLY

Description of Savings and Profits	Saving or Profit		Total Value of Saving or Profit at End of 35 Years		
	S	P	For SBB	For MIP	For YEPP
$60 of first-year return (12% of $500 average) for SBB and MIP, resulting from the immediate investment of savings:					
1. $13 annual interest on savings account earned by year-end investor		P	$5,600	$5,600	$5,600

2. $20 annual payment of commissions on two-stock purchase	S	8,600	8,600	–
3. $5 annual odd-lot differential on two-stock purchase	S	2,200	2,200	–
4. $22 remaining first-year profit	P	9,500	9,500	–
$60 of remaining first-year return, for SBB, attributable to anticipatory investment of savings:				
5. $40 net annual interest payment on Save-by-Borrowing loan, which forces the borrower to save	S	?	–	–
6. $20 annual anticipatory investment profit	P	8,600	–	–
The high cost of purchasing stocks under MIP:				
7. $40 annual saving on commissions to invest $1,000, as compared with MIP	S	17,300	–	17,300
8. $\frac{1}{8}$% loss in return for MIP, due to 6% commission to reinvest dividends, in comparison to 1% paid by SBB and YEPP	S	10,000	–	10,000
Reinvestment profits:				
9. $\frac{17}{100}$% loss in return due to delays in reinvestment of dividends—avoidance of	P	15,300	15,300	–
10. $\frac{1}{8}$% increase in return, the anticipatory reinvestment profit	P	11,000	–	–
		$88,100	$41,200	$32,900

The preceding comparison is made from a SBB perspective. Thus, Items 1–4 under DESCRIPTION OF SAVINGS AND PROFITS allocate the same dollar values to MIP as to SBB, even though MIP's full $60 of return actually would be used to pay investment commissions, from an accounting point of view. The correcting adjustment is found in

Item 7, which charges MIP with the long-run value of the $40 difference in investment commissions.

Savings for the Save-by-Borrower will amount to the full $38,100, necessitating *no* deduction from the $431,700 accumulation value. The monthly investor achieved only a $10,800 saving; accordingly, he should deduct $27,300 ($38,100 minus $10,800). The year-end investor, having achieved savings amounting to $27,300, should deduct only $10,800 from the 35-year accumulation value ($38,100 minus $27,300).

To the $431,700, the Save-by-Borrower should add his *profits,* aggregating $50,000. The monthly investor, in comparison, should add $30,400; and the year-end investor should add $5,600.

Comparing the respective combined saving and profit values, we find that the Save-by-Borrower has a $46,900 advantage over the monthly investor, and a $55,200 advantage over the year-end investor.

To the foregoing profits for SBB, MIP, and YEPP should be added

1. the $21,600 dollar-cost averaging profit (calculated by an assumed 5% of the $431,700 accumulation value, or about a $\frac{1}{4}$% addition to the net rate of return); and

2. the $13,700 profit attributable to the dividend-exclusion loophole ($40 per year for about 33 years).

These profits are enjoyed by the followers of any of the three investment programs.

For the Save-by-Borrower, therefore, there is a total profit of $85,300, which affords him a soft cushion of about 20% of the $431,-700 accumulation value, increasing it to $517,000.

Looking at this from another angle, we see that there is a cushion of almost $\frac{4}{5}$% net return, increasing the over-all rate to about $12\frac{4}{5}$% net, after taxes.

The computations made above do assume a 12% annual compound return, after taxes, which may or may not be realized, on the average. Nobody knows what will happen. Although this return has been realized during the 14-year period ranging from 1951 to 1964, inclusive, it cannot be guaranteed or even predicted to continue. But the past return does give an indication of the trend—one can therefore expect a *high* rate of return.

A particular investor may do better or worse than the average, depending on his skill, in part, and other circumstances, such as good fortune and the quality of investment advice. But to the extent the investor takes the trouble to learn about and oversee his investments, he should be able to maintain the 12% net return—or a higher return. An individual investor does have the opportunity to seek out and invest in good companies, thereby being able to realize a high return. Thus, it is believed, use of the 12% return is justified, not necessarily as an average, but at least as a possibility for many investors.

Save-by-Borrowers will derive higher profits, on the average, than the persons following a monthly or year-end purchase program involving the same stocks and equal aggregate dollar amounts. This assumes that the average return is 5.3% or 6.3% after taxes—at least sufficient to cover the $40 net (or $50 pre-tax) cost of interest and $13 net loss of savings bank interest. Therefore, Save-by-Borrowers have a greater opportunity to reach the 10th Multiple. And the mandatory-savings feature of his program will take him to the goal, assuming his capacity to save and a sufficient life expectancy.

WHY BORROW?

When reflecting upon the Save-by-Borrowing method, the reader should bear in mind that the program involves no risk for the sake of speculation. Annual borrowing of $1,000 is done only to facilitate the saving and investment process. Although the anticipatory investment profit of $8,600 is welcome, it is not the reason for borrowing. Instead, *we borrow to obtain a forced-saving feature to our savings program, to obtain the effect of immediate investment of savings, and to reduce substantially the high cost of commissions.*

The reinvestment process, involving the purchase of stocks on margin, is non-speculative also. Borrowing will ordinarily be limited to about 3% to 5%, and will seldom exceed 6% or 7%, of the value of the investment fund. The risk is very slight in comparison to the probable rewards. Borrowing reduces the cost of reinvestment commissions to 1% and prevents costly delays in reinvestment. The anticipatory reinvestment profit of $11,000, representing the speculative profit, is small, but pleasing nevertheless.

Neither of the two borrowing operations ($1,000 annual and margin) is analogous to the evil of widespread borrowing which helped to bring on the 1929 stock market crash. The $1,000 loan is unsecured; and the margin transaction involves only a small percentage of the investment fund, with virtually no chance of being sold out in the event of a major decline in stock market prices. Furthermore, both loans are to be paid off by the end of each year, unlike loans of the late 1920s, when investors pyramided their paper profits by ever increasing amounts of borrowing.

Although the cost of borrowing the $1,000 per year will be greater by use of an unsecured loan,[1] such loan is more apt to be repaid on schedule out of current earnings. The securities purchased with the borrowed $1,000 are not pledged with the bank and, therefore, are not subject to being sold out from under the borrower in the event of a temporary decline in market prices. Under a secured-loan agreement, the lender could be calling for more collateral when the investor is least able to respond. It is during a decline in prices that the investor should be buying more stocks, to keep alive his dollar-cost averaging program, unhampered by calls for margin. Another advantage to the unsecured loan is the flexibility which it affords. The investor is free to switch from one investment to another without creating a nuisance for the lending bank.

THREE PRELIMINARY STEPS

An investor who wishes to undertake a Save-by-Borrowing program should be prepared to take the following three steps:

FIRST: The prospective Save-by-Borrower should sit down—with his spouse, if applicable—and determine the amount of money to be kept in the emergency fund. A guide may be the amount of take-home pay for an average six-month period. This fund should be kept in fixed-dollar investments such as United States Savings Bonds; checking, savings bank, or savings and loan association accounts; and the cash surrender value of "permanent" life insurance policies.

Selection of the appropriate institution for deposit of the emergency fund depends on the relative importance of various factors. Choice could be made by the convenience to deposit or, perhaps, the inconvenience to withdraw. For the latter, banking by mail may afford the desired degree of removal from the temptation of invasion.

Investment returns are always a factor to be considered, although

---

[1] 9.2% true annual interest for the signature loan in comparison to about 6% for a secured loan.

the rate of return increases at the expense of safety and availability of savings. Availability and safety of the emergency fund should be of utmost concern, bearing in mind the purpose of the fund. Some portion of the fund should be ready for use at all times.

An investor should make sure that his account in a savings bank or savings and loan association is covered by federal or other insurance. United States Government Savings Bonds have the highest degree of safety. Life insurance savings, on the other hand, are ordinarily no safer than the financial position of the particular company and for this reason selection of a life insurance company should be made with great care.

Demand deposits are most readily available; the rate of return is, however, non-existent or quite low. An example is a checking account.

Savings on deposit with savings and loan associations or savings banks, or savings represented by the cash surrender value of "permanent" life insurance ordinarily can be obtained by request, but not as of right. At the option of the particular institution, payment of the savings may be withheld for varying periods. As a practical matter, this factor probably will be disregarded by the investor when he decides where to place his money.

By allocating the emergency fund among various financial institutions, higher rates of return can be earned on some portion of the fund and with the other part greater availability can be obtained. Diversification may be as useful here as it is in the field of equity investments. As an added advantage, there is no cost to obtain diversification, except slight inconvenience.

An investor could not go wrong if he kept at least one half of his emergency fund in one or more savings banks, in accounts insured by the Federal Deposit Insurance Corporation (FDIC). The remaining portion of the fund could be deposited in an insured savings and loan account or kept with a sound life insurance company, for example.

SECOND: The Save-by-Borrower must make adequate provision for insurance (non-participating in dividends).

He could obtain decreasing (that is, reducing) term insurance, covering the period ending at his retirement. If retirement is too far away, he could combine decreasing term coverage with a 5-year renewable term policy or, perhaps, an underlying base of "permanent" insurance.

Otherwise, the Save-by-Borrower should purchase a 5-year renewable term policy, perhaps coupling it with some permanent insurance. By renewal of the policy every five years and annual reduction of the coverage (in multiples of $1,000), as of each anniversary date for the policy, he obtains insurance coverage similar to decreasing term insurance and the pure insurance aspect of a permanent insurance policy.

The cost per thousand dollars of either type of term coverage will be slightly higher than the permanent insurance premium allocable to the pure insurance coverage. There are compensations, however, which more than pay the increased cost. The savings feature of permanent life insurance passes through the hands of a salesman, who during the first years of the policy pockets an amount equivalent to about 100% of the savings for one year. In later years, this commission will be restored to the cash value of the policy. With decreasing or renewable term insurance, the salesman obtains no portion of your savings.

A guide to the initial amount of term insurance could be the amount of permanent life insurance (for example, endowment at 65 or whole life) you would need and could afford, assuming no independent program of saving and investment. You may already have some term insurance where you work (called "group insurance"). There would be a problem, however, if you left your employment. Unless you could obtain sufficient insurance at your new employment, you would have to convert your group insurance to a permanent form of insurance or let it terminate altogether.

Save-by-Borrowers should seek advice from a professional in the field of life insurance, remembering to impress upon him the conviction that they cannot be talked out of their plan to buy term and invest the difference.

Savings banks in three states—Connecticut, Massachusetts, and New York—offer (participating) life insurance, at rates generally lower than the low, non-participating rates of stock insurance companies. If lower-cost insurance of the appropriate type can be obtained from a savings bank, it would obviously be advantageous to do so. A disadvantage, however, is the probable lack of adequate professional counseling. The savings bank life insurance salesman may not have the time, ability, or incentive to advise you appropriately, although this would not necessarily be true in all or even most situations.

When buying renewable term insurance, you must make sure that the policies are renewable at least up to age 65; and that the renewals are *guaranteed,* with no medical examination required.

Convertibility into a form of permanent insurance increases the cost, although it can be of advantage, particularly for persons buying decreasing term insurance. Undoubtedly, the insurance agent or salesman, almost always permanent-insurance-oriented, will try to sell you on paying the additional premium, if the company affords you any choice at all. Ask him what the difference in total annual cost would be—then determine for yourself if convertibility is worth it.

Any renewable or reducing term policy should contain a *waiver of premium* provision, to keep the policy in force during periods of disability; and you ordinarily should obtain *disability income insurance,* to provide support and possibly allow for continuation of the monthly Save-by-Borrowing payments to the lending institution during a disability, without invading your investment or emergency fund.

Health and accident insurance are also necessary to provide coverage for any extraordinary medical expenses that may arise, expenses that, if not covered, could wipe out the results of many years of an effective savings program.

THIRD: The difference between the cost of the renewable or decreasing term policy and the "permanent" life policy in the same face amount is now available for investment in equity securities. To this amount should be added other sums which the investor is able to set aside. We assume that a Save-by-Borrower determines that he can save and invest a total of $1,000 per year.

Having determined to save $1,000 per year, he should shop around for the most favorable rate of interest on an unsecured loan of $1,000. This should be the sum actually received by the borrower, if reasonably practicable. (Probably it would not be the face amount of the promissory note evidencing the loan.)

Borrowing, as a practical matter, is best accomplished at a local commercial or industrial bank. Mutual savings banks and savings and loan associations usually are not allowed to lend on an unsecured basis.

Upon receiving the loan, the loan proceeds should be deposited in the individual's checking account, to facilitate and obtain a receipt for payment.

Prior to borrowing, the investor must have taken stock of his financial temperament, abilities, free time, interest, knowledge, and other matters bearing on the selection of the proper investment medium.

In what type of investment do you intend to place your savings? Real estate? Stock? Mutual funds? The decision should be made before taking out the $1,000 loan, to avoid the high cost of uninvested assets. Especially this is true because the $1,000 will be borrowed at a true annual interest rate of approximately 9.2% per year.

Let us take several hypothetical situations, to see how the Save-by-Borrowing program should be employed.

REAL ESTATE

Real estate investment can be done by outright purchase of specific real property or by purchase of shares in a real estate trust or syndicate. A prospective investor in real estate should study books on real estate investment and syndication to acquire the technical know-how necessary to avoid investment disaster. With the appropriate know-how and ample free time, his chances for attaining the 10th Multiple would seem to be better than his opportunity through common stock or mutual fund investments.

In outright purchase of real property, the investor would probably borrow part of the purchase price in a loan secured by the real property to be purchased. Frequently the secured borrowing will range from 75% to 90% of the value of the real property. Thus, a $1,000 investment fund at the outset could be used to acquire property valued from $4,000 to $10,000. Additional money would be needed for repairs, taxes, insurance, etc., to the extent rentals are insufficient to cover these expenses, after making payments on the mortgage. After various improvements, the investor may decide to sell out, at a profit, he hopes. The investment opportunity in real estate would increase each year, upon borrowing the annual $1,000.

Purchase of syndicate or trust shares is possible, but loaded with tricks. Be careful. The syndicators or managers frequently take for themselves a substantial portion of the profits. Returns to the investors are much lower than outright real estate investment, but rightfully so, to some extent at least; the investor has no managerial responsibility for the investment.

In spite of the drawbacks, there are two highly favorable factors to this method of real estate investment: the opportunity afforded for making relatively small investments in real estate, and certain tax advantages.

MUTUAL FUNDS

If you are interested in investing your savings in mutual funds, you should write to various no-load funds (and load funds, if still not convinced), requesting a prospectus and other sales literature. Within several days the mutual funds should respond to your request. The names and addresses of most if not all no-load funds (except those for foreign investments) currently offering to sell their shares to the public are listed in Appendix A. After comparison of the funds, on the bases discussed previously, a selection of, say, two or three funds could be made.

For Save-by-Borrowers growth (or, perhaps, income and growth) common stock funds would seem to be suitable. A review of each fund's portfolio of stocks would be in order to ensure the requisite degree of diversification. Then, to select the best two or three funds, you should look to past performance; percentage of unrealized appreciation; ratio of operating expenses (including management fees) to net asset value; management fees; and special services. Also, seek advice from friends knowledgeable about the investment business. The better funds should be well known to many members and friends of the brokerage fraternity.

After deciding which no-load mutual fund shares to buy, fill out the subscription application (ordinarily accompanying or contained in the prospectus), then mail it to the fund together with your check. All of the money will be invested for your benefit, except in a few instances. Occasionally, there will be a minimal issuance fee, of 1% or so; or a similar redemption fee. These fees, when kept by the fund, may be a more equitable method of having each mutual fund investor pay the brokerage cost allocable to his own investment.

By the end of the year, the $1,000 bank loan will be repaid, and the saving for the year will have been completed. No margin transaction is needed to effect automatic reinvestment. No-cost, automatic reinvestment of no-load distributions will be available ordinarily. All you need do is give appropriate instructions to the fund.

If a Reform Mutual Fund ever becomes available, investors will be able to avoid the annoying and recurrent task of selecting the best-performing mutual funds. Shares in a Reform Fund could be bought on the basis of the fund's stated investment policy instead of past performance, which is so difficult to ascertain and compare.

Until a Reform Fund is available, however, a mutual fund investor would do well to diversify, by purchasing $500 worth of shares in each of two funds; or, perhaps, $333⅓ worth of shares in each of three funds, assuming the funds selected would permit initial subscriptions in such minimum amount.

You may have been wondering about the net cost of investing in mutual funds. The chart below shows the difference in investment

DIFFERENCE IN INVESTMENT RESULTS BETWEEN AVERAGE COMMON STOCK AND AVERAGE MUTUAL FUND INVESTMENT

Assumes $1,000 Annual Investment During 35-Year Period and 1% Reduction from Net Rate of Return, after Taxes

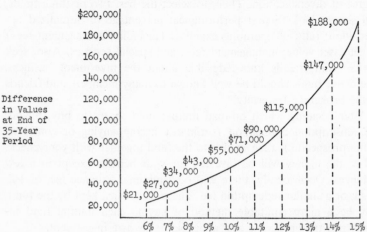

Net Annual Rate of Return, After Taxes, for Direct Common Stock Ownership (1% higher than rate of return for comparable mutual fund investment)

results between the alternatives of outright common stock ownership and indirect ownership by purchase of mutual fund shares. We assume that all relevant factors are equal except a 1% net difference in annual compound rate of return, after taxes. This difference of 1% is attributable to the management fee and other expenses of operating a mutual fund.

For load funds, the difference in results would necessarily be greater, on the average.

So, in making up your mind whether you wish to purchase the convenience of mutual fund investment (applying equally to load, no-load, and proposed Reform mutual funds), consider the costs.

A 1% difference in rate of return, after taxes, represents a substantial amount of money, bearing in mind that the 1% comes off the top of your investment return. The chart points out how important the 1% loss can be when the relative rates of return are high. As the return for an average common stock investment increases from the representative range of 6% to 15%, compounded annually, after taxes, the cost to an investor goes from $21,000 to $188,000 over the course of his 35-year program of $1,000 annual saving and investment.

For those seeking the 10th Multiple, this difference may mean non-completion of their programs. The convenience of mutual fund investment does not seem worth the high cost. But the investor will be unable to avoid it if he feels forced to purchase mutual fund shares to obtain his requisite degree of diversity. One salvation would be to invest in a mutual fund which is bound to do better than average. But just try to find such a fund.

COMMON STOCKS

To invest in common stocks by outright purchase, select a competent broker, then open up a margin account with him. To automatically reinvest dividends, you *must* purchase stocks on margin. The initial margin requirement of $2,000 can be met by the deposit of stocks (whether listed or not) valued at no less than $2,000. Some Save-by-Borrowers will not be able to meet the requirement at the outset of their programs.

Forms will have to be filled out, but this is far from a difficult task. One form will be a consent, required in conjunction with the opening of the margin account, for the broker to pledge your securities. The broker who is to lend you money may have to borrow some himself, putting up your stocks as collateral to secure the loan. This margin transaction, as stated previously, is safe, being used to secure repayment of an amount of money insubstantial in comparison to the over-all value of the investment fund.

As a new account holder, you should discuss your investment objectives with your broker. Particularly, you should ask the broker what two or three stocks look particularly promising, in light of your investment objectives. Before committing yourself to purchase any of the suggested stocks, you may wish to seek independent advice about the soundness of the proposed purchases, just to make sure you are not being led too far astray.

The Save-by-Borrower may decide to purchase two stocks with his $1,000, making a $500 investment in each stock. Brokerage commissions would amount to about 2%, exclusive of the odd-lot differential.

For persons borrowing only $500 per year, let us say, Save-by-Borrowing possibilities are diminished if they split their $500 into two stock purchases. A major purpose of the Save-by-Borrowing program is to avoid payment of the 6% commission applicable to small monthly stock investments. For small investors, there is a choice of less diversification or reduced savings on brokerage commissions.

Once the Save-by-Borrower has made all the preliminary arrangements, by opening his margin account and tentatively selecting his two stocks, he should arrange for a bank loan. A person unsure about obtaining a loan may avoid embarrassing moments by not opening his margin account until he has obtained the bank loan.

Now the moment of truth arrives. The investor communicates with his broker, instructing him to buy the proper stocks in the correct quantities. For example, you decide to invest your $1,000 in two stocks valued at $30 and $60 per share. To the $1,000 should be added the amount equivalent to the dividends expected to be received from the two stock holdings during the next twelve months. Your broker will advise you, at your request, as to the anticipated dividends for each stock. Otherwise, you could determine the amount for yourself by reference to the stock market tables in most of the leading daily newspapers.

Let us say you anticipate receiving a 3% return from one stock and 4% from the other, averaging 3.5% on an assumed $1,000 investment.[2] This would mean a $35 additional stock purchase, plus another dollar representing the anticipated dividends on the $35 purchase, for a total purchase of $36 above the $1,000. Actually, the market value of the stock has to be less, to cover brokerage costs. These costs are added to the market value of the purchased stock to arrive at the target amount of $1,036.

Now we determine the number of shares of each stock which can be purchased with $500 or so and conclude that 15 shares of the $30 stock ($540) and 8 shares of the $60 stock ($480) should be purchased. Total market value of the two stock purchases would be $1,020, leaving $16 or so to defray brokerage expenses.

We find that commissions and odd-lot differential costs would amount to $24.49, as follows:

18 Shares of the $30 Stock ($540)

18 × $.125, odd-lot differential	$ 2.25	
$5 fixed fee	5.00	
1% of $542.25 odd-lot price	5.42	
	$12.67	$12.67

8 Shares of the $60 Stock ($480)

8 × $.25, odd-lot differential	$ 2.00	
$5 fixed fee	5.00	
1% of $482.00 odd-lot price	4.82	
	$11.82	11.82
		$24.49

We see, therefore, that our brokerage expense will exceed our $16 of unexpended money by $8.49, but not enough to suggest purchase of one less share of either stock. So, we must add $8.49 to the $36 to be borrowed from the broker, to make $44.49 the total amount to be borrowed from him, by a margin purchase of stock.

[2] Income taxes on the dividends will pose no real problem for many years. The investor will probably pay the expense out of his earnings. Thereafter, he may have to make appropriate adjustments to provide for the income tax liability.

As the dividends aggregating $36 are paid to your broker, your account with him will be credited and the loan reduced. (This assumes your broker is willing to go along with your program—some brokers may not be willing, because of reduced brokerage commissions and increased administrative costs.) He receives the dividends either by reason of a *dividend order* to the dividend-disbursing agent of each dividend-paying corporation or by holding your stock certificates in street name. By the end of the twelve-month period, the loan will be reduced to about $8.49, an amount which should be deducted from anticipated dividends when calculating the appropriate amount of margin purchase for the next Save-by-Borrowing year.

By borrowing from your stockbroker, you will be able to reinvest at a cost of only 1%, avoiding the 6% cost of reinvestment normally paid by small investors under the Monthly Investment Plan of the New York Stock Exchange. (This excludes in each case the odd-lot differential, which must be paid under either method of purchase.) At the same time, you will obtain immediate reinvestment, to avoid the high cost of reinvestment delays. The advantage of this margin purchase will be of tremendous importance in a long-run saving and investment program. It is the only way to minimize or eliminate the inefficiencies in a small investor's program.

By the start of year two, you will have paid off your first Save-by-Borrowing loan from the bank and the margin loan from your broker (except for the minimal amount of $8.49). Now you should repeat the Save-by-Borrowing process.

Take out another $1,000 loan. By now, your credit rating should be excellent. Then, determine which two stocks you want to buy, probably new stocks, to achieve progressive diversification. Temporarily allocate the $1,000 on a roughly comparable basis between the stocks to be purchased; calculate the anticipated dividends from all stock holdings (including last year's purchases and the stocks to be purchased this year); then add the total anticipated dividends to the $1,000 of borrowed money; deduct anticipated brokerage expenses; deduct the $8.49 margin loan still outstanding; apportion the available amount between the two new stocks on an approximately equal basis; finally, place your stock-purchase order with your broker.

This is the Save-by-Borrowing process as applied to the outright purchase of stocks. The advantages include diversification (to a limited extent), dollar-cost averaging, brokerage commission savings, additional profits resulting from the borrowing operations, immediate reinvestment at 1% cost, and a higher rate of return, on the average, than a comparable investment in a common stock mutual fund.

LIFE INSURANCE CONVERSION PROGRAM

Save-by-Borrowers should be concerned not only with future savings but with effective employment of past savings. Obviously, fixed-dollar investments in bank accounts and government bonds are available for investment in equity securities, to the extent they are not part of the emergency fund. Less obvious are the savings found in cash surrender values of "permanent" life insurance policies.

At the outset the reader should be warned that lump-sum investment in equities when market prices are high could be disastrous and should be avoided. Instead, a program of gradual conversion could be employed.

The holder of a "permanent" life insurance policy could gradually convert any cash surrender value, by borrowing $1,000, let us say, from the insurance company each year, to invest in equities. This borrowing would be *in addition* to the annual $1,000 unsecured loan from the bank. The cost of borrowing his own money from the insurance company may approximate 1% or 2% per year, after taking into account the reserve build-up, which continues as if no borrowing occurred. The loan will not have to be repaid, and the borrower ordinarily may not want it to be repaid (unless, possibly, he follows a form of cyclical investment).

To the extent the borrowing is secured by cash surrender values built up by premium payments of prior years, the borrowed money does not represent savings out of current income; instead, he is converting *prior* savings from fixed-dollar to equity investments. (Even a portion of a current increase in cash value relates back to prior years, to enable the cash value to catch up to the reserve for the policy.) But borrowing against the annual increase in cash value and investing the proceeds in equity securities amounts to a program of "buying term and investing the difference."

Policies taken out only recently may have little or no cash surrender value, and, on the basis of tax brackets, and comparative costs and returns (which are exceedingly difficult to ascertain), it may be advisable to take out reducing or renewable term insurance and, thereafter, surrender the old, permanent policy or let it lapse. (During the first one or two years, however, the company could deny its liability under the term policy if fraud or misrepresentation were involved—such as non-disclosure of a heart attack—under a one- or two-year *"incontestable clause."*)

When dealing with your life insurance agent, be forewarned that he will not necessarily be happy with your decision to convert to the less expensive, renewable or decreasing term insurance. This will be so especially if he has *not* received a substantial part of his sales commission on the "permanent" insurance policy. On the other hand, a bright spot could come into his life if he were able to realize a greater profit by inducing you to surrender your old policy and take out a new policy, even though it be term only. He would have to protect himself, however, to avoid charges of twisting. ("Twisting" is the term applied to a senseless, costly change from one life policy to another.)

Whether borrowing against the cash surrender value or changing to term insurance is less expensive depends on the circumstances. First let the agent offer you his opinion. Then, obtain competent, unbiased advice from somebody else, to see if the agent's recommendation is sound. Remember, borrowing against life insurance may generate a tax-saving deduction for interest paid, depending on the circumstances. For some people this may be the deciding factor.

In any event, when you have life insurance problems, you must rely to a great extent on the superior knowledge of your agent. But you can always review his advice, particularly when he tells you about the absolute necessity of having liquidity in your estate upon your demise. A lawyer—perhaps with the aid of a personal trust officer in a bank—will be able to discuss your needs and work together with the life insurance agent to plan an effective program for the devolution of your property and support of your dependents, without loss of Save-by-Borrowing benefits.

ON YOUR WAY

Before starting your Save-by-Borrowing program, you should assure yourself that fears arising as a result of the 1929 crash are no longer justified. We have a new order of society, in which the federal government has assumed command of virtually all important aspects of the nation's well-being. Another 1929 crash seems highly improbable, although temporary declines will occur, such as in 1955, when President Eisenhower suffered a heart attack; and in 1962, when President Kennedy clashed with the steel industry. The market has always rebounded more quickly since the new order took firm hold.

For the investor who has adequate reserves and can maintain his program of dollar-cost averaging, the rewards for adopting a Save-by-Borrowing program should be the 10th Multiple, given a reasonable life span. All he must do is buy and hold onto fundamentally sound, diversified stocks or invest soundly in other equities.

Although particular stocks and mutual funds have been mentioned by name, no conclusion should be reached that any recommendation is being made to purchase (or not to purchase) the securities of such companies, or to purchase any securities for that matter. These investments may or may not be suitable for a particular Save-by-Borrower and, in many instances, will be less suitable than others not named. You must make your own investment decisions, after a thorough investigation of the facts.

Save-by-Borrowing is flexible enough to permit you to make your own investment decisions, provided they are reasonable. There are many good investment opportunities, even when the over-all market is retreating from a new high, unable to sustain a rapid rate of growth. Yet, who is to say that new services and products, and planned obsolescence will not help to push the market to newer highs, thus maintaining the high growth rate? Also, ever growing pension trust funds, institutional investors, and mutual funds can be expected to continue buying blue-chip and other stocks, making the market prices go higher and higher.

The truth is that we do not know where the market is going. But in playing the lifetime guessing game, which way are you inclined to go? A wrong answer either way will result in losses. If you believe the economy will expand in the long run, you would be backing your belief by adoption of the Save-by-Borrowing program. You would be forcing yourself to save and permitting yourself to avoid the high cost of saving. The goal is financial independence, known to Save-by-Borrowers as the 10th Multiple.

Acknowledgments

I express great appreciation to Philip H. Horwitz, for his valuable time and effort reviewing most of the manuscript and rendering constructive criticism. Also, I acknowledge with gratitude the contributions of John D. D'Amico, George L. Kelley, and Lewis B. Stone for reading various parts of the manuscript and offering worthwhile suggestions. Because I alone had the final word on what was to be included, the ideas and facts to the extent controversial or erroneous are my sole responsibility.

C.E.P.

APPENDIXES

Appendix A

47 NO-LOAD MUTUAL FUNDS

Leon B. Allen Fund, Inc.
120 Broadway
New York, New York 10005

American Enterprise Fund, Inc.
26 Broadway
New York, New York 10004

American Investors Fund, Inc.
1841 Palmer Avenue
Larchmont, New York 10538

American Pacific Fund, Inc.
American Pacific Life Building
Kalakaua at King
Honolulu, Hawaii

Beacon Hill Mutual Fund, Inc.
80 Federal Street
Boston, Massachusetts 02110

Bridges Investment Fund, Inc.
259 Swanson Building
8401 West Dodge Road
Omaha, Nebraska 68114

Concord Fund
630 Third Avenue
New York, New York 10017

Connecticut Western Mutual Fund, Inc.
1 Atlantic Street
Stamford, Connecticut 06901

Consultant's Mutual Investments, Inc.
211 South Broad Street
Philadelphia, Pennsylvania 19107

Counselors Investment Fund, Inc.
606 South Hill Street
Los Angeles, California 90014

de Vegh Mutual Fund, Inc.
20 Exchange Place
New York, New York 10005

Dodge & Cox Balanced Fund
Mills Tower
San Francisco, California 94104

Dodge & Cox Stock Fund
Mills Tower
San Francisco, California 94104

Drexel Equity Fund, Inc.
1500 Walnut Street
Philadelphia, Pennsylvania 19101

Energy Fund Incorporated
2 Broadway
New York, New York 10004

Fairfield Securities, Inc.
250 Park Avenue
New York, New York 10017

First National Mutual Fund, Inc.
110 Sutter Street
San Francisco, California 94104

General Securities, Inc.
133 South Seventh Street
Minneapolis, Minnesota 55402

Guardian Mutual Fund, Inc.
120 Broadway
New York, New York 10005

The Johnston Mutual Fund, Inc.
230 Park Avenue
New York, New York 10017

Loomis-Sayles Capital Development Fund, Inc.
140 Federal Street
Boston, Massachusetts 02110

Loomis-Sayles Mutual Fund, Incorporated
140 Federal Street
Boston, Massachusetts 02110

Mairs & Power Growth Fund, Inc.
W. 2062 First National Bank Building
St. Paul, Minnesota 55101

Mutual Shares Corporation
200 E. 42nd Street
New York, New York 10017

The Nassau Fund
1 Palmer Square
Princeton, New Jersey 08540

National Industries Fund, Inc.
1800 Avenue of the Stars
Los Angeles, California 90067

Nelson Fund, Inc.
37 Wall Street
New York, New York 10005

Newton Fund, Inc.
330 East Mason Street
Milwaukee, Wisconsin 53202

Northeast Investors Trust
50 Congress Street
Boston, Massachusetts 02109

The One William Street Fund, Inc.
1 William Street
New York, New York 10004

Paramount Mutual Fund, Inc.
404 North Roxbury Drive
Beverly Hills, California

Penn Square Mutual Fund
451 Penn Square
Reading, Pennsylvania 19601

Pennsylvania Mutual Fund, Inc.
40 Wall Street
New York, New York 10005

Pine Street Fund, Inc.
20 Exchange Place
New York, New York 10005

The Prudential Fund of Boston, Inc.
50 Congress Street
Boston, Massachusetts 02109

The Regency Fund, Inc.
350 Fifth Avenue
New York, New York 10001

Rittenhouse Fund
2 Penn Center Plaza
Philadelphia, Pennsylvania 19102

T. Rowe Price Growth Stock Fund, Inc.
1 Charles Center
Baltimore, Maryland 21201

Rowe Price New Horizons Fund, Inc.
1 Charles Center
Baltimore, Maryland 21201

Scudder, Stevens & Clark Balanced Fund, Inc.
10 Post Office Square
Boston, Massachusetts 02109

Scudder, Stevens & Clark Common Stock Fund, Inc.
10 Post Office Square
Boston, Massachusetts 02109

Securities Fund, Inc.
1617 John F. Kennedy Boulevard
Philadelphia, Pennsylvania 19103

Stein Roe & Farnham Balanced Fund, Inc.
135 South La Salle Street
Chicago, Illinois 60603

Stein Roe & Farnham Stock Fund, Inc.
135 South La Salle Street
Chicago, Illinois 60603

Trans American Fund, Incorporated
901 Washington Avenue
St. Louis, Missouri 63178

Variable Stock Fund, Inc.
5001 West Broad Street
Richmond, Virginia 23226

Venture Securities Fund, Inc.
860 Suburban Station Building
Philadelphia, Pennsylvania 19103

THE COMPROMISE TAX

As stated in Chapter One, it is difficult to take taxes into account properly. As a practical solution, we decided upon two assumed rates for use in this book. An assumed tax of 20% is deducted from *ordinary investment income,* such as dividends and interest; and a *Compromise Tax of 15%* is deducted from rates of return on *equity* investments, such as stocks, real estate, and mutual funds. Note that unless stated to the contrary, all interest, yields, and rates of return are *net,* having been adjusted to reflect annual payment of federal income taxes at the rate of either 15% or 20%, whichever is appropriate. The 20% ordinary income tax rate and 15% Compromise Tax rate will be higher than the tax rate to be paid by some investors (frequently persons filing a joint tax return) and lower than the actual tax rate to be paid by many others (single persons, often).

The *average* rate of tax paid on taxable income is not the rate which should be deducted from investment income. With taxable income of $5,000 (after deductions and exemptions) a couple filing a joint return will pay a tax of $810, which appears to be a tax at the rate of 16.2%. However, their next dollar of ordinary income would be taxed at the rate of 19%. Our tax system, progressive in nature, is based upon graduated rates. Their next dollar of taxable ordinary income, therefore, will generate a tax based on their highest income tax bracket; or the additional income may push them into the next highest bracket. Accordingly, their highest tax rate—19% (and not the 16.2%, average rate)—should be deducted from annual pre-tax yields when computing their net investment yield.

The compromise rate of 15% was selected to take into account the tax status of *long-term capital gains,* which ordinarily result from sale of stocks, mutual fund shares, or real estate after a holding period of more than six months. When such gains constitute part of an investor's yield, the over-all tax rate on his investment return will be lower than when such gains are not included. Federal tax law provides that the rate of tax applicable to such gains is either (1) 25% or (2) the investor's highest income tax rate, applied to only 50% of the gains, whichever alternative produces the lesser tax. The second alternative applies to most beginning investors.

Recall the assumption that the average reader's next dollar of ordinary income would be taxed at 20%. Assuming long-term capital gains equal about 50% of the investor's total return before taxes, taxable at only 10%, the effective tax rate on the total investment return would be approximately 15%.

Actually, the 15% tax, as a compromise rate, is too conservative. Long-term capital gains often amount to 70–75% of the rate of return before taxes. Also, it should be remembered that the 15% tax is assumed to be paid each year, whereas the tax on long-term capital gains is frequently postponed for many years, if paid at all. Such postponement permits the investor to have working for him a greater amount of capital than would be possible if the investor were required to make annual payment of the long-term capital-gains tax on unrealized capital appreciation.

For many persons the assumed 20% tax on ordinary income from investments will not be sufficient. The tax on ordinary income increases to a maximum of 70% (but only 25% on long-term capital gains) for a married couple in the $200,000 tax bracket filing a joint return. Accordingly, for persons in high income tax brackets, the projections of accumulation values contained throughout this book should be reduced appropriately.

Validity of the assumed 15% and 20% taxes must be judged on a case-by-case basis. At the outset of your program the assumed tax will probably be too high. Later, your investment income will increase and so may your salary. When this occurs, your long-term capital-gains tax may go as high as 25%. But, as said before, much of the long-term capital-gains tax will be deferred, making the assumed 15% tax on the annual pre-tax yield much more onerous than the actual tax payment for such years. Later—25 years from now, perhaps—when you finally sell your stocks and pay the tax, your investment capital will be reduced in value by no more than 25%. We have attempted to reflect this 25% (deferred) reduction in our estimates of accumulation values. We created, in effect, a separate investment account (called a "reserve") to which we'll turn for payment of the 25% (maximum) tax when it becomes due. (Actually, the reserve will be an unidentifiable portion of your investment fund.) The reserve is funded by that portion of the 15% Compromise Tax not required for payment of current income taxes (on unrealized capital appreciation, for the most part). Together with your investment fund, the reserve will appreciate in value—after making provision for payment of its own income taxes; and its value should ultimately equal or exceed the long-term capital-gains taxes payable, if and when you sell your stocks.

There are other considerations. An investor must take into account the possibilities of a reversal in his marital status, which may involve a change in the effective tax rate applicable to his investment income. Any state taxation of income should be reflected too. Furthermore, the federal tax structure does not remain static. Tax reductions seem less probable than increases, and more effective enforcement techniques may increase the over-all tax burden.

In view of these divergent possibilities, the assumed tax rates of 15% and 20% seem justified. These rates are used to make the predictions concerning various investment opportunities contained in the Investment Spectrum (Chapter One), and other accumulation projections in this book.

You are invited to judge for yourself whether the 15% and 20% tax rates are applicable to you, but keep in mind the foregoing considerations, especially the conservative basis on which the rates were estimated.

FEDERAL INCOME TAX RATES FOR YEARS
BEGINNING WITH 1965

Investment Income Bracket (in Thousands of Dollars)		Tax Rates for Ordinary Income		
Over	Not Over	Separate Return	Married Couple Filing Joint Return	Head of Household
0	$ .5	14%	14%	14%
$ .5	1	15	"	"
1	1.5	16	15	16
1.5	2	17	"	"
2	3	19	16	18
3	4	"	17	"
4	6	22	19	20
6	8	25	"	22
8	10	28	22	25
10	12	32	"	27
12	14	36	25	31
14	16	39	"	32
16	18	42	28	35
18	20	45	"	36
20	22	48	32	40

Investment Income Bracket (in Thousands of Dollars)		Tax Rates for Ordinary Income		
Over	Not Over	Separate Return	Married Couple Filing Joint Return	Head of Household
$ 22	$ 24	50%	„ %	41%
24	26	"	36	43
26	28	53	"	45
28	32	"	39	46
32	36	55	42	48
36	38	"	45	50
38	40	58	"	52
40	44	"	48	53
44	48	60	50	55
48	50	"	"	56
50	52	62	"	56
52	56	"	53	58
56	60	"	"	"
60	64	64	"	"
64	70	"	55	61
70	76	66	"	"
76	80	"	58	63
80	88	68	"	"
88	90	"	60	64
90	100	69	"	"
100	120	70	62	66
120	140	"	64	67
140	160	"	66	68
160	180	"	68	69
180	200	"	69	70
200	up	"	70	"

Lower tax rates applicable to a married couple filing a joint tax return result from a splitting of the combined income of the spouses. Each spouse is deemed to have income amounting to 50% of the combined income, which 50% is taxed at the rate applicable to individual tax returns. This results in a lower over-all tax rate than if the combined income were taxed at individual rates without a split. If an individual's taxable investment income of $2,000 places him in the $10,000 to $12,000 income tax bracket, a tax rate of 32%, his investment income would generate a tax of $640. If, however, the individual is married and chooses to file a joint return with his spouse (who, it is now assumed, has no taxable income) the $2,000 of investment income would be split into two parts, both falling in the $4,000 to $6,000 income tax bracket for an individual return. Total tax, at the rate of 22%, would amount to $440, for a total tax saving of $200. The conclusion: Marriage maximizes Multiples.

Appendix C

1960 LIFE EXPECTANCY TABLE
FOR THE UNITED STATES
AGES 21–50

Life Expectancy in Years

Present Age in Years	Whole Population	White Male	White Female	Non-White Male	Non-White Female
21	51.5	49.2	55.3	44.6	49.0
22	50.6	48.2	54.3	43.7	48.0
23	49.6	47.3	53.3	42.8	47.1
24	48.7	46.4	52.3	41.9	46.2
25	47.7	45.5	51.4	41.1	45.2
26	46.8	44.5	50.4	40.2	44.3
27	45.9	43.6	49.5	39.3	43.4
28	44.9	42.7	48.5	38.5	42.5
29	44.0	41.7	47.5	37.6	41.6
30	43.0	40.8	46.6	36.7	40.7
31	42.1	39.9	45.6	35.9	39.8
32	41.2	38.9	44.6	35.0	38.9
33	40.2	38.0	43.7	34.2	38.0
34	39.3	37.1	42.7	33.3	37.2
35	38.4	36.1	41.8	32.5	36.3
36	37.4	35.2	40.8	31.6	35.4
37	36.5	34.3	39.9	30.8	34.6
38	35.6	33.4	38.9	30.0	33.7
39	34.7	32.5	38.0	29.2	32.9
40	33.8	31.6	37.1	28.4	32.1
41	32.9	30.7	36.1	27.6	31.2
42	32.0	29.8	35.2	26.8	30.4
43	31.1	28.9	34.3	26.1	29.6
44	30.2	28.0	33.4	25.3	28.8
45	29.4	27.2	32.5	24.6	28.0
46	28.5	26.3	31.6	23.8	27.3
47	27.7	25.5	30.7	23.1	26.5
48	26.8	24.7	29.8	22.4	25.7
49	26.0	23.9	28.9	21.7	25.0
50	25.2	23.1	28.0	21.0	24.3

Appendix D

TOTAL VALUE OF ANNUAL ACCUMULATIONS OF $1,000* INVESTED, AT YEAR'S END, AT ALTERNATIVE NET RETURNS RANGING FROM 8% TO 15%, COMPOUNDED ANNUALLY

Total Accumulation Values for Alternative Net Returns

No. of Years	8%	9%	10%	11%	12%	13%	14%	15%
5	$ 5,867	$ 5,985	$ 6,105	$ 6,228	$ 6,353	$ 6,480	$ 6,610	$ 6,742
10	14,487	15,193	15,937	16,722	17,549	18,420	19,337	20,304
15	27,152	29,361	31,772	34,405	37,280	40,417	43,842	47,580
20	45,762	51,160	57,275	64,203	72,052	80,947	91,025	102,444
25	73,106	84,701	98,347	114,413	133,334	155,620	181,871	212,793
30	113,283	136,308	164,494	199,021	241,333	293,199	356,787	434,745
35	172,317	215,711	271,024	341,590	431,663	546,681	693,573	881,170
40	259,057	337,882	442,593	581,826	767,091	1,013,704	1,342,025	1,779,090

* For an Annual Accumulation other than $1,000, say $50, multiply the Total Accumulation Value by the $50, then divide the result by $1,000. Thus, the Total Accumulation Value for $50 per year invested at an 8% net return for 40 years would be $12,953 ($259,057 multiplied by $50 and divided by $1,000).

BIBLIOGRAPHY
OF RECOMMENDED READINGS

Listed by topic below are books I recommend as supplemental reading for persons desiring to learn more about the fields of personal finance, estate planning, saving, investment, and speculation. Your interest and experience will lead you to other worthwhile books.

Borrowing:

Black, Hillel. *Buy Now, Pay Later*. New York: William Morrow and Company, 1961.

Cobleigh, Ira U. *How and Where to Borrow Money*. New York: Avon Books, 1965.

Definitions:

Low, Janet. *The Investor's Dictionary*. New York: Simon and Schuster, 1964.

Economics:

Hazlitt, Henry. *What You Should Know about Inflation*. Princeton, N.J.: D. Van Nostrand Company, 1965, 2nd ed.

Samuelson, Paul A. *Economics*. New York: McGraw-Hill Book Company, 1961, 5th ed.

Estate Planning:

Wormser, René A. *Wormser's Guide to Estate Planning*. Englewood Cliffs, N.J.: Prentice-Hall, 1958.

Formula Purchase of Stocks:

Tomlinson, Lucile. *Practical Formulas for Successful Investing*. New York: Wilfred Funk, 1953.

Wycoff, Peter. *The Psychology of Stock Market Timing.* Englewood Cliffs, N.J.: Prentice-Hall, 1963.

Fundamental Analysis of Stocks:

Graham, Benjamin; Dodd, David L.; and Cottle, Sidney. *Security Analysis.* New York: McGraw-Hill Book Company, 1962, 4th ed.

Stabler, C. Norman. *How to Read the Financial News.* New York: Harper & Row, 1965, 10th ed.

Insurance:

Angell, Frank Joseph. *Health Insurance.* New York: The Ronald Press Company, 1963.

Dacey, Norman F. *What's Wrong with Your Life Insurance.* New York: The Crowell-Collier Press, 1963.

Hendershot, Ralph. *The Grim Truth about Life Insurance.* New York: G. P. Putnam's Sons, 1957.

Linton, M. Albert. *How Life Insurance Can Serve You.* New York: Harper and Brothers, 1958.

Maclean, Joseph B. *Life Insurance.* New York: McGraw-Hill Book Company, 1962.

Money and Banking:

Whittlesey, Charles R.; Freedman, Arthur M.; and Herman, Edward S. *Money and Banking: Analysis and Policy.* New York: The Macmillan Company, 1963.

Mutual Funds and Other Investment Companies:

Palance, Dean. *Mutual Funds . . . Legal Pickpockets?* New York: Vantage Press, 1963.

Securities and Exchange Commission. *Report of the Special Study of the Securities Markets,* Pt. 4, Ch. XI entitled "Open-End Investment Companies (Mutual Funds)." Pub. by House Comm. on Interstate and Foreign Commerce, H. R. Doc. No. 95, Pt. 4, 88th Cong., 1st Sess. (1963).

Smith, Ralph Lee. *The Grim Truth about Mutual Funds.* New York: G. P. Putnam's Sons, 1963.

Wharton School of Finance and Commerce. *A Study of Mutual Funds.* Prepared for the Securities and Exchange Commission and pub. by House Comm. on Interstate and Foreign Commerce, H. R. Rep. No. 2274, 87th Cong., 2d Sess. (1962).

Personal Finances:

Lasser, J. K. and Porter, Sylvia F. *Managing Your Money.* New York: Holt, Rinehart and Winston, 1961, rev. ed.

Rodda, William H. and Nelson, Edward A. *Managing Personal Finances.* Englewood Cliffs, N.J.: Prentice-Hall, 1965.

Rates of Return:

Fisher, L. and Lorie, J. H. "Rates of Return on Investments in Common Stocks." *The Journal of Business of the University of Chicago,* Vol. 37, No. 1, January 1964 (1–21).

Real Estate:

McMichael, Stanley L. and O'Keefe, Paul T. *How to Finance Real Estate.* Englewood Cliffs, N.J.: Prentice-Hall, 1953, 2nd ed.

Nickerson, William. *How I Turned $1,000 into a Million in Real Estate in My Spare Time.* New York: Simon and Schuster, 1959.

Rothschild, Hugo; revised by Berman, Daniel S. *How to Invest & Protect Your Profits in Real Estate Syndicates.* Garden City, N.Y.: Doubleday & Company, 1964, rev. ed.

Savings and Loan Associations:

Cobleigh, Ira U. *$100 Billion Can't Be Wrong!* New York: Cobleigh & Gordon, 1964.

Prather, William C. *Savings Accounts.* Chicago: American Savings and Loan Institute Press, 1961, 2nd ed.

Securities and Exchange Commission:

de Bedts, Ralph F. *The New Deal's SEC: The Formative Years.* New York: The Columbia University Press, 1964.

Speculation:

Cadwallader, Clyde T. *How to Make Money Speculating in Real Estate.* Englewood Cliffs, N.J.: Prentice-Hall, 1960.

Darvas, Nicolas. *How I Made $2,000,000 in the Stock Market.* Larchmont, N.Y.: American Research Council, 1960.

Filer, Herbert. *Understanding Put and Call Options.* New York: Crown Publishers, 1959.

Fried, Sidney. *The Speculative Merits of Common Stock Warrants.* New York: R.H.M. Associates, 1957.

Gold, Gerald. *Modern Commodity Futures Trading.* New York: Commodity Research Bureau, 1963, 3rd ed. (rev.).

Stocks and Stock Markets:

Barnes, Leo. *Your Investments.* Larchmont, N.Y.: American Research Council, 1966 or later ed.

Crane, Burton; revised by Eisenlohr, Sylvia Crane. *The Sophisticated Investor.* New York: Simon and Schuster, 1964, rev. ed.

Engel, Louis. *How to Buy Stocks.* Boston: Little, Brown and Company, 1953, 3rd ed. (rev.).

Leffler, George L.; revised by Farwell, Loring C. *The Stock Market.* New York: The Ronald Press Company, 1963, 3rd ed.

Loeb, Gerald M. *The Battle for Investment Survival.* New York: Simon and Schuster, 1965, rev. ed.

Taxation:

Lasser, J. K. *J. K. Lasser's Your Income Tax.* New York: Simon and Schuster, 1966 or later ed.

Technical Analysis of Stocks:

Edwards, Robert D. and Magee, John. *Technical Analysis of Stock Trends.* Springfield, Mass.: John Magee, 1957, 4th ed.

Granville, Joseph E. *A Strategy of Daily Stock Market Timing for Maximum Profit.* Englewood Cliffs, N.J.: Prentice-Hall, 1960.

INDEX